THE HISTORIAN AND THE CLIMATE OF OPINION

Edited by

ROBERT ALLEN SKOTHEIM
University of Colorado

ADDISON-WESLEY PUBLISHING COMPANY
Reading, Massachusetts
Menlo Park, California • London • Don Mills, Ontario

THEMES AND SOCIAL FORCES IN AMERICAN HISTORY SERIES
Under the editorship of Robin W. Winks

Purpose: To explore major influences on the development of American society and character.

ANTIDEMOCRATIC TRENDS IN TWENTIETH CENTURY AMERICA
Roland L. DeLorme and Raymond G. McInnis

ALLEGIANCE IN AMERICA: THE CASE OF THE LOYALISTS
Geraint N. D. Evans

PURITANISM AND THE AMERICAN EXPERIENCE
Michael McGiffert

THE AMERICAN ENVIRONMENT:
READINGS IN THE HISTORY OF CONSERVATION
Roderick Nash

THE HISTORIAN AND THE CLIMATE OF OPINION
Robert A. Skotheim

THE AMERICAN MILITARY:
READINGS IN THE HISTORY OF THE MILITARY IN AMERICAN SOCIETY
Russell F. Weigley

Printed in the United States of America. Published simultaneously in Canada. Library of Congress Catalog Card No. 73-78501.

This collection of writings by outstanding
twentieth-century American historians
is dedicated to
W. Stull Holt, historiographer

CONTENTS

Introduction

The greatest problem in historical scholarship, theoretically and practically, is the relation between the historian and his subject matter. The past is gone, and the historian can study only its remnants. Although there is no way to recapture the past in entirety, the historian can reconstruct aspects of it from the remaining records and from the inferences, deductions, and guesses he can make using these records. But even though the totality of the past is lost, the records for all except remote periods of history are so numerous that the scholar cannot possibly reproduce them. Even if he could, with the help of modern technology, collect and arrange chronologically all the factual remains of the past, his efforts would be futile. The records by themselves are meaningless. They cannot speak; the historian who interprets them must speak for them. Yet the historian is finite and fallible as he confronts the infinite, immutable past.

On what basis does the scholar select certain facts from the mass of data left from the past? How does he explain the interrelationship of the facts he selects? What criteria does he use to evaluate his subject, if he does evaluate it? These are the essential questions faced by the historian.

This volume of writings by outstanding twentieth-century American historians presents one aspect of the problem which results from the conflict between the subjectivity of the historian and the objectivity of the past. The particular part of this general problem which will be examined is the relationship between the historian and the climate of opinion in which he does his work.

The concept of a climate of opinion is central to our purpose and needs to be defined, however loosely, at the outset. Climate of opinion, like other similar phrases which are sometimes used such as the spirit of an age, refers to the fundamental assumptions and attitudes shared by significant elements of a population at a given time. We may speak of the climate of opinion or the spirit of an age as a basic intellectual outlook which is shared by people in several nations over a span of centuries; such an example is the modern, rationalist, scientific spirit of western civilization since the eighteenth century. In the present case we mean to highlight recent common assumptions concerning God, nature, reason, and the possibility of man's progress through control of his environment. In this context, we may also talk of the common intellectual climate shared by "hippies" of the 1960s in the United States who assume that older generations have nothing to teach them and that they must find their individual identities through personal relationships. Whether a few people during a short period or millions over the centuries are involved, and whether ideas of the nature of the world or personal fulfillment are involved, our attempt to locate the climate of opinion is an attempt to describe the basic intellectual viewpoint of the group in question.

In this volume, the climate of opinion ordinarily refers to the attitudes toward society shared by most members of the educated American public during a period of three or four decades. For example, the progressive climate of the earlier twentieth century refers to the pervasive belief in man's ability to reform society. By contrast, the years following World War II brought an intellectual temper which was more pessimistic about the possibility of significantly improving the human condition, and which instead emphasized the value of traditional American society. A single intellectual climate does not necessarily, of course, envelop every group or individual in a society at any particular time, and often there are competing basic outlooks. For instance, in the United States during the 1960s a minority dissent from the prevailing post-war mood has emerged in the young people born during and after the Great Depression. This dissenting frame of mind, with its critical stance toward the American status quo and its demand for social reform, is described in this volume as a return to the earlier progressivism.

What does the climate of opinion have to do with the way a scholar writes history? From the mass of records left by the past, the historian selects and interprets data on the basis of what is meaningful and important to him. In this process, he is reflecting his climate of opinion, for he studies the past from the perspective of the present. His sense of what is meaningful and important significantly derives from the climate of opinion in which he lives. This is not to deny that he honestly tries to understand the past, or to suggest that he intentionally distorts the past because of his present interests. It is only to insist that the historian cannot jump out of his intellectual skin. The same human limitation naturally applies to scholars in other fields of study, including scientists, as well as to historians. But historical scholarship is more thoroughly and obviously sensitive to the climate of opinion in which it is created than is scientific scholarship. One reason for this sensitivity is that historians study the socially significant ideas and patterns of behavior of people in past generations. Historians are apt to derive their understanding of human nature and of what constitutes social significance in part from the climate of opinion in which they live. Further, because historians do not employ esoteric techniques in their research or write their histories in technical language, and because they direct their scholarship not only to a small professional audience of experts, but also to the general educated public, historians are more prone than scientists to be affected by the attitudes of the public. And by their usual willingness to pass moral judgments upon the past and their tendency to make evaluations of the present, historians are, in a sense, literary statesmen as well as antiquarians.

As this characterization of the nature of historical scholarship might suggest, the relation between the historian and the climate of opinion in which he works is reciprocal. Precisely because the historian is so integrally related to his society's intellectual temper, he influences it even as it influences him. The historian informs his contemporaries of their historical development and in so doing provides them with a memory extending back before their own lives, a memory of their aspirations, difficulties, and achievements. Just as each individual's memory is essential for daily life, so a collective memory is necessary for a community to maintain a sense of direction. Because of his efforts to make his scholarship on the past of interest and relevance to the present generation, the historian, in his role as historian, has greater inherent reason to try to affect current social thought than does a scientist, in his role as a scientist.

Since historians have generally been influencers of, as well as having been influenced by, the prevalent social thought of their own times, it is no surprise to find that they have become variously involved in public affairs throughout American history. Admittedly rare is the case of Woodrow Wilson, who wrote several volumes of political history before becoming president of Princeton University and then embarking upon a life in politics which quickly reached the White House. More common are those scholars who did not permanently change careers, but whose historical writings were accompanied by brief or part-time political involvement. George Bancroft, one of the greatest of American historians in the nineteenth century, became a leading Democrat in Massachusetts and writer of policies for the party; he was rewarded by cabinet positions and Ministerships to European countries. More recently the Democratic party has often turned to historians for advice and the writing of speeches. Arthur Schlesinger, Jr., a distinguished contemporary historian who for more than two decades has been an active participant in national affairs, was President Kennedy's special assistant at the White House. Another outstanding scholar, Eric Goldman, occupied a similar formal position under Lyndon Johnson, without being as close to the President. And of course, there are those public figures who pursue the writing of history as an avocation. In the seventeenth century, the leading figures of Massachusetts Bay and Plymouth colonies, John Winthrop and William Bradford, respectively, wrote chronicles of their wilderness communities even as they governed them. In the twentieth century, Theodore Roosevelt wrote several volumes of history as a hobby, and John F. Kennedy, the author of *Profiles of Courage* as a young politician, reportedly planned to devote time to historical scholarship when he left the Presidency.

These examples of historians who emerged as public figures and public figures who became historians suggest the easy relationship between the two fields of endeavor. Of course, such examples touch only superficially, however dramatically, upon the question of the historian's possible impact on the climate of opinion. Most historians remain historians and do not become presidential advisors. It is through their scholarship that they affect social thought. The histories of George Bancroft, without regard to his career in the Democratic party, stand as a celebration of the nineteenth-century common man in the United States, insofar as they traced the victory of Protestantism and democracy over historic superstition and aristrocracy during the seventeenth and eighteenth centuries in America. This view of the past was Bancroft's contribution to affecting the way his contemporaries looked at the world. Similarly in our own time, Arthur Schlesinger, Jr. has written histories of the political reform tradition, from Andrew Jackson through Franklin Roosevelt to John Kennedy, which attempt to portray a reformer's past that can be admired and emulated in the present. From these writings, rather than from his brief official relationship with the nation's Chief Executive, stems Schlesinger's influence upon the post-war climate of opinion.

In summary, granting that the historian has to select and interpret the data, and granting that he influences and is influenced by the prevailing climate of opinion, in what sense can a problem be said to exist? Does his situation not allow for a healthy interplay between scholarship and life? In a world of increasing specialization and fragmentation of knowledge, is it not fortunate such interplay exists so that historical scholarship can continue to affect and be affected by, the society of which it is a part?

The problem lies precisely in the fact that, despite the impossibility of recapturing the past in totality, the historian and his readers expect something more than a history based upon a complete capitulation to the interests of the present. The historian and his readers demand obedience to the integrity of the past, even though they recognize the necessity of viewing the past through the lens of the present. The dual obligation to past and present is inescapable. Consequently historians attempt to protect the claims of the past by accepting as legitimate scholarship only those histories which are based upon apparently valid data and whose interpretations seem coherent and consistent. At the same time, historians honor the claims of the present by praising histories that possess broad or contemporary significance in addition to factual accuracy and logical consistency.

Despite the efforts of historians to erect canons for defining scholarly worth, the problem of the relation of the historian to his subject matter remains. What the collection of writings in this volume suggests is that over the course of the twentieth century the facts selected for emphasis and the interpretations drawn from these facts, in the histories generally accepted to be outstanding, have significantly changed. The changes have coincided with alterations in the prevailing climate of opinion which existed at the time the histories were written. Thus the outstanding American historians since the early 1900s have not simply improved upon each other, progressing toward the attainment of true historical omniscience. Rather they have set out interpretations in their histories, contradicted them, and returned again to modify their original versions, all in conjunction with changes in the country's intellectual temper.

Everyone who accepts the conflicting claims of past and present will recognize that a problem exists in the close relationship between the historian and the climate of opinion which surrounds him. However, readers will define that problem differently as they read the volume. Some, horrified at the changes of interpretation, will conclude that histories should be called tracts instead of scholarship, and that climate of opinion constitutes an obstacle to a historian's understanding of the past. These readers may sympathize with the pleas of those recent "scientific" historians presented in Part Four who want to establish methods to minimize the extent of vagueness, guess-work, moral judgment, and influence of the climate of opinion in written histories. Other readers will accept the dramatic changes in historical interpretations as legitimate and conclude that the flexibility excercised in interpreting history testifies to the continuing opportunity each climate of opinion affords for new insight into the past.

Part One

Historians of the Earlier 1900s

1

Written History as an Act of Faith

CHARLES BEARD (1934)

To understand the connections between the climate of opinion during the first four decades of the twentieth century and the writings of historians represented in Part One, it is necessary to know the nature of the "progressive" and "pragmatic" intellectual temper which dominated most of those years. It was progressive insofar as it assumed that the world was becoming a better place in which to live, and that man himself was the agent of his progress. Two related ideas played a part in developing the particular form which this belief in progress took. One was an assumption that man was basically good, and the second was a conviction that by changing man's environment, human nature itself would be changed. Improvement of society could therefore be effected by bettering the environment of potentially good mankind. This concept was the generating force behind such reform enterprises, both before and after World War I, as campaigns for tenement house legislation, child labor laws, improvement of working conditions (particularly for women), and various social security plans.

The contribution of pragmatism to social thought was twofold. First, pragmatism led to emphasis on the specific historical conditions which gave rise to established beliefs, laws, and public policies. Using this approach, existing beliefs, laws, and public policies could be recognized as being at one time relevant to certain past circumstances but perhaps as being now irrelevant to the present. Thus pragmatism undermined the authority of the status quo and by its insistence that the human thought process functioned as a device to solve problems, encouraged reform. Second, by its insistence that one could not know the real meaning of a belief, law, or public policy except by ascertaining their practical consequences, pragmatism encouraged an experimental approach to social affairs, a method of trial-and-error.

Reprinted by permission from *The American Historical Review,* XXXIX, January 1934, pp. 219-229. The essay was read as a presidential address to the American Historical Association in 1933.

These pragmatic interpretations concerning the problem-solving origin of ideas and the meaning of ideas in terms of their actual consequences implicitly challenged traditional policies, allegedly eternal "truths," and old laws. But pragmatism was congenial to reformers not merely because it helped attack the status quo. The enthusiasm for pragmatism's ability to destroy was closely linked to the pervasive belief in progress. Precisely because reformers assumed the probability of constant betterment, they embraced pragmatism's cutting analysis of the established order.

Charles Beard's (1874-1948) presidential address to the American Historical Association in 1933, in which he outlined his view of the function of a historian and of the nature of written histories, affords an opportunity to see how one famous scholar expressed a blend of philosophic pragmatism and progressive faith. Beard opened his address by undermining the "objective" or scientific pretensions of those who thought that written histories were simply carbon copies of the past as it actually happened, or that they were omniscient revelations of deterministic laws of human behavior. On the contrary, he argued, written histories have always been in the form of contemporary thought concerning the past, and as such they have been intellectual responses to specific conditions prevalent at the time they were written. Even the idea of scientific or objective history, according to Beard, was itself a reflection of the nineteenth-century desire for peace and preservation of the status quo. By relegating the claims of scientific history to specific cultural conditions in the past which were no longer relevant to the present, Beard freed historical scholarship for his own purposes. However, he admitted that if all histories were relative to their particular circumstances, then this relativism applied to his own scholarship as well as to the histories of others in previous ages. Beard then declared that it was only logical that the idea of relativity itself be relative, and that there had to be an irreducible absolute: "the totality of history as actuality which embraces all times and circumstances and all relativities." This exercise in logic brought Beard back to the point at which he had started, of trying to decide how the historian should organize his histories; but he now envisioned himself as "more or less a guesser in this vale of tears."

Beard's conclusion was that the historian had to adopt a philosophy of history, or a criterion for selection of data, before he could write a history. Regardless of which scheme the historian chose to adopt, he would discover that no one formula would encompass all the available evidence. Whether the chosen interpretation was that of a chaotic, or cyclical, or progressive past, the wise historian had to admit that his choice was an act of faith. And in strikingly pragmatic fashion, Beard added that the profundity of the historian's choice would depend upon whether the future corroborated or contradicted what he said about the movement of history. In this sense, the writing of history was a prediction as much as a recollection. In the next-to-last sentence in the next-to-last paragraph of his address Beard indicated that his own act of faith was that history was moving progressively toward a collectivist democracy. Thus, to Beard, the historian's function was to create the past pragmatically in the interest of creating a progressive future.

The significance of Beard's position was great. The historian was not simply a nostalgic archivist who lived in the present and dreamed of the past. Instead, the historian was a scholar who used his knowledge of the past to improve the present. Beard spoke to the young, the hopeful, and to all those who wanted to believe that the world could be molded into a better form. "Written History as an Act of Faith" provided what was, in effect, a defense for the use of historical scholarship in the cause of reform.

History has been called a science, an art, an illustration of theology, a phase of philosophy, a branch of literature. It is none of these things, nor all of them combined. On the contrary, science, art, theology, and literature are themselves merely phases of history as past actuality and their particular forms at given periods and places are to be explained, if explained at all, by history as knowledge and thought. The philosopher, possessing little or no acquaintance with history, sometimes pretends to expound the inner secret of history,* but the historian turns upon him and expounds the secret of the philosopher, as far as it may be expounded at all, by placing him in relation to the movement of ideas and interests in which he stands or floats, by giving to his scheme of thought its appropriate relativity. So it is with systems of science, art, theology, and literature. All the light on these subjects that can be discovered by the human mind comes from history as past actuality.

What, then, is this manifestation of omniscience called history? It is, as Croce says, contemporary thought about the past. History as past actuality includes, to be sure, all that has been done, said, felt, and thought by human beings on this planet since humanity began its long career. History as record embraces the monuments, documents, and symbols which provide such knowledge as we have or can find respecting past actuality. But it is history as thought, not as actuality, record, or specific knowledge, that is really meant when the term history is used in its widest and most general significance. It is thought about past actuality, instructed and delimited by history as record and knowledge–record and knowledge authenticated by criticism and ordered with the help of the scientific method. This is the final, positive, inescapable definition. It contains all the exactness that is

*For a beautiful example, see the passages on America in the introduction to Hegel's *Philosophy of History.*

possible and all the bewildering problems inherent in the nature of thought and the relation of the thinker to the thing thought about.

Although this definition of history may appear, at first glance, distressing to those who have been writing lightly about "the science of history" and "the scientific method" in historical research and construction, it is in fact in accordance with the most profound contemporary thought about history, represented by Croce, Riezler, Karl Mannheim, Mueller-Armack, and Heussi, for example. It is in keeping also with the obvious and commonplace. Has it not been said for a century or more that each historian who writes history is a product of his age, and that his work reflects the spirit of the times, of a nation, race, group, class, or section? No contemporary student of history really believes that Bossuet, Gibbon, Mommsen, or Bancroft could be duplicated today. Every student of history knows that his colleagues have been influenced in their selection and ordering of materials by their biases, prejudices, beliefs, affections, general upbringing, and experience, particularly social and economic; and if he has a sense of propriety, to say nothing of humor, he applies the canon to himself, leaving no exceptions to the rule. The pallor of waning time, if not of death, rests upon the latest volume of history, fresh from the roaring press.

Why do we believe this to be true? The answer is that every written history–of a village, town, county, state, nation, race, group, class, idea, or the wide world–is a selection and arrangement of facts, of recorded fragments of past actuality. And the selection and arrangement of facts–a combined and complex intellectual operation–is an act of choice, conviction, and interpretation respecting values, is an act of thought. Facts, multitudinous and beyond calculation, are known, but they do not select themselves or force themselves automatically into any fixed scheme of arrangement in the mind of the historian. They are selected and ordered by him as he thinks. True enough, where the records pertaining to a small segment of history are few and presumably all known, the historian may produce a fragment having an aspect of completeness, as, for example, some pieces by Fustel de Coulanges; but the completeness is one of documentation, not of history. True enough also, many historians are pleased to say of their writings that their facts are selected and ordered only with reference to inner necessities, but none who takes this position will allow the same exactitude and certainty to the works of others, except when the predilections of the latter conform to his own pattern.

Contemporary thought about history, therefore, repudiates the conception dominant among the schoolmen during the latter part of the nineteenth century and the opening years of the twentieth century–the conception that it is possible to describe the past as it actually was, somewhat as the engineer describes a single machine. The formula itself was a passing phase of thought about the past. Its author, Ranke, a German conservative, writing after the storm and stress of the French Revolution, was weary of history written for, or permeated by, the purposes of revolutionary propaganda. He wanted peace. The ruling classes in Germany, with which he was affiliated, having secured a breathing spell in the settlement of 1815, wanted peace to consolidate their position. Written history that was cold, factual, and apparently undisturbed by the passions of the time served best the cause of those who did not want to be disturbed. Later the formula was fitted into the great conception of natural science—cold neutrality over against the materials and forces of the physical world. Truths of nature, ran the theory, are to be discovered by maintaining the most severe objectivity; therefore, the truth of history may be revealed by the same spirit and method. The reasoning seemed perfect to those for whom it was satisfactory. But the movement of ideas and interests continued, and bondage to conservative and scientific thought was broken by criticism and events. As Croce and Heussi have demonstrated, so-called neutral or scientific history reached a crisis in its thought before the twentieth century had advanced far on the way.

This crisis in historical thought sprang from internal criticism—from conflicts of thought within historiography itself—and from the movement of history as actuality; for historians are always engaged, more or less, in thinking about their own work and are disturbed, like their fellow citizens, by crises and revolutions occuring in the world about them. As an outcome of this crisis in historiography, the assumption that the actuality of history is identical with or closely akin to that of the physical world, and the assumption that any historian can be a disembodied spirit as coldly neutral to human affairs as the engineer to an automobile have both been challenged and rejected. Thus, owing to internal criticism and the movement of external events, the Ranke formula of history has been discarded and laid away in the museum of antiquities. It has ceased to satisfy the human spirit in its historical needs. Once more, historians recognize formally the obvious, long known informally, namely, that any written history inevitably reflects the thought of the author in his time and cultural setting.

That this crisis in thought presents a distressing dilemma to many historians is beyond question. It is almost a confession of inexpiable sin to admit in academic circles that one is not a man of science working in a scientific manner with things open to deterministic and inexorable treatment, to admit that one is more or less a guesser in this vale of tears. But the only escape from the dust and storm of the present conflict, and from the hazards of taking thought, now before the historian, is silence or refuge in some minute particularity of history as actuality. He may edit documents, although there are perils in the choice of documents to be edited, and in any case the choice of documents will bear some reference to an interpretation of values and importance–subjective considerations. To avoid this difficulty, the historian may confine his attention to some very remote and microscopic area of time and place, such as the price of cotton in Alabama between 1850 and 1860, or the length of wigs in the reign of Charles II, on the pleasing but false assumption that he is really describing an isolated particularity as it actually was, an isolated area having no wide-reaching ramifications of relations. But even then the historian would be a strange creature if he never asked himself why he regarded these matters as worthy of his labor and love, or why society provides a living for him during his excursions and explorations.

The other alternative before the student of history as immense actuality is to face boldly, in the spirit of Cato's soliloquy, the wreck of matter and the crush of worlds–the dissolution of that solid assurance which rested on the formula bequeathed by Ranke and embroidered by a thousand hands during the intervening years. And when he confronts without avoidance contemporary thought about the nature of written history, what commands does he hear?

The supreme command is that he must cast off his servitude to the assumptions of natural science and return to his own subject matter–to history as actuality. The hour for this final declaration of independence has arrived: the contingency is here and thought resolves it. Natural science is only one small subdivision of history as actuality with which history as thought is concerned. Its dominance in the thought of the Western World for a brief period can be explained, if at all, by history; perhaps in part by reference to the great conflict that raged between the theologians and scientists after the dawn of the sixteenth century–an intellectual conflict associated with the economic conflict between landed aristocracies, lay and clerical, on the one side, and the rising bourgeois on the other.

The intellectual formulas borrowed from natural science, which have cramped and distorted the operations of history as thought, have taken two forms: physical and biological. The first of these rests upon what may be called, for convenience, the assumption of causation: everything that happens in the world of human affairs is determined by antecedent occurrences, and events of history are the illustrations or data of laws to be discovered, laws such as are found in hydraulics. It is true that no historian has ever been able to array the fullness of history as actuality in any such deterministic order; Karl Marx has gone further than any other. But under the hypothesis that it is possible, historians have been arranging events in neat little chains of causation which explain, to their satisfaction, why succeeding events happen; and they have attributed any shortcomings in result to the inadequacy of their known data, not to the falsity of the assumption on which they have been operating. Undiscouraged by their inability to bring all history within a single law, such as the law of gravitation, they have gone on working in the belief that the Newtonian trick will be turned some time, if the scientific method is applied long and rigorously enough and facts are heaped up high enough, as the succeeding grists of doctors of philosophy are ground out by the universities, turned loose on "research projects," and amply supplied by funds.

Growing rightly suspicious of this procedure in physico-historiography, a number of historians, still bent on servitude to natural science, turned from physics to biology. The difficulties and failures involved in all efforts to arrange the occurrences of history in a neat system of historical mechanics were evident to them. But on he other side, the achievements of the Darwinians were impressive. If the totality of history could not be brought into a deterministic system without doing violence to historical knowledge, perhaps the biological analogy of the organism could be applied. And this was done, apparently without any realization of the fact that thinking by analogy is a form of primitive animism. So under the biological analogy, history was conceived as a succession of cultural organisms rising, growing, competing, and declining. To this fantastic morphological assumption Spengler chained his powerful mind. Thus freed from self-imposed slavery to physics, the historian passed to self-imposed subservience to biology. Painfully aware of the perplexities encountered as long as he stuck to his own business, the historian sought escape by employing the method and thought of others whose operations he did not understand and could not control, on the simple, almost childlike, faith that the biologist, if not the physicist, really knew what he was about and could furnish the clue to the mystery.

But the shadow of the organismic conception of history had scarcely fallen on the turbulent actuality of history when it was scrutinized by historians who were thinking in terms of their own subject as distinguished from the terms of a mere subdivision of history. By an inescapable demonstration Kurt Riezler has made it clear that the organismic theory of history is really the old determinism of physics covered with murky words. The rise, growth, competition, and decline of cultural organisms is meaningless unless fitted into some overarching hypothesis—either the hypothesis of the divine drama or the hypothesis of causation in the deterministic sense. Is each cultural organism in history, each national or racial culture, an isolated particularity governed by its own mystical or physical laws? Knowledge of history as actuality forbids any such conclusion. If, in sheer desperation, the historian clings to the biological analogy, which school is he to follow–the mechanistic or the vitalistic? In either case he is caught in the deterministic sequence, if he thinks long enough and hard enough.

Hence the fate of the scientific school of historiography turns finally upon the applicability of the deterministic sequence to the totality of history as actuality. Natural science in a strict sense, as distinguished from mere knowledge of facts, can discover system and law only where occurrences are in reality arranged objectively in deterministic sequences. It can describe these sequences and draw from them laws, so-called. From a given number of the occurrences in any such sequence, science can predict what will happen when the remainder appear.

With respect to certain areas of human occurrences, something akin to deterministic sequences is found by the historian, but the perdurance of any sequence depends upon the perdurance in time of surrounding circumstances which cannot be brought within any scheme of deterministic relevancies. Certainly all the occurrences of history as actuality cannot be so ordered; most of them are unknown and owing to the paucity of records must forever remain unknown.

If a science of history were achieved, it would, like the science of celestial mechanics, make possible the calculable prediction of the future in history. It would bring the totality of historical occurrences within a single field and reveal the unfolding future to its last end, including all the apparent choices made and to be made. It would be omniscience. The creator of it would possess the attributes ascribed by the theologians to God. The future once revealed, humanity would have nothing to do except to await its doom.

To state the case is to dispose of it. The occurrences of history–the unfolding of ideas and interests in time-motion–are not identical in nature with the data of physics, and hence in their totality they are beyond the reach of that necessary instrument of natural science–mathematics–which cannot assign meaningful values to the imponderables, immeasurables, and contingencies of history as actuality.

Having broken the tyranny of physics and biology, contemporary thought in historiography turns its engines of verification upon the formula of historical relativity–the formula that makes all written history merely relative to time and circumstance, a passing shadow, an illusion. Contemporary criticism shows that the apostle of relativity is destined to be destroyed by the child of his own brain. If all historical conceptions are merely relative to passing events, to transitory phases of ideas and interests, then the conception of relativity is itself relative. When absolutes in history are rejected the absolutism of relativity is also rejected. So we must inquire: To what spirit of the times, to the ideas and interests of what class, group, nation, race, or region does the conception of relativity correspond? As the actuality of history moves forward into the future, the conception of relativity will also pass, as previous conceptions and interpretations of events have passed. Hence, according to the very doctrine of relativity, the skeptic of relativity will disappear in due course, beneath the ever-tossing waves of changing relativities. If he does not suffer this fate soon, the apostle of relativity will surely be executed by his own logic. Every conception of history, he says, is relative to time and circumstances. But by his own reasoning he is then compelled to ask: To what are these particular times and circumstances relative? And he must go on with receding sets of times and circumstances until he confronts an absolute: the totality of history as actuality which embraces all times and circumstances and all relativities.

Contemporary historical thought is, accordingly, returning upon itself and its subject matter. The historian is casting off his servitude to physics and biology, as he formerly cast off the shackles of theology and its metaphysics. He likewise sees the doctrine of relativity crumble in the cold light of historical knowledge. When he accepts none of the assumptions made by theology, physics, and biology, as applied to history, when he passes out from under the fleeting shadow of relativity, he confronts the absolute in his field—the absolute totality of all historical occurrences past, present, and becoming to the end of all things. Then he finds it necessary to bring the occurrences of history as actuality under one or another of three broad conceptions.

The first is that history as total actuality is chaos, perhaps with little islands of congruous relativities floating on the surface, and that the human mind cannot bring them objectively into any all-embracing order or subjectively into any consistent system. The second is that history as actuality is a part of some order of nature and revolves in cycles eternally—spring, summer, autumn, and winter, democracy, aristocracy, and monarchy, or their variants, as imagined by Spengler. The third is that history as actuality is moving in some direction away from the low level of primitive beginnings, on an upward gradient toward a more ideal order—as imagined by Condorcet, Adam Smith, Karl Marx, or Herbert Spencer.

Abundant evidence can be marshaled, has been marshaled, in support of each of these conceptions of history as actuality, but all the available evidence will not fit any one of them. The hypothesis of chaos admits of no ordering at all; hence those who operate under it cannot write history, although they may comment *on* history. The second admits of an ordering of events only by arbitrarily leaving out of account all the contradictions in the evidence. The third admits of an ordering of events, also by leaving contradictions out of consideration. The historian who writes history, therefore, consciously or unconsciously performs an act of faith, as to order and movement, for certainty as to order and movement is denied to him by knowledge of the actuality with which he is concerned. He is thus in the position of a statesman dealing with public affairs; in writing he acts and in acting he makes choices, large or small, timid or bold, with respect to some conception of the nature of things. And the degree of his influence and immortality will depend upon the length and correctness of his forecast—upon the verdict of history yet to come. His faith is at bottom a conviction that something true can be known about the movement of history and his conviction is a subjective decision, not a purely objective discovery.

But members of the passing generation will ask: Has our work done in the scientific spirit been useless? Must we abandon the scientific method? The answer is an emphatic negative. During the past fifty years historical scholarship, carried on with judicial calm, has wrought achievements of value beyond calculation. Particular phases of history once dark and confused have been illuminated by research, authentication, scrutiny, and the ordering of immediate relevancies. Nor is the empirical or scientific method to be abandoned. It is the only method that can be employed in obtaining accurate knowledge of historical facts, personalities, situations, and movements. It alone can disclose conditions that made possible what happened. It has a value in itself—a value high in the hierarchy of values indispensable to the life of a democracy. The inquiring spirit of science, using the scientific method, is the chief safeguard against the tyranny of authority, bureaucracy, and brute power. It can reveal by investigation necessities and possibilities in any social scene and also offerings with respect to desirabilities to be achieved within the limits of the possible.

The scientific method is, therefore, a precious and indispensable instrument of the human mind; without it society would sink down into primitive animism and barbarism. It is when this method, a child of the human brain, is exalted into a master and a tyrant that historical thought must enter a caveat. So the historian is bound by his craft to recognize the nature and limitations of the scientific method and to dispel the illusion that it can produce a science of history embracing the fullness of history, or of any large phase, as past actuality.

This means no abandonment of the tireless inquiry into objective realities, especially economic realities and relations; not enough emphasis has been laid upon the conditioning and determining influences of biological and economic necessities or upon researches designed to disclose them in their deepest and widest ramifications. This means no abandonment of the inquiry into the forms and development of ideas as conditioning and determining influences; not enough emphasis has been laid on this phase of history by American scholars.

But the upshot to which this argument is directed is more fundamental than any aspect of historical method.

It is that any selection and arrangement of facts pertaining to any large area of history, either local or world, race or class, is controlled inexorably by the frame of reference in the mind of the selector and arranger. This frame of reference includes things deemed necessary, things deemed possible, and things deemed desirable. It may be large, informed by deep knowledge, and illuminated by wide experience; or it may be small, uninformed, and unilluminated. It may be a grand conception of history or a mere aggregation of confusions. But it is there in the mind, inexorably. To borrow from Croce, when grand philosophy is ostentatiously put out at the front door of the mind, then narrow, class, provincial, and regional prejudices come in at the back door and dominate, perhaps only half-consciously, the thinking of the historian.

The supreme issue before the historian now is the determination of his attitude to the disclosures of contemporary thought. He may deliberately evade them for reasons pertaining to personal, economic and intellectual comfort, thus joining the innumerable throng of those who might have been but were not. Or he may proceed to examine his own frame of reference, clarify it, enlarge it by acquiring knowledge of greater areas of thought and events, and give it consistency of structure by a deliberate conjecture respecting the nature or direction of the vast movements of ideas and interests called world history.

This operation will cause discomfort to individual historians but all, according to the vows of their office, are under obligation to perform it, as Henry Adams warned the members of this Association in his letter of 1894. And as Adams then said, it will have to be carried out under the scrutiny of four great tribunals for the suppression of unwelcome knowledge and opinion: the church, the state, property, and labor. Does the world move and, if so, in what direction? If he believes that the world does not move, the historian must offer the pessimism of chaos to the inquiring spirit of mankind. If it does move, does it move backward toward some old arrangement, let us say, to 1928, 1896, 1815, 1789, or 1295? Or does it move forward to some other arrangement which can be only dimly divined—a capitalist dictatorship, a proletarian dictatorship, or a collectivist democracy? The last of these is my own guess, founded on a study of long trends and on a faith in the indomitable spirit of mankind. In any case, if the historian cannot know or explain history as actuality, he helps to make history, petty or grand.

To sum up contemporary thought in historiography, any written history involves the selection of a topic and an arbitrary delimitation of its borders—cutting off connections with the universal. Within the borders arbitrarily established, there is a selection and organization of facts by the processes of thought. This selection and organization—a single act—will be controlled by the historian's frame of reference composed of things deemed necessary and of things deemed desirable. The frame may be a narrow class, sectional, national, or group conception of history, clear and frank or confused and half-conscious, or it may be a large, generous conception, clarified by association with the great spirits of all ages. Whatever its nature the frame is inexorably there, in the mind. And in the frame only three broad conceptions of all history as actuality are possible. History is chaos and every attempt to interpret it otherwise is an illusion. History moves around in a kind of cycle. History moves in a line, straight or spiral, and in some direction. The historian may seek to escape these issues by silence or by a confession of avoidance or he may face them boldly, aware of the intellectual and moral perils inherent in any decision—in his act of faith.

2

The Rise of American Civilization

CHARLES AND MARY BEARD (1927)

Charles Beard has published more than any other American historian, in part because he resigned his Columbia professorship in his early forties and, in association with his wife, devoted the last thirty years of his life exclusively to research and writing. Beard became the best-known and most-read historian in the United States during the first half of the twentieth century. Although he produced books and articles over a span of five decades, and to some extent changed his views, it is nevertheless accurate to say that most of Beard's scholarship exemplified the precepts he

---

Reprinted by permission from *The Rise of American Civilization,* Macmillan, New York, 1930, one-volume edition, "The Agricultural Era," pp. 266-267, 291-296, 303-307, 309-311.

offered in "Written History as an Act of Faith." His writings provided a historical map of the terrain of reform, as he showed how progress had fought its way through jungles of opposition.

Beard's personal background was similar to many reformers of his generation: son of a "conservative" businessman, raised in a small midwestern town; a member of the great white, Anglo-Saxon, Protestant middle class, whose social conscience was awakened in the 1890s by first-hand observation of the tremendous poverty and suffering in big cities. After doing undergraduate work at a small Indiana school, at the turn of the century he studied in England where he helped organize the first Oxford college for workingmen, and he wrote and spoke in support of increased benefits for laborers. Beard's early subscription to the progressive faith which he expressed in his 1934 presidential address can be seen to derive from statements he made while in England in 1901. "The central theme of history," he wrote, was mankind's triumph over "priestcraft, feudal tyrants, and warring elements." Beard expressed the hope that, as the industrial revolution continued, "the people, instead of a few capitalists, would reap the benefits," and that modern technology would give "the material key to man's spiritual progress."

Beard returned to the United States in the early 1900s and began to write histories which documented the long struggle between the forces of light and darkness. His overall interpretation of America's past was that progress had occurred through social and intellectual conflict rooted ultimately in economic conflict. Clashes of opinion concerning social philosophy, domestic politics, and foreign policy were seen to be reflections of economic divisions. Beard viewed economic "have-not" groups, "liberal" social thinkers, political reformers, and supporters of a nonbelligerent foreign policy as agents of progress working toward a better society. He viewed economic "have" groups, "conservative" social thinkers, opponents of reform, and foreign policy imperialists as agents of reaction. Because the theme of conflict was central to Beard, he explored the defeats and obstacles of reformers as well as their victories. Indeed, if past defeats were to be avoided in the future, it was imperative to understand why they had occurred.

His characteristic interpretation can be seen in the following passages on the patriots during the American Revolution and on the background of the making of the Constitution. In the discussion of the Revolution, Beard accented differences among the colonists as to whether a domestic social revolution should accompany the external revolt against Great Britain. On the side of domestic reform were the common men whereas the men of large means resisted any alteration of the status quo except national independence. Beard concluded that in the end the Revolution effected progressive social reform as well as external freedom from England. He was sympathetic to the period of the Articles of Confederation because of the extent to which the various state governments were controlled by the masses of the people, and he denied the fact that without a strong centralized government the country would have been on the brink of ruin. When Beard moved to a discussion of the background of the making of the Constitution in the 1780s, he emphasized that those who were most dissatisfied with the Articles of Confederation were the business and financial interests. These dissatisfied economic interests represented "conservative" social classes who feared the democratic impulses which had been released by the Revolution and which were allowed to develop under the decentralized state governments of the Articles. The movement to make a more centralized, less democratic Constitution was therefore in effect a successful counter-revolt against the spirit of the egalitarian Declaration of Independence and the Revolution.

...Everywhere the supporters of the Revolution were divided into conservative and radical wings, the former composed mainly of merchants and men of substance and the latter of mechanics and yeomen-farmers, sometimes led by men of the other group. In Massachusetts an insurgent left wing drew up a state constitution pleasing to the politicians but was not strong enough to force its adoption. By a skillful combination, the aristocracy of "wealth and talents" defeated the plan and substituted a system which safeguarded the rights and privileges of property at every bastion. Morison describes the instrument briefly: "The Constitution of 1780 was a lawyers' and merchants' constitution, directed toward something like quarterdeck efficiency in government and the protection of property against democratic pirates."

Pennsylvania was harassed by similar factions–sharply marked in their divisions and violent in their relations–which engaged in long and unseemly wrangles on every issue of the hour. At one time the revolutionary government itself was assailed by a still more revolutionary group and blood was shed. Even after astute management had restored calm among the patriots, local conflicts continued to consume the energies of their leaders until independence was finally won. For this reason, among others, Pennsylvania, though ranking among the largest and richest states, was constantly hampered in complying with the requests of the Continental Congress.

Nor were the Southern States any more fortunate. Throughout the war a desperate struggle was waged in Virginia between planters on the seaboard and small farmers of the interior–"a struggle which involved nothing less than a revolution in the social order of the Old Dominion with its Established Church and its landed aristocracy." As a result many historic families on the coastal plain hated Thomas Jefferson and Patrick Henry far more than they did the Englishmen who served as the king's officers.

A kindred spirit flamed out in South Carolina, where slave-owners of the lowlands and merchants of the towns engaged in almost daily contests with mechanics from the shops and farmers from the back country. On one occasion, the heat of the dispute moved even Gadsden, a leader of the radicals, to inquire "whether there is not a danger amongst us far more dangerous than anything that can arise from the whole herd of Contemptible, exportable Tories." So threatening in fact was the menace–a group of "levelers" bent on overthrowing the aristocracy of "wealth and talents"–that the notables of the state had to exercise considerable skill in saving their privileges and prestige. . . .

Within each state, no less than in external relations, the Revolution started a dislocation of authority–a phase of the eventful years which the historians, too long concentrating on spectacular episodes, have just begun to appreciate. The shifts and cracks in the social structure produced by the cataclysm were not all immediately evident; half a century passed before the leveling democracy proclaimed in Jefferson's Declaration of Independence came flooding into power. But still the states of the confederation differed as much from the colonial provinces of Governor Shirley's time as the France of Louis Philippe, hero of the green umbrella, did from the régime of Louis XV. Just as the French Revolution sent émigrés fleeing into Germany and England, so the American Revolution drove out about one hundred thousand high Tories of the old school. By breaking the grip of English economic and political adventurers on the spoils of America, it brought into power new men with new principles and standards of conduct.

It is true that, in the severe and sometimes savage contests between the conservative and radical supporters of the Revolution, the former were generally the victors for the moment and were able to write large their views of economic rights in the first state constitutions. Broadly speaking, only taxpayers or property owners were given the ballot as in colonial times and only men of substantial wealth were made eligible to public office. But in many cases the qualifications were lowered and the structure of the old social system seriously undermined.

Above all, the spirit of domestic politics, especially in the royal provinces, was distinctly altered by the sudden removal of the British ruling class–a class accustomed to a barbarous criminal code, a narrow and intolerant university system, a government conceived as a huge aggregation of jobs and privileges, a contempt for men and women who toiled in field and shop, a denial of education to the masses, an Established religion forced alike on Dissenters and Catholics, a dominion of squire and parson in counties and villages, callous brutality in army and navy, a scheme of primogeniture buttressing the rule of the landed gentry, a swarm of hungry placemen offering sycophancy to the king in exchange for offices, sinecures, and pensions, and a constitution of church and state so ordered as to fasten upon the masses this immense pile of pride and plunder. From the weight of this mountain the American revolutionists delivered the colonial subjects of the British Crown. Within a decade or two after that emancipation they accomplished reforms in law and policy which required a hundred years or more of persistent agitation to effect in the mother country—reforms which gave to the statesmen who led in the agitation their title to immortality in English history.

Naturally the American Revolution, a movement carried to its bitter end by the bayonets of fighting farmers, even though it was started by protesting merchants and rioting mechanics, wrought a far-reaching transformation in the land system that had been developed under British inspiration and control. With engaging conciseness, these changes have been summarized in J. Franklin Jameson's admirable little book on The American Revolution Considered as a Social Movement. First of all, royal limitations on the seizure and enjoyment of vacant lands—notably the prohibition upon the free settlement of regions beyond the Alleghenies contained in the proclamation of 1763—were swept away; and at the same time the "vast domains of the Crown" were vested in the hands of the state legislatures to be dedicated to the uses of their constituents.

Secondly, the quitrents paid to the king and to proprietary families, the Penns and the Baltimores, by farmers and planters according to their acreage were simply abolished, relieving Americans of an annual charge approximating a hundred thousand dollars a year. Thirdly, the rule and the practice of reserving for the royal navy white pine trees suitable for masts were abrogated without ceremony, releasing landowners from an irksome restriction. In the fourth place, there was a smashing confiscation of Tory estates, including Sir William Pepperell's Maine holdings extending thirty miles along the coast, the Phillipse heritage in New York embracing about three hundred square miles, the property of the Penn family worth in round numbers five million dollars, and the Fairfax estate in Virginia stretching out like a province. All in all, the Tories reckoned their losses at no less than forty million dollars and the British Parliament, after scaling their demands to the minimum, granted the claimants fifteen million dollars by way of compensation.

In harmony with their principles, the Revolutionists who made this huge sequestration of property distributed the land by sales in small lots on generous terms to enterprising farmers. The principality of Roger Morris in New York, for example, was divided into no less than two hundred and fifty parcels, while a still larger number of farms was created out of the confiscated holdings of James De Lancey.

Finally, among the effects of the Revolution on agricultural economy, must be reckoned the abolition of the system of entails and primogeniture. Whereas it took a century of debate and then the corroding taxes of a World War to drive a wedge into the concentrated land monopoly of England, the American Revolutionists brought many an ancient structure to earth by swift and telling blows. Three months after he penned the Declaration of Independence, Jefferson opened a war on the entailed estates of the Old Dominion, to the horror of the best people; and before the lapse of a year he pushed through the legislature an act which accomplished his radical design, releasing from entail "at least half, and possibly three-quarters of the entire 'seated' area of Virginia." Within ten years "every state had abolished entails excepting two, and those were two in which entails were rare. In fifteen years every state, without exception, abolished primogeniture"–all save four placing daughters on an equality with sons in the distribution of landed inheritances.

Considered relatively, therefore, the destruction of landed privilege in America by the forces unchained in the War for Independence was perhaps as great and as significant as the change wrought in the economic status of the clergy and nobility during the holocaust of the French Revolution. As in France country lawyers and newly rich merchants swarmed over the seats of the once proud aristocracy, so in the United States during and after the cataclysm a host of groundlings fresh from the plow and counting house surged over the domains of the Jessups, De Lanceys, and Morrises. When members of the best families of France turned to tutoring and translating in London for a livelihood or to teaching dancing and manners in America, in the days of Danton, Marat, and Robespierre, they found ladies and gentlemen who sighed for good old colonial days ready to join them in cursing the rights of man.

The clergy as well as the landed gentry felt the shocks of the American Revolution. When the crisis opened, nine of the thirteen colonies had established churches. In New Hampshire, Massachusetts, and Connecticut it was the Congregationalists that enjoyed this legal privilege, while in Virginia Maryland, New York, the Carolinas, and Georgia it was the Episcopalians who claimed a monopoly on religion supported by taxes. Before the echoes of Lexington and Concord had died away, an attack on ecclesiastical establishments was launched, and in five of the states where the Anglican clergy possessed privileges and immunities under the law dissenters, outnumbering their opponents, were quickly victorious. In Virginia, however, where the Anglican party was strong, and in New England, where the Congregationalists enjoyed a supremacy, every clerical redoubt was stubbornly defended.

It took a struggle of more than half a century in the mother country to win political equality for Catholics and Dissenters, and to sweep away tithes for the support of an official religion. The twentieth century opened before France, going beyond England in her evolution, could put asunder Church and State. Only ten years sufficed to carry through the legislature Jefferson's "Statute of Virginia for Religious Freedom," and before the nineteenth century had far advanced, the Congregationalists were finally disestablished–in New Hampshire in 1817, in Connecticut the following year, and in Massachusetts in 1833. So before Jefferson's death Episcopalians could enjoy in Connecticut liberties they had once withheld in Virginia.

In law as in religion the light of reason was being turned on ancient customs. During this stirring period of intellectual and spiritual awakening, the British government was making its penal code more and more savage; when George III came to the throne in 1760 there were about one hundred and sixty offenses for which men, women, and children were put to death; before the end of his reign nearly one hundred new offenses were added to this appalling list.

Although the American colonists had never been so sweeping in their vengeful passions as English lawmakers, they too had adopted penal codes of shocking brutality–codes that loomed black and ominous against the new faith in the common run of mankind. Deeply moved by this incongruity, the impetuous Jefferson, to whom at least his Declaration was no mere mass of glittering generalities, hastened away from Philadelphia soon after independence to start the revolution in the legal system of Virginia. On his arrival he announced that the law must be reformed root and branch "with a single eye to reason and the good of those for whose government it was framed," so alarming the bench and bar by his rashness that it took him twenty years to gain his principal points. In the other states a similar campaign was waged against the barbarities of the statute books, now swiftly, now tardily casting into oblivion great fragments of the cruel heritage. Even at the worst the emancipated colonists were in most matters respecting criminal legislation half a century ahead of the mother country.

Indeed, in nearly every branch of enlightened activity, in every sphere of liberal thought, the American Revolution marked the opening of a new humane epoch. Slavery, of course, afforded a glaring contrast to the grand doctrines of the Revolution, but still it must be noted that Jefferson and his friends were painfully aware of the anachronism; that Virginia prohibited the slave trade in 1778–a measure which the British Crown had vetoed twenty years before; that a movement for the abolition of slavery appeared among the new social forces of the age; and that it was the lofty doctrines of the Revolution which were invoked by Lincoln when in the fullness of time chattel bondage was to be finally broken. If a balance sheet is struck and the rhetoric of the Fourth of July celebrations is discounted, if the externals of the conflict are given a proper perspective in the background, then it is seen that the American Revolution was more than a war on England. It was in truth an economic, social, and intellectual transformation of prime significance–the first of those modern world-shaking reconstructions in which mankind has sought to cut and fashion the tough and stubborn web of fact to fit the pattern of its dreams. . . .

[After the survey above of the Revolution, Beard summarized the state of government under the Articles of Confederation. Although he admitted the lack of centralized authority under the Articles, Beard denied that chaos was imminent.]

Undoubtedly the period that followed the close of the Revolutionary War was one of dissolution and reconstruction; that is the story of every great social dislocation. Still there is much evidence to show that the country was in many respects steadily recovering order and prosperity even under the despised Articles of Confederation. If seven of the thirteen states made hazardous experiments with paper money, six clung to more practical methods and two or three of those that had embarked on unlimited inflation showed signs of turning back on their course. While a few states displayed a heartless negligence in paying their revolutionary debts, others gave serious attention to the matter. Though the efforts of the Congress to secure larger powers over taxation and commerce were defeated, an agreement on some control over foreign trade was almost in sight when the constitutional convention was summoned by men impatient with delay. The very fact that the convention could be assembled was in itself evidence of a changing spirit in the country.

On the whole, the economic condition of the country seemed to be improving. No doubt shipping in New England and manufacturing in general suffered from the conflicting tariff policies, domestic and foreign, which followed the war, but, at the opening of 1787, Benjamin Franklin declared that the prosperity of the nation was so great as to call for thanksgiving. According to his judgment, the market reports then showed that the farmers were never better paid for their produce, that farm lands were continually rising in value, and that in no part of Europe were the laboring poor in such a fortunate state. Admitting that there were economic grievances in some quarters, Franklin expressed a conviction that the country at large was in a sound condition.

Nearly a hundred years after Franklin's time a learned, if controversial, historian, Henry B. Dawson, on the basis of minute researches, made out a very good argument to the effect that the "chaos" of the "critical period" was largely a figment of political imagination. Whatever the verdict on this point may be, the difficulty with which the Constitution was "wrung" from a reluctant people and the existence of a large body of voters aggressively opposed to the change will put the prudent inquirer on his guard against the easy assumption that the entire country was seized with a poignant sense of impending calamity.

Nevertheless, when the best possible case is made for the critical period, there remain standing in the record of those years certain impressive facts that cannot be denied or explained away. Beyond all question the financiers had grounds for complaint. Though the principal of the continental debt was slightly reduced under the confederation, the arrears of interest increased nearly fourfold and the unpaid interest on the foreign obligations piled steadily higher. In an equally chaotic condition were the current finances. The Congress in due course made requisitions on the states to pay its bills, but it was fortunate if it received in any year one-fourth of the amount demanded, and during the last fourteen months of its life less than half a million in paper money was paid into the treasury—not enough to meet the interest on the foreign debt alone.

Hence all who held claims against the confederacy had sufficient cause for discontent. Holders of government bonds, both original subscribers who had made sacrifices and speculators who had bought up depreciated paper by the ream, had good reasons for desiring a change in the existing form of government. To them were added the soldiers of the late revolutionary army, especially the officers whose bonus of full pay for five years still remained in the form of paper promises.

Industry and commerce as well as government finances were in a state of depression. When peace came and the pent-up flood of British goods burst in upon the local market, greatly to the joy of the farmers and planters, American manufacturers, who had built up enterprises of no little importance during the suspension of British trade, found their monopoly of domestic business rudely broken. Nothing but a protective tariff, they thought, could save them from ruin. In the same category of the distressed were American shipowners and factors engaged in foreign trade, especially the ubiquitous Yankees who now suffered from discriminations as aliens in the ports of the British empire. In spite of heroic efforts they could not effect a return to prosperity; nor was there any sign of relief in sight as long as the Congress under the Articles of Confederation possessed no power to enact retaliatory measures calculated to bring foreign countries to terms.

In an equally unhappy position were the domestic merchants. They had at hand no national currency uniform in value through the length and breadth of the land—nothing but a curious collection of coins uncertain in weight, shaven by clippers, debased by counterfeiters, and paper notes fluctuating as new issues streamed from the press. Worse than the monetary system were the impediments in the way of interstate commerce. Under local influences legislatures put tariffs on goods coming in from neighboring states just as on foreign imports, waged commercial wars of retaliation on one another, raised and lowered rates as factional disputes oscillated, reaching such a point in New York that duties were levied on firewood from Connecticut and cabbages from New Jersey.

If a merchant surmounted the obstacles placed in his way by anarchy in the currency and confusion in tariff schedules and succeeded in building up an interstate business, he never could be sure of collections, for he was always at the mercy of local courts and juries—agencies that were seldom tender in dealing with the claims and rights of distant creditors as against the clamors of their immediate neighbors. While the Articles of Confederation lasted there was no hope of breaching such invincible barriers to the smooth and easy transaction of interstate business.

Other economic groups likewise had powerful motives for desiring a change in the form of government. Money lenders who held outstanding notes and mortgages objected to receiving in payment paper bills emitted by the treasuries of the agrarian states and demanded a limitation on their right to issue such legal tenders. In a plight no less distressing were the British creditors and Americans to whom British claims had been transferred. Checked by the hostility of state legislatures and local courts, they were usually unable to collect debts solemnly recognized by the treaty of peace and they could hope for no adequate settlement, especially in the South, while the confederation endured. Loyalists who had lost property during the Revolution suffered similar handicaps in the presence of local judges and jurors. Finally, the officers and soldiers, who held land warrants issued to them in return for their war services, and capitalists engaged in western land speculation could count on no realization of their claims until there was a national army strong enough to suppress the hostile Indians on the frontier.

In short, the financial, creditor, commercial, and speculating classes in the new confederate republic were harassed during the critical period just as such classes had been harassed by rebellious patriots on the eve of the

Revolution. From every point of view, as they saw the matter, they had valid reasons for wanting to establish under their own auspices on American soil a system of centralized political, judicial, and economic control similar in character to that formerly exercised by Great Britain. They wanted debts paid, a sound currency established, commerce regulated, paper money struck down, and western lands properly distributed; they desired these things quite as much as the governing classes of England had desired them in colonial times. No more than the stoutest Tory of London or Boston did they relish agrarian politics; commerce simply could not thrive in that economic atmosphere. Those who sponsored business enterprise accordingly demanded new central organs of power and control and fresh restraints on the leveling tendencies of local legislatures generally dominated by farmers . . . .

Such were the circumstances in which rose and flourished a movement for a drastic revision of the Articles of Confederation . . . .

Among the many historic assemblies which have wrought revolutions in the affairs of mankind, it seems safe to say that there has never been one that commanded more political talent, practical experience, and sound substance than the Philadelphia convention of 1787 [which met to revise the Articles of Confederation]. In all, sixty-two delegates were formally appointed by the states; fifty-five attended the sessions with more or less regularity; and thirty-nine signed the final draft of the new Constitution. On the list were men trained in war and diplomacy, skilled in legislation and administration, versed in finance and commerce, and learned in the political philosophy of their own and earlier times. Seven had been governors of states and at least twenty-eight had served in the Congress of the union either during the Revolution or under the Articles of Confederation. Eight had been signers of the Declaration of Independence. At the head stood Washington, who, with one voice, was chosen president of the convention. Among those who sat under him were such men as the two Morrises, the two Pinckneys, Madison, Hamilton, Franklin, Rutledge, Gerry, Ellsworth, Wilson, Randolph, Wythe, Dickinson, and Sherman, nearly all of whom represented the conservative wing of the old revolutionary party.

At all events none of the fiery radicals of 1774 was present. Jefferson, then serving as the American minister in Paris, was out of the country, Patrick Henry was elected but refused to attend because, he said, he "smellt a rat"; Samuel Adams was not chosen; Thomas Paine left for Europe that very year to exhibit an iron bridge which he had designed and to wage war on tyranny across the sea. So the Philadelphia assembly, instead of being composed of left-wing theorists, was made up of practical men of affairs—holders of state and continental bonds, money lenders, merchants, lawyers, and speculators in the public land—who could speak with knowledge and feeling about federation. More than half the delegates in attendance were either investors or speculators in the public securities which were to be buoyed up by the new Constitution. All knew by experience the relation of property to government.

[The result of the Philadelphia convention, according to Beard, was a Constitution designed to protect the interests of the "conservative" well-to-do few rather than the masses of the people.]

3

Main Currents in American Thought

VERNON LOUIS PARRINGTON (1927-1930)

Vernon Louis Parrington (1871-1929) was a virtually unknown professor of English at the University of Washington in Seattle in his late fifties when he published the first two volumes of what quickly became the most popular history of ideas ever written in the United States. Colorfully written, and saturated with vehement moral judgments, Parrington's interpretation of American thought strikingly complemented Beard's political history. Parrington agreed with Beard that history was a series of conflicts between rival social groups and ideas which were rooted in economic conditions. Parrington was even more emphatic than Beard in concluding that these conflicts generally pitted the forces of justice and humanitarianism against those of selfishness. However, Parrington was much gloomier than was Beard during the 1920s in assessing the success of democracy in America.

Parrington's personal background was much like Beard's. He was raised in Kansas, was the son of a Republican lawyer and judge, and was an undergraduate at the College of Emporia prior to transferring to Harvard in 1891. After graduation, he taught English at Emporia, the University of Oklahoma, and for the last two decades of his life at the University of Washington. More aesthetic than political as a student and young professor,

---

Parrington became politically interested and sympathetic to reform in the late 1890s. By the early 1900s he had started to develop his economic interpretation of the growth of American ideas and literature which was to be expressed finally in *Main Currents in American Thought.* "The past five years," Parrington wrote in a letter in 1918, "I have spent in study and writing, up to my ears in the economic interpretation of American history and literature, getting the last lingering Harvard prejudices out of my system." As Parrington continued the letter to his former Harvard classmates, he made it clear that his economic interpretation was closely related to strong sentiments favoring democratic reform. "I become more radical with each year," he wrote, "and more impatient with the smug Tory culture which we were fed on as undergraduates." By 1918 Harvard appeared to Parrington to be "a liability rather than an asset to the cause of democracy," because the school seemed to him "the apologist and advocate of capitalistic exploitation." Clearly, Parrington's sympathies were on the side of reform.

His economic interpretation was part of his pragmatic conception of the role of ideas in history. "[Ideas] are weapons hammered out on the anvil of human needs," Parrington wrote, "not godlings that spring perfect-winged from the head of Jove." Consequently, Parrington argued that it was necessary not only to examine the ideas in history, but also to investigate the "social forces" which conditioned ideas. The most important of all the social forces, said Parrington, in agreement with Beard, was the economic.

The first two volumes of *Main Currents in American Thought,* which were published in 1927, covered the years from colonial settlement to the Civil War, with an incomplete third volume published posthumously in 1930 containing fragments touching upon the late 1800s and early 1900s. Parrington's theme was the conflict between progress and reaction, in which reason, optimism, democracy, and intellectual freedom were joined in combat with irrationality, pessimism, aristocracy, and religious dogmatism. Parrington characterized Puritan religious ideas as inert and useless mountains of rock serving mainly as a bastion to wall New England in and close from its sight the expanded horizons of a changing post-Renaissance world. The eighteenth century happily developed an ampler body of thought, with a more generous view of man's ability to shape his institutions anew in order to promote justice and liberalize his society. After arriving at a Jeffersonian and Jacksonian zenith, American democracy was confronted by a new acquisitive spirit in the nineteenth century. According to Parrington, private self-interest and consolidation largely smothered the liberating impulses set loose by Revolutionary thought. The Civil War era was unfortunately a continuation of this licentious acquisitive spirit, in which the Northern "imperialistic" industrial capitalism vanquished the Southern "imperialistic" agrarian slavocracy.

In the following passages, selected from his final, uncompleted third volume, Parrington expressed his criticism of the materialism and political selfishness of the dominant late-nineteenth-century mood, and he explained the lack of social idealism in terms of the capitalistic environment. Political thought came to be nothing more than a rationalization of dominant economic interests. The bright side of the Gilded Age was the agrarian protest against the politics of plutocracy which perpetuated Jeffersonian and Jacksonian idealism and which laid the foundations for the successful democratic progressive reforms of the early twentieth century.

It is, perhaps, not extreme to interpret the political history of America since 1790 as largely a struggle between the spirit of the Declaration of Independence and the spirit of the Constitution, the one primarily concerned with the rights of men, the other more practically concerned with the rights of property. The humanitarian idealism of the Declaration has always echoed as a battle-cry in the hearts of those who dream of an America dedicated to democratic ends. It cannot be long ignored or repudiated, for sooner or later it returns to plague the councils of practical politics. It is constantly breaking out in fresh revolt. When the major parties have grown callous and indifferent to the wishes of the common people, it has reformulated its principles in third-party platforms. Without its freshening influence our political history would have been much more sordid and materialistic. With the exception of such sporadic outbursts as Antimasonry and Know-nothingism, the third-party movements of the nineteenth century were democratic movements, inspired by a sense of social justice, founded on the Declaration of Independence, and promulgated to recall the American people to their heritage of idealism. The Locofoco party, the Freesoil party, the early Republican party, the Greenback party, the Populist party, the Progressive party, however they differed in immediate programs, have had a common objective, namely to set man above property as the great object of governmental concern, and preserve in America the democratic principle of equal opportunity.

Despite the fact that they failed in their immediate objectives they served the larger purpose of reminding the major parties that America professes to be a democratic country, and that party platforms must be brought to square with that fact. Thus interpreted the history of party struggle since 1790 falls into three broad phases: the Jeffersonian movement that established the ideal of political democracy; the Jacksonian movement that established equalitarianism crudely in practice; and the successive third-party movements that attempted, in successive reactions, to regain such ground as had been lost, to extend the field, and to perfect the machinery of democratic government. Since the rise of the slavery controversy the major parties, allied with masterful economic groups, have persistently ignored the Declaration of Independence, and repudiated in practice the spirit of democracy. To prevent if possible so grave a treason to our traditional ideals, to assert the rights of the common man against the encroachments of a class, has been therefore the common mission of the third-party movements. The significance of their somewhat scanty success is something the thoughtful American may interpret as he will. . . .

In 1865 the Republican party was no other than a war machine that had accomplished its purpose. It was a political mongrel, without logical cohesion, and it seemed doomed to break up as the Whig party had broken up and the Federalist party had broken up. But fate was now on the side of the Whigs as it had not been earlier. The democratic forces had lost strength from the war, and democratic principles were in ill repute. The drift to centralization, the enormous development of capitalism, the spirit of exploitation, were prophetic of a changing temper that was preparing to exalt the doctrine of manifest destiny which the Whig party stood sponsor for. The middle class was in the saddle and it was time to bring the political state under its control. The practical problem of the moment was to transform the mongrel Republican party into a strong cohesive instrument, and to accomplish that it was necessary to hold the loyalty of its Democratic voters amongst the farmers and working-classes whilst putting into effect its Whig program.

Under normal conditions the thing would have been impossible, but the times were wrought up and blindly passionate and the politicians skillful. The revolt of Andrew Johnson came near to bringing the party on the rocks; but the undisciplined Jacksonians were overthrown by the appeal to the Bloody Flag and put to flight by the nomination of General Grant for the presidency. The rebellion of the Independent Republicans under Horace Greeley in 1872 was brought to nothing by the skillful use of Grant's military prestige, and the party passed definitely under the control of capitalism, and became such an instrument for exploitation as Henry Clay dreamed of but could not perfect. Under the nominal leadership of the easy-going Grant a loose rein was given to Whiggish ambitions and the Republican party became a political instrument worthy of the Gilded Age. . . .

It is plain as a pikestaff why the spirit of Whiggery should have taken riotous possession of the Gilded Age. With its booming industrial cities America in 1870 was fast becoming capitalistic, and in every capitalistic society Whiggery springs up as naturally as pigweed in a garden. However attractive the disguises it may assume, it is in essence the logical creed of the profit philosophy. It is the expression in politics of the acquisitive instinct and it assumes as the greatest good the shaping of public policy to promote private interests. It asserts that it is a duty of the state to help its citizens to make money, and it conceives of the political state as a useful instrument for effective exploitation. How otherwise? The public good cannot be served apart from business interests, for business interests are the public good and in serving business the state is serving society. Everybody's eggs are in the basket and they must not be broken. For a capitalistic society Whiggery is the only rational politics, for it exalts the profit-motive as the sole object of parlimentary concern. Government has only to wave its wand and fairy gifts descend upon business like the golden sands of Pactolus. It graciously bestows its tariffs and subsidies, and streams of wealth flow into private wells.

But unhappily there is a fly in the Whiggish honey. In a competitive order, government is forced to make its choices. It cannot serve both Peter and Paul. If it gives with one hand it must take away with the other. And so the persuasive ideal of paternalism in the common interest degenerates in practice into legalized favoritism. Governmental gifts go to the largest investments. Lesser interests are sacrificed to greater interests and Whiggery comes finally to serve the lords of the earth without whose good will the wheels of business will not turn. To him that hath shall be given. If the few do not prosper the many will starve, and if the many have bread who would begrudge the few their abundance? In Whiggery is the fulfillment of the Scriptures.

Henry Clay had been a prophetic figure pointing the way America was to travel; but he came a generation too soon. A son of the Gilded Age, he was doomed to live in a world of Jacksonian democracy. But the spirit of Henry Clay survived his death and his followers were everywhere in the land. The plain citizen who wanted a slice of the rich prairie land of Iowa or Kansas, with a railway convenient to his homestead, had learned to look to the government for a gift, and if he got his quarter-section and his transportation he was careless about what the other fellow got. A little more or less could make no difference to a country inexhaustible in resources. America belonged to the American people and not to the government, and resources in private hands paid taxes and increased the national wealth. In his favorite newspaper, the *New York Tribune,* he read daily appeals for the adoption of a patriotic national economy, by means of which an infant industrialism, made prosperous by a protective tariff, would provide a home market for the produce of the farmer and render the country self-sufficient. Money would thus be put in everybody's pocket. Protection was not robbing Peter to pay Paul, but paying both Peter and Paul out of the augmented wealth of the whole.

The seductive arguments that Horace Greeley disseminated amongst the plain people, Henry Carey purveyed to more intelligent ears. The most distinguished American economist of the time, Carey had abandoned his earlier *laissez-faire* position, and having convinced himself that only through a close-knit national economy could the country develop a well-rounded economic program, he had become the most ardent of protectionists. During the fifties and later he was tireless in popularizing the doctrine of a natural harmony of interests between agriculture and manufacturing, and to a generation expanding rapidly in both fields his able presentation made great appeal. It was but a step from protectionism to governmental subsidies. . . .

When the social fabric is being torn rudely across by a changing economics, political theory and practice will suffer from the attendant confusions. The America of the Gilded Age accounted itself a democracy and was outwardly content to make use of the familiar democratic machinery; but until it was determined whether majority or minority rule should prevail, whether the well-being of the many or the property of the few should be the chief object of government, there would be no serious effort to create a political state for adequate social control. In the meantime the old individualisms would range the land seeking what they might devour, and the common attitude toward the political state would remain one of good-natured contempt. A shambling government, corrupt and incompetent, awakened no man's hope or pride, and amidst the slovenly anarchisms of the times, with a crude exploitation in the saddle, the state would be pretty much ignored except when its services might prove useful to such exploitation. The plutocracy would oppose the erection of a vigorous state until such time as it felt strong enough to control its activities. The principle of the majority-will held grave potentialities that might threaten the eventual mastership of wealth, and until the plutocracy had created its strongholds within the framework of the democracy it would bitterly oppose any extension of democratic control.

Broadly two great movements were going forward side by side in the unconscious drift of political tendency—the democratic and the plutocratic. The former, drawn chiefly from agrarian and labor elements with a considerable following of the middle and professional classes, was determined to carry forward and supplement the Jacksonian movement. It was honestly concerned for the development of the democratic principle. It would purify government by the application of civil service reform, it would steadily enlarge the bounds of social control of economic forces, and it would strengthen the political state to enable it to cope with corporate wealth and constrain the ambitions of the plutocracy into conformity with democratic ends. To such a democratic program the plutocracy was necessarily opposed. It professed the warmest loyalty to the abstract principle of democracy while bending every energy to emasculate effective democratic control. The problem confronting it was the familiar Federalistic problem–how to protect the minority from the majority and set property interests above human interests; but the problem had been immensely complicated by the strategic advances made by democracy. The democratic principle could not be easily thrust aside, it must be undermined. And so while awaiting the time when it should be strong enough to set up boldly its mastery of society, plutocracy took refuge in two principles, the superman theory and the *laissez-faire* theory, both of which it asserted to be democratic, the very essence of democracy. The former was "The public be damned" theory, which held that the economic leaders of society must be left free to manage their properties as they saw fit; and the latter was the familiar doctrine of individual initiative, that looked with suspicion on any interference by the political state with economic activity. If a bureaucracy may stick its nose into the citizen's private affairs what becomes of individual liberty?

But the plutocracy was building its real defenses elsewhere. Shrewdly aware of the potentialities of a Constitution that had been designed for the protection of property interests, it followed two main lines of development: it furthered the popular development of a cult of the Constitution by praising the excellence of a system of checks and balances, and spreading the view that to tamper with any provisions of the instrument was little short of sacrilege; and at the same time it bent every energy to extend the range of judicial prerogative and bring the legislative branch under control of the judiciary. It sought extra-constitutional indulgences that were dispensed by the courts in the name of the police power. The way had been prepared by Marbury vs. Madison and Dred Scott vs. Sanford, and during the Gilded Age a broad path to judicial control was opened by the elaboration of the "due process of law" principle discovered in the fourteenth amendment. With the development of the plutocracy the extension of the doctrine of judicial review went forward rapidly, providing an impregnable defense for property interests that promised ill for the principle of democratic control in the interests of the common well-being. The democracy was being driven from the inner keep of the castle. . . .

The quarter-century between the panic of 1873 that rudely disturbed the revelry of the Great Barbecue, and the campaign of 1896 that broke the agrarian opposition to capitalism, was marked by a fierce agrarian attempt to nullify in America the law of concentration. The silent drift toward plutocracy was too evident to escape comment even in the Gilded Age, and the ideal of plutocracy was too repugnant to a people drenched in Jeffersonian and Jacksonian prejudices to escape bitter hostility. The pursuit of wealth was an accepted democratic right, but it was assumed to be a fair race and no favors. The use of the political state by greater wealth to lay handicaps on lesser wealth had not been in the reckoning, and the law of progress that diminished the number of beneficiaries from the national policy of preëmption and exploitation had not been so interpreted. Something was wrong with a progress that augmented poverty as it increased wealth, and with the alarmist cry in their ears—the rich are growing richer and the poor poorer—the untutored democracy of the seventies and the eighties turned to question the drift of tendency that quite evidently was transforming a democratic people into a vast engulfing plutocracy. An older agrarian America was confronted by a younger capitalistic one, and the conflict of ideals and purposes was certain to bring on a bitter debate.

In the fierce struggle that turmoiled the politics of three decades the democracy went into battle as ill-equipped intellectually as it had been a hundred years before in the struggle over the Constitution. It was reaping the harvest of the long Jacksonian slackness that, content with the vote, had given no thought to the ultimate program of democracy but had suffered the lawyers to have their way. The Enlightenment had long since been submerged by Whiggish ambitions, and since the days of the Abolition Movement there had been no serious consideration of political theory. The success of the Jacksonian revolution had brought about its undoing. The abstract principle of democracy having won common acceptance, it was assumed to be competent to shift for itself. But unfortunately a supposedly democratic state was functioning under a Constitution designed to thwart democracy, and, interpreted by lawyers, it buttressed the rights of property far more securely than the rights of man. Within this fundamental law capitalism had long been entrenching itself. Its stronghold could not be taken by frontal attack and its flanks were protected by the courts that had assumed the high prerogative of voiding statutory enactments by judicial decree. As a result in no other country was capitalism so safeguarded from hostile attack; it plowed its fields and gathered its harvests secure from disturbance.

Unfortunately the political state did not realize that it was not in reality the democracy it professed to be. The most intelligent liberalism of the times, failing to take into account the economic basis of politics, was satisfied to spend its energy in Civil Service Reform and similar tinkering with the political machinery, convinced that it was only necessary to recover the old aristocratic sense of responsibility in political agents to perfect a democratic government. Not till another generation did liberalism come to understand that the democratic program was still largely unfulfilled, and set about in all earnestness to complete it; but that did not happen till the philosophy of democracy had been far more adequately explored and the simple faith of Jacksonianism had been instructed by the experience of other lands. Popular discontent with the drift toward plutocracy was intensified by the successive economic crises that marked the transition from agrarianism to capitalism. The gospel of progress, it seems, had not taken due account of the price that must be paid in social disturbances, and the breakdowns of 1873-1879 and 1887-1896 with their harsh dislocations aroused a spirit of revolt that issued in broad popular movements. Those movements spun the thread of liberalism that runs through the years from the Gilded Age to the World War–a thread woven by the earlier liberalism that came from the frontier, and the new collectivistic theories that came from Europe. In the eighties and nineties it was still largely native agrarian, but in the early years of the new century it drew heavily on the proletarian philosophies of Europe–seeking to apply old-world experience to American problems. Through it all runs increasingly a note of sobering realism. After a hundred years political romanticism was slowly dying in America. . . .

With its heritage of Jacksonianism it was natural for the agrarian movement to attempt to carry further the exploration of the democratic principle, seeking to complete the program that had been left unfulfilled by the Fathers. There were few as yet who questioned the finality of democracy as a political system or its adequacy to all social needs. The growing evils of American life were traced unhesitatingly to an imperfect democratic control of the forces of exploitation. If the plutocracy were making gains at the expense of the plain people it was due to defective governmental machinery, and the immediate problem was the readjustment of that machinery. There must be an extension of democratic control over the economics of society. The great principle of *laissez faire,* that had proved so useful in the earlier struggle against aristocratic paternalisms, was become a shield and buckler for the plutocracy that was rising from the freedoms of a let-alone policy. To curb the ambitions of that plutocracy and preserve the democratic bequest for the common benefit of all, was therefore the immediate problem of the times.

To this end two things remained to be achieved: to wrest possession of the government from the hands of the plutocracy that was befouling it, and to use it for democratic rather than plutocratic ends. The difficulties in the way were many. Entrenched behind the checks and balances of a complex constitution the plutocracy could not easily be dislodged from power; even if it were driven out of the legislative and executive branches of government it would find aid and succor in the judiciary, where a masterful corporation law was interpreted by a bench tender toward all property rights, and jealous of its sovereign prerogative of reviewing all legislative enactments. A surprising change had come over the attitude of the governing class towards democracy. Having gained control of the machinery of government the plutocracy found no cause to quarrel with a situation wholly to its liking. It had mastered the gentle art of guiding the majority will, and secure—as it believed—in its control of the political state, it counted on an indefinite continuation of the policy of preëmption and exploitation. From such a group, whether in Wall Street or at Washington, no new theories of government were to be expected. Business men wanted to be let alone. They clung to the anarchism of the Enlightenment and were stout in defense of the principle of individual initiative. So late as 1916 a group of confirmed individualists reissued Spender's *Man Versus the State,* with an introduction by Elihu Root, to combat the rising spirit of governmental control. They regarded the American system of government as adequate and final, and wanted no subversive changes. The Constitution had been completed by the post-war enactments that fixed the status of the negro, and for a generation thereafter—except for the silent changes wrought by the judiciary—it remained static. East of the Allegheny Mountains popular interest in political theory had come to an end. A group of academic thinkers like John W. Burgess and Woodrow Wilson, an occasional intellectual like Brooks Adams, isolated radicals like Johann Most and small Marxian groups in Chicago and New York, and leaders of the new proletarian movement like Terence V. Powderly, were still acutely concerned about political theory; but these men and their theories counted for little in the stodgy mass of capitalistic America. The political phase had passed over into the economic; politics was wholly divorced from reality.

But throughout the Middle Border and on to the Pacific Coast the spirit of political democracy was alive and vigorous. There the older frontier

Jacksonianism still lingered. For upwards of a half a century creative political thinking in America was largely western agrarian, and from this source came those democratic ideas that were to provide the staple of a later liberalism. The conscious objective of this great movement was to complete the work begun by Jacksonianism, and create a political machinery that should enable the democracy to withstand the shock of the Industrial Revolution. Many thinkers contributed to the work–U'Ren of Oregon, Jerry Simpson of Kansas, Tom Watson of Georgia, "Coin" Harvey of Arkansas, General Weaver of Iowa, Ignatius Donnelly of Minnesota, Henry D. Lloyd of Chicago, to name a handful out of the mass–homespun realists who have been forgotten by a later generation, but whose labors were given to the necessary work of refashioning the political machinery of America, and whose program provided the materials for the later Progressive party. They were commoners, men of the people, unversed in the dogmas of the schools, idealists who drew their inspiration from the Declaration of Independence; they spoke for an older America that feared the rising plutocracy, and they were casting about for ways and means to cut its claws. From their labors came the Greenback Movement, the Farmers' Alliance, Populism; and from them came in turn the Progressive Movement that reaped what they had sown.

4

Commentary on Progressive Histories

CHARLES CROWE (1966)

In the following essay Charles Crowe (b. 1922), professor of history at the University of Georgia, placed the writings of Beard and Parrington in the context of other histories during the early twentieth century and in the perspective of the climate of opinion generally.

Crowe explained that the philosophers of pragmatism, the political reformers, and the progressive historians all shared the same fundamental outlook. They refused to accept the world as it was, and asserted that man could change it to better satisfy his needs. Theoretical relativism, for example, was common to the thinking of them all, but only in that it was

---

Reprinted by permission, with the omission of the final three paragraphs, from Charles Crowe, "The Emergence of Progressive History," *Journal of the History of Ideas,* XXVII, January-March 1966, pp. 109-124.

related to their hopes for a creative future. Although the progressive historians related events of previous ages and earlier historical interpretations to various specific environmental factors, these historians were not fatalistic about the possibility for change in their own times. The contemporary economic, social, political, and psychological environment had been transformed from what it had been in the past, and, the progressives argued, ideas, laws, and public policies likewise could be changed.

The discipline of history came to maturity in America during the golden age of Pragmatism and Progressivism, and historians shared many basic attitudes with political reformers and philosophers. Pragmatic philosophers[1] devised arguments for setting aside the "closed" Newtonian universe of determinism for a cosmos with possibility, novelty, chance, and change; Oliver Wendell Holmes and his disciples replaced the implacable logic of the law with the complexity and relativism of "experience"; and intellectuals and publicists in virtually every field of thought strove mightily to "bust" the intellectual trusts, to establish an "open shop" of ideas. Around the turn of the present century a chasm developed for scholars and politicians between "real" experience and the dominant abstractions of "ruling interests." Opinion makers bridged the gap with a theory of conspiracy. Presumably, economists and their natural allies conspired to conceal the realities of power behind the masks of natural law, due process, liberty of contract, and so on. As Richard Hofstadter has suggested, *real* social forces were "rough and sordid; hidden and neglected, and, so to speak, off-stage; . . . a stream of external and material events of which psychic events were a kind of pale reflex."[2] Reality to the emerging Progressive mentality did indeed seem to be the conspiratorial and corrupt "fix." Historians played their part in the general movement by gradually piecing together a national past appropriate to the progressive movement; the scholars helped in dozens of ways, particularly by tracing the roots of social conspiracy to national origins after a fashion which revealed how the golden accomplishments of "76" had led to the painful industrial and political realities of the early XXth century. Vernon Parrington, who epitomized the Progressive approach, explained prevailing distortions of American history by "partisan interpretation" and "arid constitutionalism." Parrington also noted that the muckrakers[3] had preceded the scholars in discovering that "America was not in fact the equalitarian democracy it professed to be,' and that democracy and property had been at odds through the Constitutional Convention, the struggles of Jefferson and Hamilton, Jackson and Clay, and during all the generations afterwards.[4]

Progressive history[5]–created by Frederick Jackson Turner, Charles A. Beard, Parrington, their associates and disciples–cannot be studied in a single work or in the thoughts of any one scholar; it was not a philosophy of history, nor even a scrupulously delineated, minutely defined interpretation of the American past.[6] Rather it was a set of related impressions, a framework of Pragmatic and Progressive assumptions and attitudes, which inspired the first great flowering of professional American scholarship in history. Progressive history was characterized by: (1) a vivid sense of social, economic, and intellectual process which placed man, his institutions, and his ideas firmly in the stream of evolution; (2) a "Pragmatic" determination which sought to deal only with concrete situations and to avoid both "barren" empiricism and "grandiose" abstraction; (3) an anti-intellectualism which regarded ideas as secondary and derivative from the really important forces in history, which were primarily economic and geographical; (4) an epistemological relativism which generally denied scientific history and sometimes even scholarly objectivity; (5) a "presentism" which stressed the continuity of past, present, and future and sharply subordinated the past to the present; (6) an emphasis on the moral and social utility of history; (7) a tendency to see politics as a conspiratorial process in which dominant abstractions masked the play of "real" historical forces; (8) an interpretation of American history which stressed economic or geographical forces–or a combination of the two–and found a central theme in the conflict of agrarianism with commercialism and capitalism.

Few intellectuals at the turn of the century could escape the evolutionary ideologies and the intense awareness of social process which dominated the age. Spencer, Darwin, and Comte found many eager students and influenced the education of the young historians in a variety of ways. At least two textbooks used by Turner as a student at the Johns Hopkins University during 1888 and 1889 explained much of the human past in terms of evolutionary development through hunting, pastoral, agricultural, commercial, and industrial stages. This approach seems to have influenced Turner's application of a similar scheme to the development of the American West: "The history of our political institutions . . . is a history of the evolution and adoption of organs in response to changes in environment." In *The Rise of American Civilization,* Beard made a sort of evolutionary dialectic out of the agrarian-commercial clashes and in the introduction to *An Economic Interpretation of the Constitution* even linked historical interpretations to this evolving interplay of "social antagonisms." Along with John Dewey, both Beard and Carl Becker indicated that ideas could be evolutionary instruments of adjustment and conquest.[7]

With past and present in never-ending flux, old "static" theories and techniques of inquiry no longer seemed appropriate to historical investigation. Because "facts" did not "speak for themselves," the Progressive historians saw little point in a purely Baconian acquisition of facts. (Becker pointed out that Bacon himself, for that matter, had spoken of theories needed to "put nature to the question.") Mere fact-blinded empiricism was barren of significant results and hardly more useful than the sweeping abstract generalizations which Beard and Becker also criticized. The Progressive historians were drawn to "experience," the concrete, the non-ideological; they sought the leading idea which "emerged" from experience and explained its context, rather than devices such as the Bancroftian hand of God or the "germ" theory of institutional origins; they sought "operational" ideas which would elucidate the economic interests of the Jeffersonians or reveal the effect of frontier mobility on democratic institutions rather than an omni-comprehensive *Zeitgeist* or an all-explaining second law of thermodynamics.[8] Since Turner and Beard regarded ideas as derivative from economic and geographical factors they were clearly headed for the anti-intellectual camp. Becker's case was a little more complex, since a substantial portion of his best work was devoted to the analysis of ideas. Nevertheless, on several occasions he indicated that ideas were subordinate to more "powerful" forces, and there certainly is nothing obscure about his denial of intellectual objectivity. He insisted that any historian who "opened his mouth" (even the presumably "neutral" collector of documents) always said essentially one thing: "I exist, therefore, I am right."[9]

Becker gave the most extreme analysis of the grounds for epistemological relativism, but his conclusions were substantially shared by Turner, who advanced these views in an early essay:

Those who insist that history is simply the effort to tell the thing as it was, to state the facts, are confronted with the difficulty that the fact which they represent is not planted on the solid ground of fixed conditions; it is in the midst and is itself a part of the changing currents, the complex and interacting influences of the time, deriving its significance as a fact from its relations to the deeper-seated movements of the age, movements so gradual that often only the passing years can reveal the truth about the fact and its right to a place on the historian's page.[10]

Although Beard took a similar position during his most creative decades, it is true that he held various opinions ranging from the early hints of "scientism" to the extremes of the celebrated "act of faith" speech to the American Historical Association of 1933, in which he flatly denied the possibility of rational procedure for the historian. During the 1930's Beard was deeply influenced by Karl Mannheim, Benedetto Croce, and other European philosophers of history whom he believed to have destroyed all "illusions" about "objective" history. The historian could only surrender to faith and hope that the future would vindicate both his facts and his theories.

The notion that the historian served as the willing or unwilling spokesman of his time was an idea common to all three scholars throughout their lives. Turner's first essays are sprinkled with comments such as: "Each age writes the history of the past anew with reference to the condition uppermost in its mind"; "the historical study of the first half of the XIXth century reflected the thought of the age"; "the conceptions of history have been almost as numerous as the men who write history." All the Progressive historians echoed the Pragmatists in their conceptions of motivation and inquiry (Charles Peirce had spoken of the "irritation of doubt" and the emotional "security" of belief); the Progressives could not accept the notion of the historian's will moved by some kind of pure reason and oblivious of emotion, desire, purpose, and plans. Becker would not even allow the "scientific" historian the luxury of the detached catalogue of facts; "Caesar crossed the Rubicon" was not a simple fact but a symbol standing in a complex context for a series of events. John Dewey once remarked that problems were not solvable as "marbles in a box but as events . . . in a history, in a never finished process," and Becker asserted that even if history were like "marbles in a box," the historian, of necessity, collected the marbles and placed them in a box of his own making. Although he did not specifically refer to either John Locke's or William James's psychology in discussing the issue, Becker seems to have been protesting against the idea of mind as a passive blank slate and advocating some kind of depth psychology in which perceptions were made in a pattern, a context, a "Gestalt."[11]

A strong impulse toward "presentism" was often the natural companion of relativism. According to Turner, "the present is simply the developing past, the past the undeveloped present . . . . Historical study has for its end to let the community see itself in the light of the past, to give it new thoughts and feelings, new aspirations and energies." Although Beard never went quite so far as several proponents of the "new history"–James Harvey Robinson and Harry Elmer Barnes in their extreme moments expressed an almost open contempt for the past–he did in a book written with Robinson confess, indeed boast, that they had "consistently subordinated the past to the present" because of an "ever-conscious aim to enable the reader to catch up with his own times; to read intelligently the foreign news in the morning paper." The central goal of history was the "historical explanation of the present." Becker's ideas were more sophisticated, originating as they did with William James's concept of the "specious present": before one can utter the word "present" it has become "a thing of the past," since it is only the forward edge of the thrust by the past into the future. "Present," "past," and "future" torn from their context, the unified human consciousness, were only artificial abstractions. An original contribution of Becker's was to combine James's idea with A. N. Whitehead's notion of "climate of opinion" in order to create the idea of a "collective specious present" in which the historian as well as "everyman" lived and moved and had his being. From this collective specious present the historian drew his values, choice-making tendencies, and so on. In a significant sense and whether he wished it or not the historian must serve the "present."[12]

This presentism led the Progressive historians to stress the utility of history. Becker in his most sceptical moments was inclined to exalt the element of private and personal utility: "The value of History is, indeed, not scientific but moral; by liberalizing the mind, by deepening the sympathies, by fortifying the will, it enables us to control not society, but ourselves."[13] During the larger part of his life, however, he recognized the possibilities for human progress and granted a definite and constructive social task to the historian. Beard, a more active citizen with little aversion to controversy, pursued civic commitment more energetically, with a consciousness of the part history could play in reform. None of the Progressive historians conceded much to history as the plaything of the idle curiosity, a field studied for its own sake and nothing more.[14]

Given their tendency to regard economic and geographical forces as primary and to see ideas as instruments, it is not surprising that Progressive historians regarded so many dominant concepts and interpretations as masks for deeper realities. Turner, Beard, and Becker all sought the "real" stuff of history. Becker's pioneer monograph, *Political Parties in New York, 1760-66,* suggested that the Revolutionary struggle was not merely a chapter in the abstract history of the rights of man but primarily an economic and political struggle among merchants, mechanics, and farmers for "home rule" *and* to decide who "would rule at home." Turner believed that concern with the states, interstate relations, sectional boundaries, and abstract forces–all at best beside the main point–blinded Americans to the important springs of their history.[15] Turner emerged on the national scene with a growing interest in sectionalism, and sought to find the forces that separated and distinguished sections. Turner, William A. Schaper, Charles H. Ambler, and Orin Libby all made important contributions to this movement. Libby's study, *The Geographical Distribution of the Vote of the*

Thirteen States on the Federal Constitution, for example, stressed the conflict of debtors and creditors. Turner in an introduction to Libby's book urged that the scholarly limelight be taken from the study of institutional and constitutional forms since "behind institutions, behind constitutional forms and modifications lie the vital forces that call these organs into life . . . the economic interpretation has been neglected . . . it is much more important to note the existence of the great social and economic areas."

Turner himself, of course, found the basic stuff of American history in "the existence of an area of free land, its continuous recession, and the advance of American settlement Westward."[16] Official ideologies which proclaimed the primacy of the Atlantic Coast, the European origins of American democracy and national character, and the fundamental importance of political history, masked the realities and interfered with the serious analysis of American history. The truly vital center of the American past was the Mississippi Valley. Democracy emerged along the frontier line, and the essential part of American history consisted of the evolution of the frontier. Turner's interpretation stressed a combination of economic and geographical forces, while Beard's point of view was a more purely economic one.

Just as Turnerian notions were current before Turner's celebrated essay, so the essentials of Beard's economic interpretation were around for two decades before the publication of his most famous work. As early as 1893, in a remarkable book which Beard, Turner, and Becker were all to praise, Woodrow Wilson described the Constitution of 1787 as one designed to "check the sweep and power of popular majorities . . . [a government] originated and organized upon the initiative and primarily in the interests of the mercantile classes . . . urged to adoption by a minority under the concerted and aggressive leadership of able men representing a ruling class . . . strong and intelligent . . . possessed of unity . . . and informed by a conscious solidarity of material interests."[17] Beard's work represented a systematic elaboration of the same basic idea and its extension to other areas of American history. On this crucial issue of the Constitution the Progressive-Pragmatic approach and the theory of history as conspiracy came to a creative focal point which startled a generation of historians and social thinkers. No one has described the response to *An Economic Interpretation of the Constitution* more effectively than Parrington:

From a critical study of the Constitution came a discovery that struck home like a submarine torpedo—the discovery that the drift toward plutocracy was not a drift away from the spirit of the Constitution but an inevitable unfolding from its premises . . . [not] a democratic instrument [but a force] designedly hostile to democracy.... It was a startling discovery... [yet] it is not so easy to understand why since Civil War days intelligent Americans should have so strangely confused the Declaration of Independence and the Constitution and have come to accept them as complementary statements of the democratic purpose of America.[18]

Beard believed the major currents in American history to be "in the main, economic and realistic–a conquest of material things," and American "development," a "mass progress" toward a great abundance of material goods in a "collectivistic democracy." Despite his insistence that the notion of scientific history was "a dream of omniscience" and that history must be written as "an act of faith," Beard was from time to time haunted by the vision of the grand generalization. The great scholar, he remarked in 1919, was the one who reflected "the master current" of his age.[19] Beard wished to arrive at the faith necessary for the man of affairs who proposed to act on the world, and in the economic interpretation he believed that he had found both his approach and the "master current" of the times. In four books written and published between 1911 and 1915–*Contemporary American History* (1913), *The Supreme Court and the Constitution* (1912), *An Economic Interpretation of the Constitution* (1913), and *The Economic Origins of Jeffersonian Democracy* (1915)–Beard developed the basic ideas which he later spread across the entire panorama of United States history in *The Rise of American Civilization* (1927).[20] *The Supreme Court and the Constitution* contained much praise for the abilities of the founding fathers but still presented a characteristic Beardian point of view: the convention was dominated by "the solid conservative, commercial and financial interests" while the "debtor and paper money" interests of the majority were hardly represented at all; Revolutionary "radicals" such as Samuel Adams, Patrick Henry, and Thomas Jefferson were conspicuous by their absence; the delegates were not seeking to establish "fine notions about democracy" but realistic economic gains, order, and stability; if Caesar or Napoleon had acted as the delegates did in brushing aside the Articles of Confederation the event would have been described as a *"coup d'etat"* or even a "revolution"; and so on.

The tone of the book was almost polemical, but it aroused less indignation and controversy than the allegedly more detached book on *An Economic Interpretation of the Constitution,* which was presented as an objective and scholarly attempt to test "the economic interpretation" by examining the economic interests of the men involved in constitution making. Nevertheless, Beard associated his point of view with the approach of Holmes and Pound to the Constitution, with the Lochner dissent, the reformist approach to economics and politics of E. A. Seligman and Arthur

F. Bentley, and the muckraking histories of Gustav Myers and Algie Simons.[21] Beard objected to the notion that "law is made of some abstract stuff known as 'justice' " and the apparently absurd idea that the delegates were spurred to action by vague notions about "justice" and "advancement of the general welfare." It was no use for modern jurists to say that the Constitution emerged from the whole people since it obviously represented the work of a small minority who stood to profit from their labors. Beard proposed to leave aside conventional and "barren" political history to find the "real substance" of the past which generations had concealed from view through masks such as the "juristic" interpretation of the Constitution.

Contemporary America (1877-1913) began with a sigh of relief over leaving behind the "arid" abstractions of the Civil War era for the "real staples of politics," industrial and commercial forces. The heroes of this volume were unconventional ones unconventionally described–Leland Stanford, Roscoe Conkling, Boss Platt, rough and realistic movers and doers who guided the almost explosive growth of the industrial-urban giant. Even in *The Economic Origins of Jeffersonian Democracy* there are premonitions of the dynamo and the labor union. As if to set a theme for all of American history and to underscore the basic unity of Progressive history, Beard's frontispiece used a quotation from Turner, "We may trace the contest between the capitalist and the democratic pioneer from the earliest colonial days," and a prediction by Becker, "American history . . . [will] shortly be rewritten along economic lines." *Jeffersonian Democracy* traced the agrarian-capitalist conflicts from the 1770's to the triumph of the "agrarian" masses in 1800. Although Beard treated Jefferson as a moderate rather than a radical and underestimated the curious rôle of Southern slave owners in the leadership of the Democratic Party, there was much in the book to cheer the reformer; a vivid contrast between the democratic agrarianism of John Taylor and the commercial, capitalistic, and aristocratic views of the Hamiltonians; introductory remarks which made the American Revolution the work of an energetic minority; and intimations of the place of Jacksonian Democracy and the Civil War in the agrarian-capitalist conflicts.[22] All in all, Beard's books made of American history something far beyond the conceptions and categories of any XIXth-century historian (with the possible exception of Richard Hildreth).

Beard, Turner, and Becker pointed out a way which many followed. Arthur Schlesinger extended Becker's study on the New York merchants to all of the colonies and continued the tale of conflict between merchants and and masses. Later, Louis Hacker developed an elaborate theory of rival capitalisms to explain the Revolutionary struggle, and J. Franklin Jameson came closer to liberal hearts than any of his colleagues in stressing the elements of social revolution. In the hands of Merrill Jensen, John Fiske's "Critical Period" became a liberal epoch unnecessarily ended by constitutional reaction.[23] The Jacksonian period attracted the greatest concentration of scholarly energies. Beard and Turner gave Jackson sympathetic attention and Turner associated the man and the movement with his romantic conception of frontier democracy emerging "strong and stark and full of life from the American forest." As early as 1893 Woodrow Wilson described Jackson as the great champion of Western agrarianism, a portrait accepted by a whole generation of scholars including William E. Dodd, John Spencer Bassett, J. W. Burgess, William McDonald, Carl Fish, and others. Fish even went so far as to make something like a virtue of the spoils system. In 1946, Arthur Schlesinger, Jr., more in the spirit of Beard than of Turner, brought Progressive assumptions into sharper focus and altered the emphasis by dwelling on class conflict and by defining the Jacksonians as a coalition of Eastern mechanics and Western agrarians, a point of view which built a bridge between the New Deal and the Jacksonian era and brought Progressive history up to date.[24] With similar scholarship on Populism and Progressive politics, Theodore Roosevelt and Woodrow Wilson, the Progressive historical structure was complete.

Virtually all assumptions and presuppositions were made completely overt in the Summa Theologica of Progressive history, V. L. Parrington's *Main Currents in American Thought,* a book which thrust a systematic and formalized account of Progressive notions into all the major aspects of American thought and into every corner of national life. Parrington's pages bristled with "liberal" and "conservative," "capitalist" and "agrarian." Volume I began with "Puritanism and Liberalism" and quickly identified Thomas Hooker and Roger Williams as liberals, and Connecticut and Rhode Island as "liberal Commonwealths" in contrast to "conservative" Massachusetts under the leadership of men such as John Cotton and the Mathers. The XVIIIth Century was marked by the gradual separation of "the liberal doctrine of natural rights" which was "unfortunately entangled in . . . an absolutist theology" and by the clash between "a liberal political philosophy and a reactionary theology." The American Revolution was at least a temporary victory for the liberalism of Williams, Hooker, Franklin, and Jefferson over the conservatism of Cotton, the Mathers, Jonathan Edwards, Alexander Hamilton, and Fisher Ames. The victory, however, was short-lived and next came "The Agrarian Defeat, 1783-1787," the conspiracy of the Constitution, and the agrarian-capitalist struggles of Hamiltonians and Jeffersonians.

If Volume I bore the strong imprint of certain Beardian notions, Volume II owed more to the spirit of Turner. Beginning with the triumph of

Jeffersonian "liberalism" and "The Romance of the West," American democracy proceeded triumphantly in the hands of "Andrew Jackson–Agrarian Liberal" and "Abraham Lincoln–Free Soil Liberal." Unhappily the Civil War and the rise of industrialism brought "The Great Revolution," the conflicts of "Western Agrarianism and Eastern Capitalism," and "The Great Barbecue" of "The Gilded Age." The "conspiracy of capital," the "rising plutocracy," "like some hidden cesspool," "poisoned" American political and social life; provided "the hidden hand that was pulling the strings of the political puppets"; and even worked for "The Conscription of Economics . . . and Political Theory" until muckrakers and historians unmasked conspiracy and aided Progressive political victory.[25] Later "liberal" historians and journalists were to extend Parrington's analysis into the New Deal era and for a generation progressive history stood triumphantly as the central source of explanatory patterns, the inspiration for hundreds of textbooks and possibly thousands of scholarly articles. . . .

FOOTNOTES

1. To pursue the philosophers very far would be to range beyond the scope of this article, but a few remarks about them are needed in order to suggest one way of looking at the general community of belief. According to Charles Peirce the universe was evolving from chaos toward a distant deterministic order which would draw increasingly near but never actually arrive; meanwhile, the universe was still "open," chance and coincidence were "objective causal factors," and even the "laws" of nature were merely "habits" more systematic than the patterns according to which the human mind worked. For William James, meaning and truth were relationships between the knower and the object known rather than fixed, implacable things "out there," unaffected by the investigator; in a significant sense, the truth was "made." To John Dewey ideas were primarily "instruments" with biological and social value for survival, adjustment, and conquest. The student of Pragmatism could find new grounds for advocating political and social change; perhaps the mechanistic psychology of Locke, the Newtonian world-picture, and the alleged immutability of knowledge, meaning, and truth, were all merely intellectual devices to insure the comfort of dominant groups in different areas of life from politics to philosophy. In an "open" universe, it was impossible to speak confidently of "iron" economic laws. Moreover, if dominant abstractions were instruments of power, reformers could surely forge new tools from the new logic. For discussions of "Pragmatic" thought in philosophy, economics, legal thought, and so on, a few references will be cited: Philip P. Wiener, *Evolution and the Founders of Pragmatism* (Cambridge, Mass., 1949, New York, 1965); Richard Hofstadter, *Social Darwinism in America* (New York, 1944); and Peirce's very suggestive autobiographical essay in Justus Buchler, ed., *The Selected Papers of Charles Peirce* (London and New York, 1940). For relevant works by James and Dewey, see Horace M. Kallen, ed., *The Philosophy of William James* (New York, 1939), esp. 158-196, and Joseph Ratner, ed., *The Philosophy of John Dewey* (New York, 1939),

esp. 435-461. For examples of the economists, see Richard T. Ely, *Monopolies and Trusts* (New York, 1900); and E. A. Seligman, *The Economic Interpretation of History* (New York, 1902). On Veblen, see Joseph Dorfman, *Thorstein Veblen and his America* (New York, 1934), and J. A. Hobson, *Veblen* (London, 1936). For legal thought, see Holmes, *Dissenting Opinions,* ed., Alfred Lief (New York, 1920).

2. See Hofstadter, "Charles Beard and the Constitution," in Howard K. Beale, ed., *Charles A. Beard: An Appraisal* (Lexington, 1954), 75-92. The Hofstadter article also appeared in *The American Quarterly,* II (1950), 195-213. See also Hofstadter, *The Age of Reform* (New York, 1958).

3. On muckrakers and progressives, see Harold U. Faulkner, *The Quest for Social Justice* (New York, 1931); C. C. Regier, *The Era of the Muckrakers* (New York, 1932); and Louis Filler, *Crusaders for American Liberalism* (New York, 1950).

4. Parrington, *The Beginnings of Critical Realism in America* (New York, 1930), 410.

5. Progressive presuppositions began to conquer at a time when professional historians were emerging from the university seminars to capture control of historical writing from the gifted and patriotic amateurs of the XIXth century who tended to rely heavily upon a few grand abstractions such as "democracy," "God," "progress," and "destiny." The new historians needed both guiding ideologies and effective methods of practical procedure. The ideological storms of Darwinism, Marxism, cosmic materialism, and "scientific" history captured some of the abler young historians before passing from the center of the intellectual stage. Even Charles Beard in the beginning toyed with the popular notion of "scientific" history based on von Ranke's alleged dictum that historical analysis dealt with things "as they actually happened." This point of view inspired A. B. Hart to state that the great generalizations would follow a generation of patient, monographic, "scientific" labors and Albert J. Beveridge to insist that "the facts when justly arranged interpret themselves." Frederick Jackson Turner, as an apprentice scholar, also gave lip service to the scientific school and more than passing tribute to that form of Social Darwinism which was called the "germ theory" of social institutions. (In Turner's master's thesis on the Wisconsin fur trade he traced the institution back to Phoenician times and a short time later did a doctoral dissertation on the New England town meeting in characteristic "Teutonic" terms.) Nevertheless, when all was said and done, none of these ideologies captured scholarly imaginations in any central way. It was left to the Progressive *Zeitgeist* to win a majority of the most influential young scholars. The progressive impact on historical writings was all the greater for the lack of a rival dynamic ideology which might firmly lead the investigator. On "scientific" history and on the "germ theory" of institutional origins, see A. B. Hart, "Imagination in History," *ibid.,* XV (1910), 232-233; William A. Dunning, "Truth in History," *ibid.,* XIX (1914), esp. 219; George Burton Adams, "History and the Philosophy of History," *ibid.,* XIV (1909), esp. 236; W. Stull Holt, "The Idea of Scientific History," *Journal of the History of Ideas,* I (1940), esp. 352. For discussions on the new history and Pragmatism, see Charles Crowe, "Pragmatic and Progressive Characteristics of Modern American Historical Writing," *Il Politico,* XXVI (1961). On Turner's early life and thought, see Turner, *Early Writings,* Fulmer Mood, ed., (Madison, 1938), esp. 43; and Mood, "The Development of Frederick Jackson Turner as a Historical Thinker," *Transactions of the Colonial Society of Massachusetts,* XXXIV (1939), 29. Professor John Braeman of Brooklyn College, after reading the manuscript of this article, commented on the fact that the two major Progressive politicians who also wrote history seriously were certainly not "Progressive" historians. I can only plead that Beveridge was devoted to the ideal of scientific history and was in scholarship and politics a complex and often contradictory personality; at any rate he was not the only likely fish to escape the

Progressive net. As for TR, most of his writing was done during the 1880's under the guidance of "Whig" training and education at a time when neither "Progressive" history nor a strong reformist bent in TR's mind existed.

6. For a generation after the Civil War, protest had largely been limited to small alienated groups such as the Molly McGuires or the immigrant anarchists, to the upper-class patrician reformers alarmed by the rising economic buccaneers who threatened their position, or to Granger and Populist, labor and Greenback factions which were for a year or a decade out of economic joint with the times. By the end of the XIXth century, however, it had become almost impossible for the great middle-class majority to ignore the growing chasm between traditional democratic "ideals" and the new political and economic "realities." Either the social and symbolic crisis had to be resolved or the society courted the possibility of widespread social alienation. The most important attempt to solve the problem was "the Progressive movement" which made a few modifications in traditional American ideals and invented a theory of social conspiracy to explain modern evil. The Progressives clung to old notions of democracy, progress, amelioristic politics, and continued to deny the existence of enduring class conflict or *essential* corruption in society. To account for obvious evils, they developed a conspiratorial theory of reality and reform which placed the reformers in conflict with irresponsible capitalists and in alliance with their victims, a homogeneous, united majority called "the people." To explain the fact that the "irresponsibles" seemed virtually to own dominant abstractions, the muckrakers advanced the notion that certain traditional ideas and symbols were being used to hide the un-American activities of sinister interests. When Supreme Court judges insisted on their function as passive voices for an all-wise and immutable Constitution, common law, and natural law, their critics suspected the existence of vested economic and social interests. Reformers wished to penetrate the rhetoric of dominant groups to discover the realities of the situation.

7. Turner, "The Problem of the West," (1896) in *The Frontier in American History* (New York, 1920) 205-61; Beard, *An Economic Interpretation of the Constitution* (New York, 1913), 4; Becker, *The Heavenly City of the Eighteenth Century Philosophers* (New Haven, 1932), 18-19; John Dewey, *The Problems of Men* (New York, 1946), 282-6.

8. Becker, "What Are Historical Facts?" (1926), reprinted in *Western Political Quarterly,* VIII (1955), 328; Beard, Introduction to J. B. Bury's *The Idea of Progress* (New York, 1932), ix-xv.

9. Becker, "Some Aspects of the Influence of Social Problems and Ideas . . . upon the Writing of History," *Publ. of the Amer. Sociological Society,* VII (1913), 93-94.

10. Turner, *The Frontier,* 332.

11. Beard and J. H. Robinson, *The Development of Modern Europe,* 2 vols. (New York, 1907-8), I, preface; Beard, *The Nature of the Social Sciences* (New York, 1934), 50-60; Beard and Sidney Hook, "Problems of Terminology in Historical Writing," *Theory and Practice in Historical Study* (New York, 1946), 112-130; also Beard, *ibid.,* 3-44, 105-108; Peirce, "The Fixation of Belief," *Popular Science Monthly,* VII (1877), 162-168; Dewey, *The Study of Ethics* (Ann Arbor, 1894), 31-60; Dewey, *Logic: The Theory of Inquiry* (New York, 1938), 238; Becker, "Detachment and the Writing of History," *Atlantic Monthly,* C (1910), 527; Becker, "The Problem of Historical Knowledge," *Philosophical Review,* XXII (1940), 363-364.

12. Turner, *Early Writings,* 52; J. H. Robinson, *The New History* (New York, 1912), 20; Harry Elmer Barnes, *The New History and the Social Sciences* (New York, 1926); Robinson and Beard, *Modern Europe,* I, preface; Becker, *Everyman His Own Historian* (New York, 1935), 233-256.

13. Becker, "A New Philosophy of History," *The Dial,* LIX (1915), 148.

14. Beard, "That Promise of American Life," *New Republic,* LXXXI (1935), 35-38; Beard, Introduction to J. B. Bury's *Idea of Progress.* Two points ought to be made clear about the Progressive historians. First, each had a different idea about practical reform politics: Becker lived largely within the conventional confines of university life and tended to view party battles with a certain detachment and irony; Turner was an optimistic and not overly critical soul who, for example, trusted that the robber barons as children of frontier culture would not betray frontier democratic ideals; and even Beard was a maverick in reform circles, apparently voting Republican in several elections when it was not the liberal fashion to do so. Secondly, none of the three were consistent throughout their lives: the contours of Turner's basic concepts were all softened and changed during his later life; Becker's scepticism about history and society deepened toward despair in the 1930's, leading him to think that liberalism might be only a "way station" in modern times; and the curious twistings and turnings of Beard's latest writings shocked many readers. However, this article is concerned neither with the private politics of the Progressives nor with their intellectual heresies after the completion of the Progressive historical edifice.

15. Becker, *Political Parties in New York, 1760-66* (New York, 1909).

16. Schaper, *Sectionalism and Representation in South Carolina,* Annual Report of the Amer. Hist. Assoc. for 1900 (Washington, 1901), I, 237-463; Charles H. Ambler, *Sectionalism in Virginia* (Chicago, 1910); Orin Libby, *The Geographical Distribution of the Vote of the Thirteen States on the Federal Constitution* (Madison, 1894); Turner, *The Frontier,* 1.

17. Wilson, *Division and Reunion* (New York, 1893), 12-13. See also Henry Jones Ford, *The Rise and Growth of American Politics* (New York, 1898), 59; Alexander Johnson, "Convention of 1787," *Labor's Cyclopedia of Political Science* (New York, 1882), I, 638; and John Fiske, *The Critical Period of American History* (Boston, 1897), 243.

18. Parrington, *Critical Realism,* 410.

19. Beard, "That Promise of American Life," 358; Beard, "Written History as an Act of Faith," *American Historical Review,* XXXIX (1934), 219-229; Beard, "That Noble Dream," *American Historical Review,* XLI (1935), 74-87; Lee Benson, *Turner and Beard* (Glencoe, Ill., 1960), 79-91.

20. For the impact of Beard's book, see Maurice Blinkoff, *The Influence of Charles A. Beard Upon American Historiography* (Buffalo, 1936).

21. See Beard's introductions to the 1913 and the 1935 editions of *Economic Interpretation.* Beard has been savagely attacked by Robert Brown in *Charles Beard and the Constitution* (Princeton, 1956), for the statement of his thesis and more gently criticized by Lee Benson in *Turner and Beard* for confusing "economic interpretation" and "economic determinism."

22. For all of Parrington's admiration of Beard's works, he flatly rejected Beard's portrait of Jefferson.

23. Becker, *Eve of the Revolution* (New York, 1911); Schlesinger, *Colonial Merchants and the American Revolution* (Boston, 1918); Hacker, "The First American Revolution," *Columbia University Quarterly,* XXVII (1935), esp. 239; Jameson, *The American Revolution Considered as a Social Movement* (New York, 1940); and Jensen, *The Articles of Confederation* (Madison, 1948).

24. Turner, *Frontier,* 216; Wilson, *Division and Reunion;* Burgess, *The Middle Period 1817-1858* (New York, 1905); Dodd, *Expansion and Conflict* (Boston, 1915); Bassett, *The Life and Times of Andrew Jackson,* 2 vols. (Garden City, N. Y., 1911); McDonald, *Jacksonian Democracy, 1829-1837* (New York, 1906); Schlesinger, Jr., *The Age of Jackson* (Boston, 1946).

25. Despite all of this self-conscious liberalism, one historian detected, perceptively and correctly, a powerful note of implicit pessimism in Parrington; see Arthur A. Ekirch, "Parrington and the Decline of American Liberalism," *The American Quarterly,* III (1951), 295-308.

Part Two

Historians Since World War II

5

The Liberal Tradition in America

LOUIS HARTZ (1955)

The 1940s and 1950s brought a climate of opinion to the United States very different from the dominant one of the earlier 1900s. With the new mood came historical interpretations which were in marked contrast to those of Beard and Parrington. The three historians whose writings are selected in Part Two represent various emphases of the new post-war scholarship, but they stand together in their explicit criticism and conscious reformulation of the interpretations put forth by the progressive historians.

Americans have always viewed themselves in part from a European perspective; but the conclusions they have drawn using this perspective have not always been the same. Beard and Parrington took for granted that American history paralleled European history in the sense that both histories were characterized by similar conflicts. The battles between the enlightened and the vested interests were not peculiar to the New World alone. Beard and Parrington interpreted the period of the American Revolution and the making of the Constitution, for instance, as a version of the era of the French Revolution. They described reform movements generally in the United States as being parallel to those which originated out of European radicalism, and viewed American opponents of reform as being similar to European conservatives or reactionaries. The similarities between American history and European history were underlined during the earlier 1900s when, consistent with the progressive outlook, it seemed that the whole world was advancing toward a humane and democratic future. This was not to detract from the reality of the conflicts, or to deny that some countries were advancing ahead of others, but to point out that the world was sharing in an historical process which included progressive development.

 Abridgment is from pp. 3-4, 27-32, 228-232, 236-237, 240, 259, 261-264, 270-271.

Challenges to this optimistic view of universal betterment came with the Great War, and the antidemocratic seizures of power by both the Bolsheviks in Russia during the war and the Fascists in Italy in the early 1920s. However, to a remarkable extent the American progressive and pragmatic climate of opinion persisted despite these challenges through the 1920s. World War I tended to be interpreted at worst as simply a mistake from which lessons could be learned in order to make improvement in the future. The dictatorships tended to be at first either discounted in significance or even optimistically interpreted as social "experiments" which, according to the progressive law of history, would be abandoned if they were not ultimately beneficial. The 1930s however finally brought challenges which could not be minimized. The Great Depression, the continuing permanence of Stalin's and Mussolini's rule even as they became more tyrannical, the emergence of new despotisms such as Adolf Hitler's, and the continuation of worldwide military aggressiveness, all combined to make a mockery of progressive hopes. The assumption by Americans that human nature was basically good was increasingly undermined during the 1930s by the apparent acquiescence of masses of civilized Europeans to their governments' unspeakable cruelties against minority groups and critics of the regime. Even more discouraging was the seeming willingness of the same peoples to exchange their own former freedoms and individual autonomy for total subjugation of self to state.

The violence of the world in the 1930s, and particularly the violence of Europe, constituted a devastating and ultimately successful challenge to the dominance of the progressive climate of opinion in the United States. The world had not turned out as Americans in the earlier twentieth century had expected. Furthermore, what had happened in Europe had cast a new light on the United States. Despite the Depression, which all governments had faced, the United States emerged from the 1930s relatively unscarred, having avoided the resort to dictatorship which strangled the Soviet Union, Germany, Italy, and Spain. Franklin Roosevelt's New Deal was called by some a version of dictatorial state planning, but it was so weak a version as to highlight the contrasts rather than the similarities in the comparison. The New Deal moved slowly toward moderate goals. Important too was the large measure of consensus enjoyed by Roosevelt's program. Both the radical left and the reactionary Right lacked the support they had in European countries. What this suggested was that perhaps America was far more different from Europe than historians had previously thought. Perhaps there was something about American history which freed it from the violent extremism of European history.

Following World War II American historians began to concern themselves more than they had previously with the contrasts between American and European history. It was obvious that part of the background for this concern was the relative tranquillity of recent American political history as opposed to the violence of modern European history. Another part of the background, which stemmed from the post-war years, and which was particularly important in the case of Louis Hartz (b. 1919), was the new relationship of the United States to emerging nations and to the rest of the world generally. Hartz, a historian of political thought at Harvard University, made the most sweeping statement of the differences between American and European history in *The Liberal Tradition in America,* a sometimes extravagant and difficult, but still exceedingly stimulating and important, book. He argued that the big questions of European history had from the beginning been resolved for Americans. Whereas rival claims of feudalism or aristocracy, on one side, and socialism or democracy, on the other side, had torn Europe asunder for centuries, America had always been unquestioningly individualistic, capitalistic, and middle class. This liberal tradition was the only significant one in the United States, according to Hartz. Although he never precisely defined the word liberal (or liberal society, or liberalism) except by the examples and discussions presented in the book itself, it was clear that Hartz would have included in his definition a commitment to the middle class, individualism, capitalism, and the pursuit of self-interest through acquisition of property with a minimum of governmental restraint. Hartz suggested that because most Americans took liberalism for granted and because it had seldom if ever confronted serious challenges from the extreme Left or Right, the liberal tradition in America had escaped popular or scholarly scrutiny. Instead of focusing upon the large areas of liberal agreement between a Jefferson and a Hamilton, or a Franklin Roosevelt and a Hoover, American historians had dwelled almost exclusively on the relatively minor issues which divided these men.

Since Hart wrote *The Liberal Tradition in America,* he has gone on to conceive a yet larger explanatory framework in which to place the American experience. Proceeding with the comparative analysis which he initiated in *The Liberal Tradition in America,* he collaborated with specialists in several other modern colonial societies to explore a theory of colonial history. In *The Founding of New Societies* (1964), Hartz argued that the European colonies founded in Canada, Latin America, Australia, South Africa, and the United States were all best understood, even in their later development, as fragments of European culture. In a bow to a kind of Hegelian dialectic, Hartz insisted that as soon as the fragment escaped from the society of which it had been a part and was freed from the process of conflict and growth which had characterized the whole, the colonial fragment would remain relatively static. Thus Hartz furnished in retrospect an explanation for *The Liberal Tradition in America.* When founded, the United States comprised basically a liberal fragment of early modern British society, and since it was removed from the conflicts of Europe, it perpetuated the liberalism of its birth. The conflicting claims of aristocrats and leveling revolutionaries were left behind in Europe.

In the selection from *The Liberal Tradition in America* which follows, Hartz criticized progressive historians for failing to see the liberal consensus which marked America's past, and he illustrated the nature of the consensus by contrasting it with the dramatic conflicts in European history. Hartz suggested that precisely because so little was at issue in American politics, Americans tended to make so much over it. Beard and Parrington were themselves involved intellectually and emotionally in early twentieth-century reform crusades, and as they exaggerated the significance of the battles of their own time, so they exaggerated the political battles of the past. In this sense, Hartz said, Beard and Parrington were looking at American history as participants rather than as observers. Only an objective observer could perceive that even during the early 1900s the political reformers were proposing essentially a purification of the traditional liberalism which was so widely supported. At that time, it was difficult for an American to realize that the difference between Theodore Roosevelt's New Nationalism and Woodrow Wilson's New Freedom was not significant. And because faith in capitalism, individualism, and the Horatio Alger myth was so pervasive, serious consideration of socialism as an alternative was out of the question. Despite the innovations of the New Deal, according to Hartz, Roosevelt's program further exemplified society's traditional liberalism by refusing to draw radical conclusions from the facts of the Depression. Instead of a confrontation of extreme alternatives during the 1930s, there was a confrontation of two liberals, Roosevelt and Hoover, whose similarities have been obscured by the exclusive attention paid to their differences. If there had been a strong socialist challenge to the New Deal, Hartz hypothesized, so strong that Roosevelt had found it necessary to reply to it, his defense of liberalism would have made clear how close his position was to Hoover's. Hartz declared that the triumph of American liberalism in the Depression was the way in which it managed to ignore radical alternatives and, to a remarkable extent, do business as usual.

The implications of Hartz's argument that Americans could understand their country's history only through an act of detachment suggested a role for the scholar which was significantly different from that of Beard and Parrington. Partisan participation in the present was not only moral citizenship, according to Beard and Parrington, but it guided their scholarship. Hartz, by contrast, suggested that the scholar had to disengage himself from partisan American conflicts or he would not be able to understand them.

The analysis which this book contains is based on what might be called the storybook truth about American history: that America was settled by men who fled from the feudal and clerical oppressions of the Old World. If there is anything in this view, as old as the national folklore itself, then the outstanding thing about the American community in Western history ought to be the non-existence of those oppressions, or since the reaction against them was in the broadest sense liberal, that the American community is a liberal community. We are confronted, as it were, with a kind of inverted Trotskyite law of combined development, America skipping the feudal stage of history as Russia presumably skipped the liberal stage. I know that I am using broad terms broadly here. "Feudalism" refers technically to the institutions of the medieval era, and it is well known that aspects of the decadent feudalism of the later period, such as primogeniture, entail, and quitrents, were present in America even in the eighteenth century.[1] "Liberalism" is an even vaguer term, clouded as it is by all sorts of modern social reform connotations, and even when one insists on using it in the classic Lockian sense, as I shall insist here, there are aspects of our original life in the Puritan colonies and the South which hardly fit its meaning. But these are the liabilities of any large generalization, danger points but not insuperable barriers. What in the end is more interesting is the curious failure of American historians, after repeating endlessly that America was grounded in escape from the European past, to interpret our history in the light of that fact. There are a number of reasons for this which we shall encounter before we are through, but one is obvious at the outset: the separation of the study of American from European history and politics. Any attempt to uncover the nature of an American society without feudalism can only be accomplished by studying it in conjunction with a European society where the feudal structure and the feudal ethos did in fact survive. This is not to deny our national uniqueness, one of the reasons curiously given for studying America alone, but actually to affirm it. How can we know the uniqueness of anything except by contrasting it with what is not unique? The rationale for a separate American study, once you begin to think about it explodes the study itself. . . .

In American social studies we still live in the shadow of the Progressive era. Historians have openly assailed Beard, challenging economic motivations here and there and often transforming "radicals" into "conservatives." But after all is said and done Beard somehow stays alive, and the reason for this is that, as in the case of Marx, you merely demonstrate your subservience to a thinker when you spend your time attempting to disprove him. The way to fully refute a man is to ignore him for the most part, and the only way you can do this is to substitute new fundamental categories for his own, so that you are simply pursuing a different path. Such categories represent the only hope for a genuine escape from the pervasive frustration that the persistence of the Progressive analysis of America has inspired.

It is not unreasonable to suspect that our own time will discover such categories and that they may well lie in the relation of America to other nations. Everyone knows the old saw about each age rewriting history from its own angle, and everyone agrees that the peculiar angle of our own age is the involvement of America with the world. What is really wrong with the Progressive analysis, insofar as the questions we want answered today are concerned, is not that it is Progressive but that it is American. And here there is an interesting paradox, for one of the advances that the Progressives thought they were making lay in the explosion of the old nationalist history, what John Spencer Bassett called the "patriotic" school of historians. No doubt they did corrode many of the premises of this school. But at the same time they carried on a profound nationalism of their own. Even the "objectivists" among American historical writers, who rejected theses of any kind, did the same thing, for they did not, as Jameson urged, look at American history "from the standpoint of the outsider."[2] Rankian fact-gathering is not the same as getting "outside" your subject. The truth is, the American historian at practically every stage has functioned quite inside the nation: he has tended to be an erudite reflection of the limited social perspectives of the average American himself.

Where then lay the nativism of Beard and J. Allen Smith? It is not simply in the fact that they did not attempt the European correlations. This hid something deeper: their theory was a projection of the Progressive social orientation, which was [a] compact of America's irrational liberalism. The agitation of Brandeis and Wilson was the agitation of Western Liberal Reform altered by the fact that, fighting only Whiggery, rather than Toryism and socialism too, it was able no more than Whiggery to perceive the nature of its liberalism. It was as if Lloyd George were fighting only the reactionary members of the Liberal party who, in any case, had no Tory party to enter if they were dissatisfied with him. Hence, with the whole scheme of liberal unity blacked out, Whiggery became for the Progressives a frightful "conservatism," whereas it itself became "progressive" or "radical," a set of terms which meant nothing insofar as Western history of Western political alignments as a whole went. Armed with these intellectual tools, and as blind as the Progressives themselves to the natural liberalism of the nation, Beard and Smith went back to the origins of American history, splitting it up into two warring camps, discovering a "social revolution" in the eighteenth century, and in general making it impossible to understand the American liberal community. Their treatment of the Constitution may have lacked the piety of the "patriotic" historians, but it was as "American" as anything those historians developed. Indeed one might even argue that the others, by stressing a kind of happy national family, were a shade closer to the Lockian solidarity of the nation, which indeed was flourishing as never before in a commonly accepted "Americanism." . . .

There were many comforts in the old Progressive history which the liberal society analysis can never claim. The Progressives, for one thing, always had an American hero available to match any American villain they found, a Jefferson for every Hamilton. Which meant that in their demonology the nation never really sinned: only its inferior self did, its particular will, to use the language of Rousseau. The analyst of American liberalism is not in so happy a spot, for concentrating on unities as well as conflict, he is likely to discover on occasion a national villain, such as the tyrannical force of Lockian sentiment, whose treatment requires a new experience for the whole country rather than the insurgence of a part of it. Actually there was amid all the smoke and flame of Progressive historical scholarship a continuous and almost complacent note of reassurance. A new Jefferson would arise as he had always arisen before. The "reactionaries" would be laid low again. Needless to say, when you are dealing with problems inspired by an unprecedented set of world forces, you cannot take this line. So that the liberal society analyst is destined in two ways to be a less pleasing scholar than the Progressive: he finds national weaknesses and he can offer no absolute assurance on the basis of the past that they will be remedied. He tends to criticize and then shrug his shoulders, which is no way to become popular, especially in an age like our own. But even if there were not an integrity to criticism which ought to be kept inviolate at any cost, this mood is not without constructive virtue. It reminds us of a significant fact: that instead of recapturing our past, we have got to transcend it. As for a child who is leaving adolescence, there is no going home again for America . . . .

One can use the term "Liberal Reform" to describe the Western movement which emerged toward the end of the nineteenth century to adapt classical liberalism to the purposes of small propertied interests and the laboring class and at the same time which rejected socialism. Nor is this movement without its ties to the earlier era. If there is a link between Progressivism and the Jacksonian movement, there is a link also between the Jacobinism of 1848 and that of the French Radicals. The socially conscious English Liberals at the turn of the nineteenth century had their progenitors even during the age of the First Reform Act. But the American movement, now as during that age itself, was in a unique position. For swallowing up both peasantry and proletariat into the "petit-bourgeois" scheme, America created two unusual effects. It prevented socialism from challenging its Liberal Reform in any effective way, and at the same time it enslaved its Liberal Reform to the Alger dream of democratic capitalism . . . .

. . . What sort of program did the American Progressive advance even during the vivid days of the New Freedom and the Bull Moose? The answer in general is obvious enough. He advanced a version of the national [Horatio] Alger theme itself, based on trust-busting and boss-busting, which sounded as if he were smashing the national idols but which actually meant that he was bowing before them on a different plane. Wilson, crusading Wilson, reveals even more vividly than Al Smith the pathetic enslavement of the Progressive tradition to the "Americanism" that Whiggery had uncovered. To be sure, there is a quaint academic touch in Wilson's Algerism, which inspired him to depict "what it means to rise" by reference to Princeton freshmen and priests in the Catholic Church during the middle ages, but in essence he is as sound as a chamber of commerce orator. So is Teddy Roosevelt, although here we find, if not the atypical atmosphere of the classroom, the rather unusual bombast of a frustrated Nietzschean in the American setting. Certainly the contention of Croly that there was a great and "fundamental difference" between the New Freedom and the New Nationalism can hardly be defended, when we consider their common allegiance to democratic capitalism, and William Allen White had one of his keenest insights when he described the chasm between them as the chasm between Tweedledum and Tweedledee. One need not deny, of course, that both movements called for social measures such as hours legislation and workmen's compensation which were not entirely within the ambit of "Americanism" and which in their own small way offered a hint of the European Liberal reformers. But these were loose marginalia, lacking a definite rationalization other than that which the Alger scheme afforded, and certainly without the concept of a permanent "working class" or a permanent "social debt" such as the English Liberals and the French Radicals hurled against reactionary capitalism and Toryism.[3]

Which brings us again to the crucial significance of ideology: the Algerism of the Progressives was no more due in the last analysis to the boom of the time than was the Algerism of Whiggery. Boom sustained it, as it did the other, but after the crash of 1929 it would not disappear but would go underground to serve as the secret moral cosmos on the basis of which New Deal pragmatism moved. It was an expression of the dogmatic Lockianism of the nation, which is why it has a very peculiar pathos. Essentially, though of course in modified form, the American Progressive confronted the same realities as confronted the European Liberal reformers: the irreversible rise of a proletariat, the irreversible inequity of the capitalist race. But in the irrational grip of "Americanism," and not yet having learned through the agony of the crash the New Deal technique of burying ethics and "solving problems," he could not look these frightening facts in the face. He could not speak of "proletarians" or "capitalists" or even "classes." He could not see what every Western Liberal reformer saw with ease. Come what may, he had to insist that the Alger formula would work if only given a chance.

Here we have the clue to the whole trust obsession of the time. We think of the trust as an economic creation of American history, and we fail to see that it was just as much a psychological creation of the American Progressive mind. Granted that America now superseded England as the home of the "great industry," to use the words of Ashley,[4] it is still a fact that the relative concentration of economic power was greater in almost any part of Europe than it was in America. And yet the European Liberal reformers, though they blasted "monopoly"—the English in the case of the tariff and land, the French in the case of large business in general—did not make the same fetish of the symbol that the American Progressives did. They spoke of other things, the large alignment of classes. The truth is, the trust in America was in significant part an intellectual technique for defining economic problems in terms of a Locke no one dared to transcend. If the trust were at the heart of all evil, then Locke could be kept intact simply by smashing it. It was a technique by which a compulsive "Americanism" was projected upon the real economic world. . . .

It does not take a deep analyst to see that the whole issue of "direct government," that passionate symbol of the Progressive days, was involved root and branch in this problem. Why smash bosses and elect senators directly? Why get rid of Croker and Quay? The answer was: to give every last individual an equal chance to govern, and if you throw in the initiative, referendum, recall, and long ballot, to give him a chance to govern in practically every situation. Here was the equity of the Alger world flowering into politics, a program related to the log-cabin concept of the presidency which Alger himself embroidered in the case of Garfield, although there the hero started as a canal boy. Indeed the political energies premised by Progressivism were no less astounding than the economic energies it premised, so that the good American was not only a frantic economic dynamo rising to the top after trusts were shattered but a frantic political dynamo voting by referendum and recall after bosses were shattered. . . .

One final point, a queer anticlimax to this whole age of rampant Lockian nationalism. The age produced in the ranks of American Progressivism and socialism a sparkling array of social science students of America: Beard, Smith, Parrington, Boudin, Myers. But did these men, who were to cast so long a shadow over our thinking, grasp the America in which they lived? The answer is predominantly negative in every case, but a curious distinction is involved. The Progressives failed because, being children of the American absolutism, they could not get outside of it, and so without fully seeing that Locke was involved everywhere, they built their analysis around a titanic struggle between "conservative" and "radical" which had little relevance to Western politics as a whole. They stood, as Bryan and Wilson themselves did, a unanimous age upside down and interpreted it in terms of cosmic conflict. But these men, as I say, were children of America: this was not true of the Marxists. The latter were children of Europe, "un-American" to begin with, outside of America, equipped with meaningful Western categories: feudalism, capitalism, liberalism. Why did they fail to comprehend the nature of the American liberal world, determined as it was by the absence of the primitive feudal factor in the Marxian scheme? Here lies the real intellectual tragedy of the time, but the reason for it is obvious enough. If an understanding of the American liberal world led to the grim conclusions for socialism we have uncovered here, why should hopeful activists look them squarely in the face? After all, Trotsky's law of combined development, which stressed the skipping of the liberal stage by Russia, was designed to rationalize that country's immediate plunge into the socialist revolution. Would he have developed the same law if it led to the opposite conclusion? What was needed if the Western historical orientation of Marx was to be effective was someone with that passion for gloom which characterized "frustrated aristocrats" like the Adamses all the way over at the other end of the political spectrum. But in the messianic world of Victor Berger, this was too much to ask. The age that "discovered America" in its social thought was doomed, as any other age in the national history, never to see itself. . . .

If the Great Depression of the 'thirties suggested anything, it was that the failure of socialism in America stemmed from the ideologic power of the national irrational liberalism rather than from economic circumstance. For however "objective" the conditions for the Marxian apocalypse now became, what emerged to deal with the economic problem was a movement within the framework of the liberal faith, or in other words, a movement which belonged to the genre of Western Liberal Reform. What emerged was a movement, familiar now for fifty years in Western politics, which sought to extend the sphere of the state and at the same time retain the basic principles of Locke and Bentham. We find again the European correlations we found during the Progressive period. . . .

. . . What makes the New Deal "radical" is the smothering by the American Lockian faith of the socialist challenge to it. Nor does the meaning of this lie merely in the fact that Roosevelt was not seriously compared by many Americans with Norman Thomas and Earl Browder who of course were more radical than he was. It lies mainly in the fact that he did not need to *reply* to them, as English Liberals and French Radicals had to reply to socialists and communists. This meant that he did not, as the Europeans did, have to spell out his liberal premises and hence create the atmosphere of indecision which this necessarily involved. Compelled to reply only to the dispossessed Whiggery of Hoover on the right, which of course was glad to call him "radical," he could look like the man the Hearst papers, after Hearst's change of heart, made him out to be. Poor Norman Thomas, instead of being able to deride the New Deal as indecisive, was forced to complain that many Americans accepted it as socialism itself.

Hence there is an unwritten history of New Deal social thought which, if we are speaking in Western terms, it is only fair to write. What would Roosevelt have said had he indeed been compelled to take Thomas and Browder seriously? What would he have said had the American Socialist party been the English Labor party or the American Communist party been the party of the United Front in France? Obviously under such circumstances Roosevelt would be speaking very strange language indeed. He would be defending private property, he would be assailing too much "bureaucracy," he would be criticizing the utopian mood in politics. After pleading for the TVA and the SEC and the HOLC, he would proceed to qualify his faith in the state by an attack on the larger radicalism which faced him to the left. In other words, instead of being "radical," he would be half radical and half conservative, which is precisely the unfortunate position that the Liberal reformers of Europe were compelled to occupy. Instead of enlisting the vigorous passions of youth, he might easily be described as a tired man who could not make up his mind: a liberal who tried to break with Adam Smith but could not really do so. . . .

. . . In other words, the crucial thing was that, lacking the socialist challenge and of course the old corporate challenge on the right such as the European conservatisms still embodied, he did not need to spell out any real philosophy at all. His "radicalism" could consist of what he called "bold and persistent experimentation,"[5] which of course meant nothing in terms of large social faiths and was indeed perfectly compatible with "Americanism." Good Americans like Edison and Alexander Graham Bell were experimenters. So were the pioneers. When asked concerning his social philosophy, Roosevelt once said that he was a Democrat and a Christian, which meant, needless to say, that he was as good an irrational Lockian as Grover Cleveland.

Of course, as we know, many of the bold and persistent experiments of Roosevelt involved substantive departures from the liberal faith of a considerable kind. There is no need to overwork the point. The New Deal left a lot of free enterprise standing, and much of its state action, from spending to trustbusting, was designed to fortify rather than to weaken free enterprise. But a problem still remains of liberal convictions held in the face of nonliberal innovations, best illustrated by the rugged individualism of the American farmer who is supported on all sides by the state, which must surely fascinate any social psychologist. It is what lies at the bottom of the belief many Americans even now have that America is a "free enterprise" country, an idea the rest of the world seems glad to share with them. But whatever might be said psychologically about the collectivism that pragmatism could build on Locke in America, politically it has had crucial uses, some of them quite apart from the major one of permitting the New Deal to survive in the land of "Americanism." It permitted the Democrats, when war prosperity came, to lapse back into some of the language of Harding. And it permitted the Republicans, when the New Deal "solutions" became irrevocable, to accept them. After all, neither the party of reform nor the party of conservatism need be seriously affected by mere technical gadgetry. One of the hidden uses of political pragmatism in a liberal society is thus its effectiveness as an instrument of party accommodation. . . .

What emerges then in the case of the New Deal is a liberal self that is lost from sight: a faith in property, a belief in class unity, a suspicion of too much state power, a hostility to the utopian mood, all of which were blacked out by the weakness of the socialist challenge in the American liberal community. And yet this radicalization of the New Deal, though it provided ammunition for the Hooverite attack, in the end was tied up with Roosevelt's very success. For when the moral cosmology of New Dealism sank beneath the surface, what appeared, of course, was that happy pragmatism which usually refused to concern itself with moral issues at all. And this, in turn, permitted the American democrat to go about solving his problems without the serious twinges of conscience which would surely have appeared had he felt that his Lockian "Americanism" was at stake. In one sense this put him, from the angle of experimental freedom, far ahead of the European Liberal reformers, or even the European socialists. During the 'thirties it used to be the fashion to lament with Thurman Arnold the way in which folklore and fixed ideas stood in the way of social change.[6] But the truth is, the age was much freer of fetish in America than it was in Europe where ideological categories reigned. Where in England or France or Germany could you find the free-wheeling inventiveness typified by the NRA, the TVA, the ERA, the WPA, the SEC, and all the other New Deal alphabetical combinations and recombinations? What Thurman Arnold failed to see was that the technical pragmatism he wanted was nourished by the very "folklore" he blasted. An irreversible ethics made all problems technical.

FOOTNOTES

1. There is no precise term for feudal institutions and feudal ideas as they persisted into the modern period amid the national states and economic movements which progressively undermined them. The phrases "quasi-feudal" and "ancien regime" are nebulous enough. Some historians speak of "corporate society," but since a good deal more is involved than a congeries of associational units and since "corporate" is often used to describe current fascist states, the term has disadvantages. Under the circumstances it seems best to retain the simple word "feudal," realizing that its technical meaning is stretched when one applies it in the modern era.

2. J. Jameson, *The History of Historical Writing in America* (Boston, 1891), 138.

3. European Liberal Reform was not, of course, all of a doctrinal piece, and one can refer to it as a whole only in the sense that it sought generally to transcend the earlier individualism. There is a world of difference between Mazzini's nationalist idealism, influenced by the utopian socialists, and Bourgeois' theory of solidarity, influenced by French sociology. And there is a lot of difference between both and the collective idealism of T. H. Green and his liberal followers. What is involved in all cases of the "New Liberalism" is a frank recognition of the need for collective action to solve the class problem (though in fact this action was not always taken on a comprehensive scale). The image of Horatio Alger, for all of the effort of the movement to retain the core of individualism, was alien to it.

4. W. Ashley, *Surveys Historic and Economic* (New York, 1900), 385.

5. Quoted, R. Hofstadter, *The American Political Tradition* (New York, 1951), 310.

6. T. Arnold, *The Folklore of Capitalism* (New Haven, 1937).

6

The Genius of American Politics

DANIEL BOORSTIN (1953)

The progressive temper was increasingly challenged during and after the 1930s by world events. By the late 'forties it was evident that a new mood was dominant in the United States. Whereas the characteristic inclination of the earlier twentieth century was toward change, on the assumption that change meant progress, the typical tendency during the 1940s and 1950s

Reprinted by permission from Daniel Boorstin, *The Genius of American Politics,* University of Chicago, 1953, pp. 1-7, 68-70, 73-75, 81.

was to fear social and political change. In the years after World War II Americans came to lump together Fascism and Communism as "totalitarianism," a form of government and way of life in which individuals gave up their liberty for the aggrandizement of the state. Thus the utopian Communist appeal of a classless society, which had formerly during the 1920s and 1930s attracted Americans in varying degrees, and the cynical elitist appeal of Fascism, were combined in a category of totalitarian philosophy which denied human rights. The hopes of revolution came to be soured for most Americans, in short, by the outcome of the twentieth-century Communist and Fascist revolutions. Even the appeal of reform, as distinguished from revolution, was tarred by the same brush in the minds of many Americans during the late 1940s and 1950s. Stability rather than change, existing imperfections rather than the cost of reforms, seemed to be preferred. America's expression of the post-war temper in foreign relations was to prosecute a Cold War in the name of maintaining the status quo against totalitarian aggression. In domestic affairs similarly the mood was one of conservatism, which is not to forget that this included maintenance of New Deal reforms, rather than of innovation.

The word "conservative" became more attractive to Americans during the late 1940s and 1950s than it had ever been before in the twentieth century. Progressives had typically spoken of conservatism, meaning a preference for gradual change and a resistance to attempts to remake society, as if it were a sign of ignorance or selfishness, or both. But after World War II new "conservatisms" flourished. Peter Viereck and Russell Kirk enunciated a new conservatism which revivified Edmund Burke's critique of man-made schemes for social change and his appreciation for the gradual evolution of society. In 1955 the quarterly, *Modern Age,* was founded by Russell Kirk as a forum for this Burkean conservatism. A different kind of new conservatism was that which declared laissez-faire economics and Christianity to be eternally necessary fixtures in American society, and that the clock should be turned back to an earlier time when things were presumably better in America for capitalism and Christ. William F. Buckley, Jr., began to publish the weekly *National Review* in 1955 as an organ for this nineteenth-century liberalism which the twentieth century had made into a conservatism. But whatever the complexities and even contradictions among the various new post-war conservatisms, it was clearly more respectable than previously for Americans to take conservatism seriously as a social philosophy.

Another aspect of the climate of opinion as it began to form during the 1930s and as it became dominant in the post-war years was an increased celebration of American achievements. Louis Hartz's writings constituted a partial exception in this respect for he somewhat pessimistically warned Americans that they would have to transcend their history and themselves if they were to understand and successfully deal with other countries, particularly the emerging nations of Asia and Africa. More common than Hartz's warning during the 1940s and 1950s was an emphasis upon the differences between Americans and those of other nationalities—making such distinctions was simply to praise the uniqueness of Americans. The United States had after all successfully preserved democratic constitutional government when almost everywhere else it was non-existent, overthrown, or in perilous condition. The rights and liberties of most individuals were better protected in the United States than in most countries, and the majority of citizens were thought to be better represented politically. Further, Americans enjoyed the highest standard of living in the world. Consequently, it was as characteristic of the 1940s and 1950s to congratulate America for its achievements, on the assumption that things could be much worse, as it was characteristic of the earlier 1900s to criticize America for its imperfections, on the assumption that things could be much better.

Daniel Boorstin (b. 1914), professor of history at the University of Chicago who as a young man in the 1930s had been critical of the United States and sympathetic to the political Left, expressed most fully in his post-war scholarship the national mood of self-approbation. In a multi-volume history which is still in the process of completion, Boorstin developed an interpretation which was strikingly similar to Hartz's, but which contained enthusiastic praise of Americans. Boorstin agreed with Hartz's thesis that since Americans had taken their first principles for granted from the beginning, consequently the history of the United States was mainly a story of the development of techniques and compromises devised to solve practical problems. Boorstin and Hartz shared also the view that since the American formula was unique, it could not serve as a standard to be used in the development of other countries in the world.

Within this general agreement, however, Boorstin interpreted the characteristic American practicality as a wise and flexible adaptation to the New World environment. He called this unphilosophical practicality "conservative," insofar as it ignored doctrinal schemes for remaking society in favor of a more intuitive approach which involved building upon native American institutions. Boorstin did not disagree with Hartz that the dominant American tradition was individualistic, capitalistic, middle-class, and static, or what Hartz called, in essence, "liberal"; but Boorstin labeled this tradition "conservative," as well as innovative.

In the brief selection reprinted below from *The Genius of American Politics,* Boorstin sketched out one part of the general interpretation he later detailed in his extensive history. He located the genius of American political history in its freedom from doctrinal disputes of a European sort. Explicitly invoking the tragedy that had befallen the European dictatorships as evidence that attempts to reconstruct society along theoretical lines lead to inhumanity, Boorstin attributed the distinctive quality of American life to the fact that such dogmatic principles were never advanced. When he treated the American Revolution, he criticized the view of Charles Beard, Vernon Louis Parrington, and other progressive historians who argued that deep conflicts in theory and social class had produced a genuine social revolution. By contrast, Boorstin characterized Americans during the Revolutionary era as acting from a conservative consensus.

The genius of American democracy comes not from any special virtue of the American people but from the unprecedented opportunities of this continent and from a peculiar and unrepeatable combination of historical circumstances. These circumstances have given our institutions their character and their virtues. The very same facts which explain these virtues, explain also our inability to make a "philosophy" of them. They explain our lack of interest in political theory, and why we are doomed to failure in any attempt to sum up our way of life in slogans and dogmas. They explain, therefore, why we have nothing in the line of a theory that can be exported to other peoples of the world.

The thesis of this book is that nothing could be more un-American than to urge other countries to imitate America. We should not ask them to adopt our "philosophy" because we have no philosophy which can be exported. My argument is simple. It is based on forgotten commonplaces of American history–facts so obvious that we no longer see them. I argue, in a word, that American democracy is unique. It possesses a "genius" all its own. By this I mean what the Romans might have described as the tutelary spirit assigned to our nation at its birth and presiding over its destiny. Or what we more prosaically might call a characteristic disposition of our culture.

In one sense, of course, everybody has a political theory, even if it is expressed only in hostility to theories. But this is a barren paradox, concealing more than it discovers. In our political life we have been like Moliere's M. Jourdain, who was astonished to discover that all his life he had been speaking prose. We have not been much interested in the grammar of politics. We have been more interested in the way it works than in the theory behind it. Our unique history has thus offered us those benefits which come (in Edmund Burke's words) "from considering our liberties in the light of an inheritance" and has led us away from "extravagant and presumptuous speculations."

The great political theorists–men like Plato, Aristotle, Augustine, Hobbes, Locke, and Rousseau–even when not guilty of "extravagant and presumptuous speculations," have been primarily interested in discovering and systematizing general truths about society, regardless of time and place.

However much they may have differed in other matters, they have all had in common an attempt to *abstract,* to separate the universal principles of all societies and governments from the peculiar circumstances of their own society and government. Much of what we understand comes from the light which they have thrown, from their different vantage points, on the problem of government. The United States has never produced a political philosopher of their stature or a systematic theoretical work to rank with theirs.

But I mean something more when in this book I speak of our antipathy to political theory. Especially in our own age (and at least since the French Revolution of 1789), more and more of the world has sought in social theory no mere rationale for institutions but a blueprint for remaking society. Rousseau and Marx, for example, have been put to this use. Recent European politics shows us men of all complexions seeking an explicit orthodoxy for society. Burke was one of the first to note this tendency and its dangers, when he observed, "The bulk of mankind on their part are not excessively curious concerning any theories, whilst they are really happy; and one sure symptom of an ill-conducted state is the propensity of the people to resort to them." A pretty good rule-of-thumb for us in the United States is that our national well-being is in inverse proportion to the sharpness and extent of the theoretical differences between our political parties.

The tendency to abstract the principles of political life may sharpen issues for the political philosopher. It becomes idolatry when it provides statesmen or a people with a blueprint for their society. The characteristic tyrannies of our age—naziism, fascism, and communism—have expressed precisely this idolatry. They justify their outrages because their "philosophies" require them.

One of the many good fortunes of American civilization has been the happy coincidence of circumstances which has led us away from such idolatry. It is my belief that the circumstances which have stunted our interest in political philosophy have also nourished our refusal to make our society into the graven image of any man's political philosophy. In other ages this refusal might have seemed less significant; in ours it is a hallmark of a decent, free, and God-fearing society.

If what I say is true, it has profound consequences both for our understanding of ourselves and for our relation to Europe. It speaks to those who say that what we need in this country is a clearer "philosophy" of democracy. It speaks to those who think we should try to compete with the Russians in a war of philosophies. This book adds up to a warning that, if we rely on the "philosophy of American democracy" as a weapon in the world-wide struggle, we are relying on a weapon which may prove a dud. It may prove so because, as I shall try to show in this book, the peculiar strengths of American life have saved us from the European preoccupation with political dogmas and have left us inept and uninterested in political theory.

Anyone who has recently been abroad and heard the sort of thing we are telling the world can say that it does not sound very good. The portraits of American life are sometimes admirable—of the public library, the general store, and the volunteer fire department. But the statements of what America believes (and therefore what Europe would be better by believing) make the American abroad uncomfortable, if not downright embarrassed. They say something which is not American at all, even if they are sometimes expressed with the engaging brashness of a Fourth of July oration. What is the matter with these general statements is not any weakness in our institutions or any special stupidity in our publicity writers. Actually, they are bad because of the peculiarities—and even the advantages—of our geography, our history, and our way of life.

To understand the uniqueness of American history is to begin to understand why no adequate theory of our political life can be written. It will also help us to see why our institutions cannot be transplanted to other parts of the world. In the present world struggle, therefore, we should not hope to convert peoples to an American theory of government or expect to save western Europe from communism by transplanting American institutions. I want to develop this thesis not by discussing the rest of the world but by underlining a few facts of American history.

Although I shall set out from some of the most familiar facts of our past, in the course of this argument I shall lead you to some unfamiliar—and even paradoxical—conclusions about our political life. To understand these conclusions, you will need to reject some of the most widely accepted clichés about us. These clichés have been manufactured by our European friends and enemies. They go back to propaganda about us several centuries old, the labels made by the age of George III and earlier, which have stuck with amazing effectiveness.

From the earliest days, romantic Europeans have touted America as the country of novelty, of the unexpected and the untried, of grand visions and aspirations, where man could try out his latest inventions and test all those vagaries which were impossible in a conservative Europe. At the same time, conservative Europeans have attacked us for these very same dispositions, which to them, of course, have seemed vices. For many decades we were the Utopia of radicals and the Babel of conservatives. We have been given a reputation for being a country without tradition, without wholesome continuity in institutions, where *anything* might happen. This is what Europeans have agreed on, and their unanimity has forced our not always grudging assent. Now it is my thesis that, whatever may have been our weaknesses, this is not one of them.

I shall try to show how American history has nourished in a very special way and to an extraordinary degree our feeling for that principle of social science which I shall later call the "seamlessness" of culture. It is enough for the present to say that all this denies the stock European picture of us. Our geography and history have led us to an unspoken assumption, an axiom, so basic to our thinking that we have hardly been aware of it at all. This is the axiom that institutions are not and should not be the grand creations of men toward large ends and outspoken values; rather they are organisms which grow out of the soil in which they are rooted and out of the tradition from which they have sprung. Our history has fitted us, even against our will, to understand the meaning of conservatism. We have become the exemplars of the continuity of history and of the fruits which come from cultivating institutions suited to a time and place, in continuity with the past.

This point, if it is true, has special importance today. For the first time in modern history, and to an extent not true even in the age of the French Revolution, Europe has become the noisy champion of man's power to make over his culture at will. Communism is, in one sense, the extravagances of the French Revolution rewritten on the Gargantuan scale and acting with the terrifying efficiency of the twentieth century. People all over Europe have been accustomed, since the eighteenth century, to the notion that man can better his condition by trying to remake his institutions in some colossal image. Fascism and nazism proposed this; and so does communism. Europe has not yet realized that the remedy it seeks is itself a disease. . . .

The most obvious peculiarity of our American Revolution is that, in the modern European sense of the word, it was hardly a revolution at all. The Daughters of the American Revolution, who have been understandably sensitive on this subject, have always insisted in their literature that the American Revolution was no revolution but merely a colonial rebellion. The more I have looked into the subject, the more convinced I have become of the wisdom of their naiveté. "The social condition and the Constitution of the Americans are democratic," De Tocqueville observed about a hundred years ago. "But they have not had a democratic revolution." This fact is surely one of the most important of our history.

A number of historians (J. Franklin Jameson and Merrill Jensen, for example) have pointed out the ways in which a social revolution, including a redistribution of property, accompanied the American Revolution. These are facts which no student of the period should neglect. Yet it seems to me that these historians have by no means succeeded in showing that such changes were so basic and so far-reaching as actually in themselves to have established our national republican institutions. When we speak of the Revolution therefore, we are still fully justified in referring to something other than what Jameson's disciples mean by "the American Revolution as a social movement." If we consider the American Revolution in that sense, it would not be a great deal more notable than a number of other social movements in our history, such as Jacksonianism, populism, progressivism, and the New Deal. Moreover, insofar as the American Revolution was a social movement, it was not much to be distinguished from European revolutions, and the increasing emphasis on this aspect of our history is but another example of the attempt to assimilate our history to that of Europe.

The Revolution, as the birthday of our nation, must mean something very different from all this. It is the series of events by which we separated ourselves from the British Empire and acquired a national identity. Looking at our Revolution from this point of view, what are some features which distinguish it from the French Revolution of 1789 or the other revolutions to which western European nations trace their national identity? And, especially, what are those peculiarities which have affected the place of theory in our political life?

1. First, and most important, the United States was born in a *colonial* rebellion. Our national birth certificate is a Declaration of Independence and not a Declaration of the Rights of Man. The vast significance of this simple fact is too often forgotten. Compared even with other colonial rebellions, the American Revolution is notably lacking in cultural self-consciousness and in any passion for national unity. The more familiar type of colonial rebellion–like that which recently occurred in India–is one in which a subject people vindicates its local culture against foreign rulers. But the American Revolution had very little of this character. On the contrary, ours was one of the few conservative colonial rebellions of modern times . . . .

2. Second, the American Revolution was *not* the product of a nationalistic spirit. We had no Bismarck or Cavour or any nationalist philosophy. We were singularly free from most of the philosophical baggage of modern nationalism.

Perhaps never was a new nation created with less enthusiasm. To read the history of our Revolution is to discover that the United States was a kind of *pis aller.* This fact explains many of the difficulties encountered in conducting the Revolution and in framing a federal constitution. The original creation of a United States was the work of doubly reluctant men: men reluctant, both because of their local loyalties–to Virginia, Massachusetts, Rhode Island, and New York–and because of their imperial loyalty. The story of the "critical period" of American history, of the Articles of Confederation and the Constitution, tells of the gradual overcoming of this reluctance. It was overcome not by any widespread conversion to a nationalist theory–even the *Federalist* papers are conspicuously lacking in such a theory–but by gradual realization of the need for effective union.

In the period of the American Revolution we do discover a number of enthusiasms: for the safety and prosperity of Virginia or New York, for the cause of justice, for the rights of Englishmen. What is missing is anything that might be called widespread enthusiasm for the birth of a new nation: the United States of America. Until well into the nineteenth century, Jefferson–and he was not alone in this–was using the phrase "my country" to refer to his native state of Virginia.

3. Our Revolution was successful at the first try. This is equally true whether we consider it as a revolt against British rule or as a movement for republican federalism. There was no long-drawn-out agitation, no intellectual war of attrition, of the sort which breeds dogmas and intransigence. Thomas Paine's *Common Sense,* which is generally considered "the first important republican tract to be issued in America . . . the first to present cogent arguments for independence," did not appear until January 10, 1776. Down to within six months of the break, few would have considered independence; and even then the colonists had only quite specific complaints. There had been no considerable tradition in America either of revolt against British institutions or of republican theorizing.

The political objective of the Revolution, independence from British rule, was achieved by one relatively short continuous effort. More commonly in modern history (take, for example, the European revolutions of the nineteenth century) any particular revolt has been only one in a long series. Each episode, then, ends on a note of suspense which comes from the feeling that the story is "to be continued." Under those circumstances, challenges to constituted authority follow one another, accumulating their ideological baggage.

In France, for example, 1789 was followed by 1830 and 1848 and 1870; a similar list could be made for Italy, Germany, and perhaps Russia. Such repetition creates a distinctive revolutionary tradition, with continued agitation keeping alive certain doctrines. Repeated efforts provide the dogmatic raw material for a profusion of later political parties, each of which rallies under the banner of one or another of the defeated revolutions or of a revolution yet to be made. But, properly speaking, 1776 had no sequel, and needed none. The issue was separation, and separation was accomplished . . . .

The feature to which I want to direct your attention might be called the "conservatism" of the Revolution. If we understand this characteristic, we will begin to see the Revolution as an illustration of the remarkable continuity of American history. And we will also see how the attitude of our Revolutionary thinkers has engraved more deeply in our national consciousness a belief in the inevitability of our particular institutions, or, in a word, our sense of "givenness."

The character of our Revolution has nourished our assumption that whatever institutions we happened to have here (in this case the British constitution) had the self-evident validity of anything that is "normal." We have thus casually established the tradition that it is superfluous to the American condition to produce elaborate treatises on political philosophy or to be explicit about political values and the theory of community.

7

The Age of Reform

RICHARD HOFSTADTER (1955)

Louis Hartz explored the contrasts between American and European history, and concluded that American political thought and behavior had been uniquely practical while they were simultaneously being dominated by a fixed commitment to a liberal theory of individualism and capitalism. Daniel Boorstin agreed that American political history was unique in its preoccupation with practical problems and in its willingness to compromise. But he argued that the practical American tradition was a genuine and flexible adaptation to New World conditions and was conservative in the sense of being organically related both to a past and present environment

---

without disrupting connections with either. Boorstin praised Americans for their conservatism, and he criticized progressive historians and reformers insofar as they proposed theories of remaking society.

Richard Hofstadter (b. 1916) contributed to the criticism and revision of progressive historical interpretation, and reinforced the views of Hartz and Boorstin to some extent in books and articles he wrote after World War II which, first, minimized differences between American political reformers and their opponents and, second, undermined the claims of ethical superiority on the part of reformers.

Hofstadter's sympathies in the 1930s were socialistic and it has always been a commonplace awareness of socialists that mainstream American politics operated within the confines of the American economic system. In the preface to his book on *The American Political Tradition* in 1948, Hofstadter wrote that "However much at odds on specific issues, the major political traditions [whether Jeffersonian or Hamiltonian, reformist or not] have shared a belief in the rights of property, the philosophy of economic individualism, the value of competition; they have accepted the economic virtues of capitalist culture as necessary qualities of man." In the book itself, composed mainly of separate discussions of various political figures, Hofstadter argued that, as in the case of Jacksonian reformers and their Whig opponents, the contrasts between these figures were not as great as the progressive historians would have had us believe and the nature of the contrasts, too, was different.

One particular aspect of the climate of opinion during the late 1940s and early 1950s was especially important as background to Hofstadter's discussion of Populism, which is reprinted below from *The Age of Reform.* As part of the overall American reaction to European totalitarianism, there occurred during the early years of the Cold War, and most intensely during the Korean War, a national examination of those people who earlier had been sympathetic to the Soviet Union and to Communism. On the mildest and most personal level, this examination took the form of autobiographical confessions by ex-Communists concerning the errors of their youth. With more violence and public import, certain politicians in state legislatures and Congress seized the issue of loyalty to "Americanism" and proceeded to investigate, expose, and discredit individuals whose attitudes or behavior were "un-American." From the United States Senator who led this crusade, Joseph McCarthy of Wisconsin, the name "McCarthyism" was applied to the whole era of Communist investigations and allegations.

On the one hand, the response of the American intellectual community, including scholars, to "McCarthyism" was virtually universal disgust, when not hatred. Most intellectuals, who were generally left of center politically, felt that the legislative investigations into loyalty and the talk of "Americanism" were ignorant and malicious, and ultimately constituted an attack not on treason, but on the welfare state. On the other hand, intellectuals knew that treason had in fact been committed by a few persons who were sympathetic to the Soviet Union and that questionable judgment had likely been exercised by a greater number who were Communist "fellow travelers." Above all, there was the awareness that many intellectuals had been genuinely optimistic about the Soviet Union, had then honestly become disillusioned, and had subsequently subjected themselves to self-criticism or even to feelings of guilt because of their earlier views. The result therefore was that intellectuals' reactions to "McCarthyism" went beyond simple rejection. But their criticisms were deep and real. Intellectuals were particularly critical of the seemingly massive popular support for "McCarthyism" among some groups in the population. Some intellectuals asked whether European totalitarian movements did not furnish a parallel to the McCarthy type of demagogic leadership supported by certain groups. This question, provoked by "McCarthyism," merged with the "conservative" post-war climate of opinion in Hofstadter's analysis of Populism, in which he suggested that Populist reformers themselves possessed some of the seeds of a modern, irrational, anti-semitic, demagogic movement. Hofstadter, in short, was so concerned about "McCarthyism" that, despite his basic sympathy for the American reform tradition, he looked back at it to see if it contained any characteristics of "McCarthyism." He concluded that, unfortunately, it did.

Hofstadter opened the following selection by discussing the mood of the later 1940s and early 1950s which he was well aware established the relevant climate of opinion for understanding *The Age of Reform.* Because he knew that his criticisms of American reformers for their inadequacies in approaching political problems would be eagerly seized upon by contemporary opponents of reform and interpreted as part of the post-war conservative temper, Hofstadter tried to distinguish his views from the views of those he called New Conservatives. In his reinterpretation of Populism, Hofstadter was moving on especially controversial ground because Populism had always been lauded by progressive historians as a major source of modern American reform. When he dwelled upon the limitations of the agrarian protesters, he undeniably weakened the claims of reformers to a usable Populist past. The questions Hofstadter asked of Populism were not the same ones asked by Parrington and Beard. Without denying altogether the economic grievances of the Populists and the correctness of their political proposals, although he significantly minimized them, Hofstadter asked whether the Populists made their demands for reform at too high a price in demagogy, hysteria, and even potential infringement of civil liberties. Beard and Parrington had tended to assume that since Populism was a democratic movement of common men, it was necessarily humane. Hofstadter recognized the possibility that it could be a popular mass movement and inhumane at the same time. The test which Hofstadter imposed on the Populists, and which they failed to pass, was that they maintain a balanced and intelligent view of the causes and nature of their economic condition, and that they demonstrate a tolerant and humane attitude toward their fellow man.

I find that I have been critical of the Populist-Progressive tradition—more so than I would have been had I been writing such a study fifteen years ago. I say critical, but not hostile, for I am criticizing largely from within. The tradition of Progressive reform is the one upon which I was reared and upon which my political sentiments were formed, as it is, indeed, the tradition of most intellectuals in America. Perhaps because in its politics the United States has been so reliably conservative a country during the greater part of its history, its main intellectual traditions have been, as a reaction, "liberal," as we say—that is, popular, democratic, progressive. For all our conservatism as a people, we have failed to develop a sound and supple tradition of candidly conservative thinking. As Lionel Trilling remarks in *The Liberal Imagination,* our conservatives, with only a few exceptions, have not sought to express themselves in ideas, as opposed to action; they have only manifested "irritable mental gestures which seek to resemble ideas." The American businessman is expected to be a conservative in his politics. The conservative American politician can expect widespread recognition, frequently a long tenure in office, and usually a rewarding sense of public usefulness, even though we usually reserve our highest acclaim for the politician who has in him a touch of the liberal reformer. A conservative politician who has sufficient gifts—Theodore Roosevelt is the best example—can in fact enjoy both respectability and the financial support of the great interests and all the satisfactions of the conservative role in public affairs and yet exert his maximal influence by using the rhetoric of progressivism and winning the plaudits of the reformers. In times past, however, the conservative intellectual, and with him the conservative politician who attempted to give to his actions the support of reasoned belief, has been rather out of touch with the main lines of thought and with the primary public that he wanted to reach. The flow of criticism between conservatives and liberals in the United States has been somewhat blocked, with the consequence that men on both sides have grown excessively complacent about their intellectual positions. In the absence of a formidable and reasoned body of conservative criticism, liberals have been driven, for that exercise of the mind which intellectuals seek, to self-criticism, which has been of less value to them than powerful and searching opposition.

In our own day, perhaps for the first time since the 1890's, this situation is changing, for there are some signs that liberals are beginning to find it both natural and expedient to explore the merits and employ the rhetoric of conservatism. They find themselves far more conscious of those things they would like to preserve than they are of those things they would like to change. The immense enthusiasm that was aroused among American intellectuals by such a circumspect and sober gentleman as Adlai Stevenson in 1952 is the most outstanding evidence of this conservatism. Stevenson himself remarked during the course of his campaign that the liberals have become the true conservatives of our time. This is true not because they have some sweeping ideological commitment to conservatism (indeed, their sentiments and loyalties still lie mainly in another direction) but because they feel that we can better serve ourselves in the calculable future by holding to what we have gained and learned, while trying to find some way out of the dreadful impasse of our polarized world, than by dismantling the social achievements of the past twenty years, abandoning all that is best in American traditions, and indulging in the costly pretense of repudiating what we should not and in fact cannot repudiate.

My criticisms of the Populist-Progressive tradition, in so far as they are at all tinctured by conservatism, are no doubt in part a response to this mood. I do not like to think of these criticisms as being associated with the "New Conservatism" of our time, which seems so modish that I find myself uncomfortable with it. The use of such a term as "*New* Conservatism" only suggests to me how uneasy Americans still are in the presence of candidly conservative ideas. I should have thought that anything that was good in conservatism was very old indeed, and so that finest of American conservatives, John Adams, would tell us if he could. To propagate something called "*New* Conservatism" sounds to me too much like the crasser forms of salesmanship. It is in itself a capitulation to the American demand for constant change, and hence a betrayal of conservatism at the outset. We Americans love to have everything labeled "new" and "big," and yet what is of most value in conservatism is its feeling for the past and for nuances of thought, of administration, of method, of meaning, that might be called "little." What appeals to me in the New Conservatism, insofar as anything does at all, is simply the old liberalism, chastened by adversity, tempered by time, and modulated by a growing sense of reality. Hence, to the degree that I have been critical in these pages of the Populist-Progressive tradition, it is criticism that aims to reveal some of the limitations of that tradition and to help free it of its sentimentalities and complacencies–in short, to carry on with a task so largely shirked by its opponents that it must be performed by its supporters . . . .

A great part of both the strength and the weakness of our national existence lies in the fact that Americans do not abide very quietly the evils of life. We are forever restlessly pitting ourselves against them, demanding changes, improvements, remedies, but not often with sufficient sense of the limits that the human condition will in the end insistently impose upon us. This restlessness is most valuable and has its most successful consequence wherever dealing with *things* is involved, in technology and invention, in productivity, in the ability to meet needs and provide comforts. In this sphere we have surpassed all other peoples. But in dealing with human beings and institutions, in matters of morals and politics, the limits of this undying, absolutist restlessness quickly became evident. At the so-called grass roots of American politics there is a wide and pervasive tendency to believe—I hasten to add that the majority of Americans do not habitually succumb to this tendency—that there is some great but essentially very simple struggle going on, at the heart of which there lies some single conspiratorial force, whether it be the force represented by the "gold bugs," the Catholic Church, big business, corrupt politicians, the liquor interests and the saloons, or the Communist Party, and that this evil is something that must be not merely limited, checked, and controlled but rather extirpated root and branch at the earliest possible moment. It is widely assumed that some technique can be found that will really do this, though there is always likely to be a good deal of argument as to what that technique is. All too often the assumption prevails among our political and intellectual leaders that the judgment of the people about such things must of necessity be right, and that it is therefore their own business not to educate the public or to curb its demands for the impossible but to pretend that these demands are altogether sensible and to try to find ways to placate them.

So we go off on periodical psychic sprees that purport to be moral crusades: liberate the people once and for all from the gold bugs, restore absolute popular democracy or completely honest competition in business, wipe out the saloon and liquor forever from the nation's life, destroy the political machines and put an end to corruption, or achieve absolute, total, and final security against war, espionage, and the affairs of the external world. The people who attach themselves to these several absolutisms are not always the same people, but they do create for each other a common climate of absolutist enthusiasm. Very often the evils they are troubled about do exist in some form, usually something can be done about them, and in a great many historical instances something has been done. It is the merit of our reform tradition that it has usually been the first to point to the real and serious deficiencies in our economic system and that it has taken the initiative in making improvements. It is its limitation that it often wanders over the border between reality and impossibility. This was, I believe, pre-eminently true of the Progressive generation. It is hardly an accident that the generation that wanted to bring about direct popular rule, break up the political machines, and circumvent representative government was the same generation that imposed Prohibition on the country and proposed to make the world safe for democracy.

I believe it will be clear that what I am trying to establish is not that the Populist and Progressive movements were foolish and destructive but only that they had, like so many things in life, an ambiguous character. Of their substantial net value in the main stream of American political experience I have no doubt. There has always been in the United States a struggle against those forces which were too exclusively preoccupied with the organization of economic life and the milking of our resources to give much thought to the human costs or to expend much sympathy on the victims of their work. It has been the function of the liberal tradition in American politics, from the time of Jeffersonian and Jacksonian democracy down through Populism, Progressivism, and the New Deal, at first to broaden the numbers of those who could benefit from the great American bonanza and then to humanize its workings and help heal its casualties. Without this sustained tradition of opposition and protest and reform, the American system would have been, as in times and places it was, nothing but a jungle, and would probably have failed to develop into the remarkable system for production and distribution that it is. If we were to follow the history of but one issue alone—that of taxation in all its aspects—we would be quickly reminded of the enormous debt we owe to the liberal tradition for shifting the costs of society to those who are best able to bear them. Fifty or sixty years ago our social system had hardly begun to be touched by the gentle hands of remorse or reform. Today, as a result of an unintended, intermittent, and usually hostile collaboration of the opposing forces of matter-of-fact profit-seeking, engineering, and salesmanship on one hand and dissent and reform on the other, it has been altered and softened in countless ways. The place of the progressive tradition in this achievement is so secure that it should now be possible to indulge in some critical comments without seeming to impugn its entire value.

While it is always both feasible and desirable to formulate ideal programs of reform, it is asking too much to expect that history will move, so to speak, in a straight line to realize them. Liberal intellectuals, who have rather well-rationalized systems of political beliefs, tend to expect that the masses of people, whose actions at certain moments in history coincide with some of these beliefs, will share their other convictions as a matter of logic and principle. Intellectuals, moreover, suffer from a sense of isolation which they usually seek to surmount by finding ways of getting into rapport with the people, and they readily succumb to a tendency to sentimentalize the folk. Hence they periodically exaggerate the measure of agreement that exists between movements of popular reform and the considered principles of political liberalism. They remake the image of popular rebellion closer to their heart's desire. They choose to ignore not only the elements of illiberalism that frequently seem to be an indissoluble part of popular movements but also the very complexity of the historical process itself. In theory we may feel that we can in most cases distinguish without excessive difficulty between reforms that are useful remedies for the evils and abuses of our society and changes that are in fact only additions to or aggravations of such abuses. Popular movements do not always operate with the same discrimination, and it is often hard to tell when such a movement has passed beyond the demand for important and necessary reforms to the expression of a resentment so inclusive that it embraces not only the evils and abuses of a society but the whole society itself, including some of its more liberal and humane values . . . .

There is indeed much that is good and usable in our Populist past. While the Populist tradition had defects that have been too much neglected, it does not follow that the virtues claimed for it are all fictitious. Populism was the first modern political movement of practical importance in the United States to insist that the federal government has some responsibility for the common weal; indeed, it was the first such movement to attack seriously the problems created by industrialism. The complaints and demands and prophetic denunciations of the Populists stirred the latent liberalism in many Americans and startled many conservatives into a new flexibility. Most of the "radical" reforms in the Populist program proved in later years to be either harmless or useful. In at least one important area of American life a few Populist leaders in the South attempted something profoundly radical and humane–to build a popular movement that would cut across the old barriers of race–until persistent use of the Negro bogy distracted their following. To discuss the broad ideology of the Populists does them some injustice, for it was in their concrete programs that they added most constructively to our political life, and in their more general picture of the world that they were most credulous and vulnerable. Moreover, any account of the fallibility of Populist thinking that does not acknowledge the stress and suffering out of which that thinking emerged will be seriously remiss. But anyone who enlarges our portrait of the Populist tradition is likely to bring out some unseen blemishes. In the books that have been written about the Populist movement, only passing mention has been made of its significant provincialism; little has been said of its relations with nativism and nationalism; nothing has been said of its tincture of anti-Semitism . . . .

There was something about the Populist imagination that loved the secret plot and the conspiratorial meeting. There was in fact a widespread Populist idea that all American history since the Civil War could be understood as a sustained conspiracy of the international money power.

The pervasiveness of this way of looking at things may be attributed to the common feeling that farmers and workers were not simply oppressed, but oppressed deliberately, consciously, continuously, and with wanton malice by "the interests." It would of course be misleading to imply that the Populists stand alone in thinking of the events of their time as the results of a conspiracy. This kind of thinking frequently occurs when political and social antagonisms are sharp. Certain audiences are especially susceptible to it–particularly, I believe, those who have attained only a low level of education, whose access to information is poor,[1] and who are so completely shut out from access to the centers of power that they feel themselves completely deprived of self-defense and subjected to unlimited manipulation by those who wield power. There are, moreover, certain types of popular movements of dissent that offer special opportunities to agitators with paranoid tendencies, who are able to make a vocational asset out of their psychic disturbances.[2] Such persons have an opportunity to impose their own style of thought upon the movements they lead. It would of course be misleading to imply that there are no such things as conspiracies in history. Anything that partakes of political strategy may need, for a time at least, an element of secrecy, and is thus vulnerable to being dubbed conspiratorial. Corruption itself has the character of conspiracy. In this sense the Crédit Mobilier was a conspiracy, as was the Teapot Dome affair. If we tend to be too condescending to the Populists at this point, it may be necessary to remind ourselves that they had seen so much bribery and corruption, particularly on the part of the railroads, that they had before them a convincing model of the management of affairs through conspiratorial behavior. Indeed, what makes conspiracy theories so widely acceptable is that they usually contain a germ of truth. But there is a great difference between locating conspiracies *in* history and saying that history *is*, in effect, a conspiracy, between singling out those conspiratorial acts that do on occasion occur and weaving a vast fabric of social explanation out of nothing but skeins of evil plots.

When conspiracies do not exist it is necessary for those who think in this fashion to invent them. Among the most celebrated instances in modern history are the forgery of the Protocols of the Elders of Zion and the grandiose fabrication under Stalin's regime of the Trotzkyite-Bukharinite-Zinovievite center. These inventions were cynical. In the history of American political controversy there is a tradition of conspiratorial accusations which seem to have been sincerely believed. Jefferson appears really to have believed, at one time, that the Federalists were conspiring to re-establish monarchy. Some Federalists believed that the Jeffersonians were conspiring to subvert Christianity. The movement to annex Texas and the war with Mexico were alleged by many Northerners to be a slaveholders' conspiracy. The early Republican leaders, including Lincoln, charged that there was a conspiracy on the part of Stephen A. Douglas to make slavery a nationwide institution. Such pre-Civil War parties as the Know-Nothing and Anti-Masonic movements were based almost entirely upon conspiratorial ideology. The Nye Committee, years ago, tried to prove that our entry into the first World War was the work of a conspiracy of bankers and munitions-makers. And now not only our entry into the second World War, but the entire history of the past twenty years or so is being given the color of conspiracy by the cranks and political fakirs of our own age.[3]

Nevertheless, when these qualifications have been taken into account, it remains true that Populist thought showed an unusually strong tendency to account for relatively impersonal events in highly personal terms. An overwhelming sense of grievance does not find satisfactory expression in impersonal explanations, except among those with a well-developed tradition of intellectualism. It is the city, after all, that is the home of intellectual complexity. The farmer lived in isolation from the great world in which his fate was actually decided. He was accused of being unusually suspicious,[4] and certainly his situation, trying as it was, made thinking in impersonal terms difficult. Perhaps the rural middle-class leaders of Populism (this was a movement of farmers, but it was not led by farmers) had more to do than the farmer himself with the cast of Populist thinking. At any rate, Populist thought often carries one into a world in which the simple virtues and unmitigated villainies of a rural melodrama have been projected on a national and even an international scale. In Populist thought the farmer is not a speculating businessman, victimized by the risk economy of which he is a part, but rather a wounded yeoman, preyed upon by those who are alien to the life of folkish virtue. A villain was needed, marked with the unmistakable stigmata of the villains of melodrama, and the more remote he was from the familiar scene, the more plausibly his villainies could be exaggerated . . . .

One feature of the Populist conspiracy theory that has been generally overlooked is its frequent link with a kind of rhetorical anti-Semitism. The slight current of anti-Semitism that existed in the United States before the 1890's had been associated with problems of money and credit.[5] During the closing years of the century it grew noticeably.[6] While the jocose and rather heavy-handed anti-Semitism that can be found in Henry Adams's letters of the 1890's shows that this prejudice existed outside Populist literature, it was chiefly Populist writers who expressed that identification of the Jew with the usurer and the "international gold ring" which was the central theme of the American anti-Semitism of the age. The omnipresent symbol of Shylock can hardly be taken in itself as evidence of anti-Semitism, but the frequent references to the House of Rothschild make it clear that for many silverites the Jew was an organic part of the conspiracy theory of history. Coin Harvey's Baron Rothe was clearly meant to be Rothschild; his Rogasner (Ernest Seyd?) was a dark figure out of the coarsest anti-Semitic tradition. "You are very wise in your way," Rogasner is told at the climax of the tale, "the commercial way, inbred through generations. The politic, scheming, devious way, inbred through generations also."[7] One of the cartoons in the effectively illustrated *Coin's Financial School* showed a map of the world dominated by the tentacles of an octopus at the site of the British Isles, labeled: "Rothschilds."[8] In Populist demonology, anti-Semitism and Anglophobia went hand in hand.

The note of anti-Semitism was often sounded openly in the campaign for silver. A representative of the New Jersey Grange, for instance, did not hesitate to warn the members of the Second National Silver Convention of 1892 to watch out for political candidates who represented "Wall Street, and the Jews of Europe."[9] Mary E. Lease described Grover Cleveland as "the agent of Jewish bankers and British gold."[10] Donnelly represented the leader of the governing Council of plutocrats in *Caesar's Column,* one Prince Cabano, as a powerful Jew, born Jacob Isaacs; one of the triumvirate who lead the Brotherhood of Destruction is also an exiled Russian Jew, who flees from the apocalyptic carnage with a hundred million dollars which he intends to use to "revive the ancient splendors of the Jewish race, in the midst of the ruins of the world."[11] One of the more elaborate documents of the conspiracy school traced the power of the Rothschilds over America to a transaction between Hugh McCulloch, Secretary of the Treasury under Lincoln and Johnson, and Baron James Rothschild. "The most direful part of this business between Rothschild and the United States Treasury was not the loss of money, even by hundreds of millions. It was the resignation of the country itself into the hands of England, as England had long been resigned into the hands of her Jews."[12]

Such rhetoric, which became common currency in the movement, later passed beyond Populism into the larger stream of political protest. By the time the campaign of 1896 arrived, an Associated Press reporter noticed as "one of the striking things" about the Populist convention at St. Louis "the extraordinary hatred of the Jewish race. It is not possible to go into any hotel in the city without hearing the most bitter denunciation of the Jews as a class and of the particular Jews who happen to have prospered in the world."[13] This report may have been somewhat overdone, but the identification of the silver cause with anti-Semitism did become close enough for Bryan to have to pause in the midst of his campaign to explain to the Jewish Democrats of Chicago that in denouncing the policies of the Rothschilds he and his silver friends were "not attacking a race; we are attacking greed and avarice which know no race or religion."[14]

It would be easy to misstate the character of Populist anti-Semitism or to exaggerate its intensity. For Populist anti-Semitism was entirely verbal. It was a mode of expression, a rhetorical style, not a tactic or a program. It did not lead to exclusion laws, much less to riots or pogroms. There were, after all, relatively few Jews in the United States in the late 1880's and early 1890's, most of them remote from the areas of Populist strength. It is one thing, however, to say that this prejudice did not go beyond a certain symbolic usage, quite another to say that a people's choice of symbols is of no significance. Populist anti-Semitism does have its importance—chiefly as a symptom of a certain ominous credulity in the Populist mind. It is not too much to say that the Greenback-Populist tradition activated most of what we have of modern popular anti-Semitism in the United States.[15] . . .

FOOTNOTES

1. In this respect it is worth pointing out that in later years, when facilities for realistic exposure became more adequate, popular attacks on "the money power' showed fewer elements of fantasy and more of reality.

2. See, for instance, the remarks about a mysterious series of international assassinations with which Mary E. Lease opens her book *The Problem of Civilization Solved* (Chicago, 1895).

3. One by-product of this conspiratorial mania is the myth that the recognition of Russia in 1933 was the result of a plot by the New Dealers. Paul Boller, Jr., in a highly amusing article, "The 'Great Conspiracy' of 1933: a Study in Short Memories," *Southwest Review*, Vol. XXXIX (Spring, 1954), pp. 97-112, shows that some of the same persons who have indulged in the conspiracy cry were advocates of recognition before 1933.

In reading the excellent study by Leo Lowenthal and Norbert Guterman, *Prophets of Deceit* (New York, 1949), a study of recent authoritarian agitators, I am impressed by certain similarities in the style of thought displayed by their subjects and that of a certain type of Populist writer represented by Mrs. Emery, "Coin" Harvey, Donnelly, and Mrs. Lease. There seem to be certain persistent themes in popular agitation of this sort that transcend particular historical eras. Among the themes delineated by Lowenthal and Guterman that one finds in Populist literature as well as among their agitators are the following: the conception of history as conspiracy; an obsessive concern with the fabulous enjoyments deemed to be the lot of the plutocrats; cynicism about the two-party system; the notion that the world is moving toward an immense apocalypse; the exclusive attention to the greed and other personal vices of bankers and other selected plutocrats, as opposed to a structural analysis of the social system; anti-Semitism and xenophobia, the appeal to the native simplicity and virtue of the folk. There are of course, other themes singled out by Lowenthal and Guterman that seem more peculiar to the conditions of our own time and lack cognates in the literature of Populism.

4. Frederick L. Paxson: "The Agricultural Surplus: A Problem in History," *Agricultural History*, Vol. VI (April 1932), p. 58; cf. the observations of Lord Bryce in *The American Commonwealth* (New York, ed. 1897), Vol. II, pp. 294-5.

5. Anti-Semitism as a kind of rhetorical flourish seems to have had a long underground history in the United States. During the panic of 1837, when many states defaulted on their obligations, many of which were held by foreigners, we find Governor McNutt of Mississippi defending the practice by baiting Baron Rothschild: "The blood of Judas and Shylock flows in his veins, and he unites the qualities of both his countrymen . . . ." Quoted by George W. Edwards: *The Evolution of Finance Capitalism* (New York, 1938), p. 149. Similarly, we find Thaddeus Stevens assailing "the Rothschilds, Goldsmiths, and other large money dealers" during his early appeals for greenbacks. See James A. Woodburn: *The Life of Thaddeus Stevens* (Indianapolis, 1913), pp. 576, 579.

6. See Oscar Handlin: "American Views of the Jew at the Opening of the Twentieth Century," *Publications of the American Jewish Historical Society*, no. 40 (June 1951), pp. 323-44.

7. W. H. Harvey: *A Tale of Two Nations* (Chicago, 1894), p. 289; cf. also p. 265: "Did not our ancestors . . . take whatever women of whatever race most pleased their fancy?"

8. Harvey: *Coin's Financial School* (Chicago, 1894), p. 124; for a notable polemic against the Jews, see James B. Goode: *The Modern Banker* (Chicago, 1896), chapter xii.

9. *Proceedings of the Second National Silver Convention* (Washington, 1892), p. 48.

10. Mary E. Lease: *The Problem of Civilization Solved*, pp. 319-20; cf. p. 291.

11. Ignatius Donnelly: *Caesar's Column* (Chicago, 1891), pp. 147, 172, 331.

12. Gordon Clark; *Shylock: as Banker, Bondholder, Corruptionist, Conspirator* (Washington, 1894), pp. 59-60; for the linkage between anti-Semitism and the

conspiracy theme, see pp. 2, 4, 8, 39, 55-8, 102-3, 112-13, 117. There was a somewhat self-conscious and apologetic note in populistic anti-Semitism. Remarking that "the aristocracy of the world is now almost altogether of Hebrew origin," one of Donnelly's characters explains that the terrible persecutions to which the Jews had been subjected for centuries heightened the selective process among them, leaving "only the strong of body, the cunning of brain, the long-headed, the persistent . . . and now the Christian world is paying, in tears and blood, for the sufferings inflicted by their bigoted and ignorant ancestors upon a noble race. When the time came for liberty and fair play the Jew was master in the contest with the Gentile, who hated and feared him." *Caesar's Column,* p. 37. In another fanciful tale Donnelly made amends to the Jews by restoring Palestine to them and making it very prosperous. *The Golden Bottle* (New York and St. Paul, 1892), pp. 280-1.

13. Quoted by Edward Flower: *Anti-Semitism in the Free Silver and Populist Movements and the Election of 1896,* unpublished M.A. Thesis, Columbia University, 1952, p. 27; this essay is illuminating on the development of anti-Semitism in this period and on the reaction of some of the Jewish press.

14. William Jennings Bryan: *The First Battle* (Chicago, 1897), p. 581.

8

Commentary on "Consensus and Continuity" in Post War Historical Interpretations

J. ROGERS HOLLINGSWORTH (1962)

In the following essay, J. Rogers Hollingsworth (b. 1932), professor of history at the University of Wisconsin, provided a comprehensive review of many of the new interpretations written during the 1940s and 1950s. He illustrated the post-war emphases by historians upon consensus rather than conflict, and upon continuity rather than drastic change. The American past thus became more homogeneous than it was to the progressive historians, and Hollingsworth explained the new homogeneity as a reflection of the climate of opinion in which the post-war historians were writing. Since they were living in an America different from that of the progressive scholars, so a different interpretation of the past was created. Because Hollingsworth related scholarship to climate of opinion, he accurately predicted in the essay's last paragraph that the emergence of yet another mood in the 1960s would again bring historical interpretations reminiscent of the progressives.

Reprinted by permission from J. Rogers Hollingsworth, "Consensus and Continuity in Recent American Historical Writing," *South Atlantic Quarterly,* LXI, Winter 1962, pp. 40-50.

Following the Second World War, a change in the intellectual climate of this nation took place a change reflected in the diminished appeal of New Dealers and the decline of ideology. Unlike the crusading thirties, the postwar period was favorable to a conservative position in politics. But in contrast to the conservatism of Metternich, De Maistre, Bonald, or Barrés, the outlook had a peculiarly American flavor. It was more of an attitude toward life than it was a political doctrine or economic dogma. In essence, it represented a fusion of a conservative temper with a liberal state of mind. The left and the right had merged, causing the traditional distinctions between conservatism and liberalism to become blurred. The American people had become more middle-of-the-road, more traditionalist, and more nostalgic.

The reasons for this change were many. The war had brought about a widespread disillusionment with utopias of the left and the right. Absolute utopias of fascism and communism had been tested and found wanting. But more important, American society had become more integrated and homogeneous than at any other time in its history. A more equitable distribution of wealth and the impact of mass communications caused regional, racial, religious, and class barriers throughout all America to melt. Prosperity promoted a widespread sense of complacency. Psychologically, the American people had become weary with experimentation and novelty. Desiring social and economic stability, people began to talk about the necessity for preserving the American way of life.

Meantime, a series of international events further tarnished the revolutionary enthusiasm of the thirties. Significant were the Berlin blockade, the rape of Czechoslovakia, the triumph of the Chinese Reds, the outbreak of the Korean War, and the Communist hysteria in America. As a result, doubts, worry, and pessimism replaced action and confidence.

The opposition of Congress to Truman's welfare programs and the victory of Eisenhower in 1952 were outward manifestations of the change in temper which had taken place since the crusading thirties. Demonstrating that he saw no conflict between liberalism and conservatism, Eisenhower announced to the nation that his administration would be conservative in economics and liberal in human welfare. His ambivalence was shared by such prominent Americans as Adlai Stevenson and Nelson Rockefeller. Idol of the nation's liberals, Stevenson during the campaign of 1952 stated that "the strange alchemy of our time has somehow converted the Democrats into the truly conservative party of this country."

Not only did these changes affect popular opinion, but some of the nation's most serious intellectuals began to share the new mood. The publication in 1949 of Peter Viereck's *Conservatism Revisited* seems to have been the signal for a number of books and articles which asserted a conservative creed as a guide for action in America. Other books were Russell Kirk's *The Conservative Mind,* August Heckscher's *A Pattern for Politics,* Francis Wilson's *The Case for Conservatism,* and Viereck again in his *Shame and Glory of the Intellectuals, The Unadjusted Man, and Conservatism: From John Adams to Churchill.* Writers with similar leanings were Thomas I. Cook, Raymond English, Allen Tate, and Russell Davenport.

It was not long before some of the nation's best historians became spokesmen of the new age. Reflecting their prosperous and conforming society, a number of historians began to emphasize conservatism as the dominant force in the American past. The Federalist party, George Washington, Alexander Hamilton, and John Adams became progenitors of a conservative tradition. Other conservatives pressed into service with new and impressive biographies were John Quincy Adams, John C. Calhoun, Brooks Adams, Henry Adams, William Graham Sumner, Elihu Root, and Henry Stimson.

Meanwhile, the triumvirate of Frederick Jackson Turner, Charles Beard, and Vernon Parrington no longer exercised a persuasive influence on the writing of American history. These writers had stressed conflict as a basic theme in the American past by emphasizing section versus section, class versus class, ideology versus ideology, agrarianism versus industrialism. But to a generation seeking to explain the uniqueness and essence of America, such themes appeared confusing and paradoxical. A more inspiring source has been Alexis de Tocqueville's *Democracy in America,* which emphasized uniformity, mediocrity, and the equality of condition in America.

Rather than stressing dualisms, recent historians have described an America with a unified past. As classes, sections, and ideologies have melted into myths, a history characterized by consensus and continuity has emerged. It is history attempting to unite the variety in the American past into one grand scheme, an all-encompassing thought or expression.

The leaders of this type of writing have been Louis Hartz, Clinton Rossiter, and Daniel Boorstin. Hartz's book, *The Liberal Tradition in America,* was probably the most influential work to appear during the last decade. While Hartz is no conservative, he does reflect the conservative mood in his search for unity in the American past. His ideas about the American Revolution are typical of his position. Emphasizing the continuity in the American past, Hartz denies that there was an American revolution. He points out that the Americans did not have to fight for their freedom, that they were born free. Unlike the Europeans, the American people escaped a feudal society, an aristocracy, and fixed status. The task for the Americans was to conserve the freedom they already had. The result was, Hartz argues, a property-owning, middle-class, Lockean society which has existed down to the present day. Unreceptive to new ideas, America has always been closed and impervious to any other set of values.

Reacting against the conflict thesis of American history, other recent writers have also emphasized the inherent conservatism of the American Revolution. In fact, most of the writing during the last ten years on the period between 1775 and 1787 has stressed its conservative character and the continuity of the political and constitutional aspect of the Confederation with the experiences and institutions of the colonies. Rather than writing about the upheaval during the period, such writers as Benjamin F. Wright, Daniel Boorstin, and Clinton Rossiter have stressed the existence of consensus rooted in the common life, habits, and institutions of several generations. One aspect of the conservatism imputed to the Revolutionary era is that these writers see Jefferson and the Declaration of Independence as pillars of conservatism.

Starting from a different position, but arriving at essentially the same conclusion as Louis Hartz, Rossiter tells us that the political theory of the colonial period was characterized by a "deep-rooted conservatism" because the colonists had already achieved freedom and did not have to fight for it. The goal "was simply to consolidate, then expand by cautious stages, the large measure of liberty and prosperity that was part of their established way of life." Continuing, Rossiter finds in the entire American past the conservative qualities of traditionalism, unity, and constitutionalism. He argues that Americans have been conservative in their constitutionalism, in their two-party system, in their individualistic collectivism, in their community ties and voluntary co-operation, in their class structure, and in the traditionalism of their patriotism. According to Rossiter, we have long been a "citadel of conservatism" and have been radical only in economics and technology. "The political American has been the most conservative of all."

As part of this monolithic approach to American history, other writers tell us that prior to the adoption of the federal Constitution, American society was fundamentally equalitarian and middle class, not divided sharply along economic lines; that there was never the straightforward cleavage between Hamilton and Jefferson that has frequently been depicted; that the Jacksonians, being neither radicals nor innovators, were trying to maintain the values of a bygone age; and that both the North and the South during the two decades immediately preceding the Civil War were not nearly as distinct in outlook as they have generally been portrayed. Daniel Boorstin goes further, by suggesting that the Civil War was not a second revolution, as the Beards argued. Neither side raised any basic political issues. Instead, the struggle took place within the framework of traditional legal argument and the American federal system, illustrating the continuity of American history.

The influence of the new writing is equally evident for the post-Civil War period. With the Second World War and the cold war setting in motion a new reconstruction of the South, several historians have employed the consensus and continuity themes to further their understanding of the issues raised in the Reconstruction of 1865-1877. No longer does a large school of historians subscribe to the views that carpetbaggers and southern white Republicans were wicked, that all southern Negroes were illiterate incompetents, and that the entire white South owes a debt of gratitude to the restorers of white supremacy. Some of the best of the new studies reveal that the "scalawags" were not all the ragged underlings of southern society, but included many erstwhile southern Whigs who ranked high in social status. Further, the radicals, in Congress and the South, are no longer portrayed as the purposeful and unified group of conspirators that they have previously been made out to be. Several recent writers have taken a much closer look at the corruption of the period and concluded that the corruption of Reconstruction days was not significantly different from the widespread land frauds in the sale of the public domain, the banking swindles and internal improvement bubbles of the 1830's, the state and local corruption of the Progressive period, the scandals of the Harding regime, and in our own day the much-advertised corruption in labor unions, rigged television shows, the licensing scandals, the fixing of basketball games, and tax evasion. Thus, some of our better historians contend that Reconstruction can be meaningful only if viewed in terms of the totality of American history. Maintaining that the sectional approach to the study of Reconstruction has lost its vitality, they stress the similarities of patterns which are visible in North, South, and West.

Studies of the more recent periods also reflect the historian's preoccupation with his present-day values. Nowhere is this more apparent than in Richard Hofstadter's *The Age of Reform,* which won a Pulitzer prize. Minimizing the economic and political conflicts of the late nineteenth century, Hofstadter identifies the Populist as a rural businessman motivated by a drive for higher status. The Populist was nostalgic for a social order in which the small farmer had enjoyed a more secure status. That is, he demanded a return to a more individualistic, equalitarian America–a return to an age when America was not controlled by industrial combines, business monopolies, and finance capitalism. Instead of being a radical, the Populist was a "harassed little businessman" with a conservative outlook.

The Progressive movement, likewise, has a number of new interpreters. Formerly, writers viewed the movement in dualistic terms, with the Progressives being farmers and small merchants who were devoted to the agrarian principles of a provincial, individualistic, egalitarian democracy. Their enemies were the giant corporations and eastern financiers who were transforming the country into one huge machine whereby a few industrial and financial bosses could hold the rest of the nation in poverty and subjection. In contrast, the newer interpretations are monolithic, with a minimum of emphasis on the class and ideological conflicts. Again, Hofstadter has led the way. Explaining the Progressive movement in terms of a status revolution, he argues that during the nineties and into the new century the old urban, unorganized, educated middle class became increasingly aware that it was losing its privileged position in American society. This group, which included lawyers, doctors, ministers, editors, and independent businessmen, had long supplied the intellectual, moral, and political leadership of the country. Now, its position was assaulted by both the leaders of the giant corporations and the rising labor unions. As the power of the corporations and labor unions penetrated into most sectors of society, the frustration of members of this old American group became acute. They were the victims "of an upheaval in status" which pertained not so much to their relative economic position as to "the changed pattern in the distribution of deference and power."

Other writers–particularly Daniel Aaron, Arthur A. Ekirch, John Blum, and Arthur Link–have also minimized the liberal aspects of Progressivism. For example, Ekirch maintains that the Progressive movement, while supporting some liberal causes and opposing many domestic abuses, was not a liberal movement. Instead, the Progressives almost completely abandoned the philosophy of natural rights for a kind of political instrumentalism. Ekirch emphasizes the Hamiltonian character of Progressivism, the influence of collectivist and statist views from Europe on the evolution of American Progressivism, and the close relationship between "the aggressive foreign policy of the progressives and their emphasis on nationalism in home affairs."

But no one has made a more penetrating analysis of the conservative quality of Progressivism than John Blum in his book, *The Republican Roosevelt.* His most challenging as well as most debatable argument is that

Theodore Roosevelt was a conservative. Blum maintains that a number of factors clearly place Roosevelt in the conservative tradition—his use of power, his approach to his party and the people, the methods he employed in dealing with Congress, his reverence for the past and its traditions, and his interest in the processes of government. In another work, *Woodrow Wilson and the Politics of Morality,* Blum also stresses the conservative side of Progressivism. He writes, "Wilson's was a nineteenth-century intelligence, obsolescing at a rapid rate and this obsolescence the war accelerated. Conscience and intellect . . . stood still while the race of time transfigured the world they understood." Concerning Wilson's domestic programs, Blum contends that they satisfied the yearnings of the past rather than "the needs of the future"—that Wilson's programs were "to become the pattern of normalcy" in the 1920's and that they contained something of the spirit that was, years later, to lead many to the Liberty League.

Ironically, as Progressivism has become more conservative, historians have stressed the continuity between Wilson's administrations and the twenties. Denying that the decade was a period of extraordinary reaction against idealism and reform, Arthur Link argues that the Progressive movement was far from dead during the 1920's. Link suggests that the Progressives combined in Congress to control the legislative branch during most of the twenties, to thwart the conservative executive leadership, and to push through a remarkable progressive legislative program, the most advanced parts of which were nullified by presidential vetoes. "Progressivism as an articulate expression of social and economic aspiring not only survived but also widened its horizons."

One characteristic of the continuity theme is that a reinterpretation of any one period affects all subsequent American history. Thus, as the twenties have become a decade of Progressivism, the New Deal has become more conservative. Whereas it was once quite common for writers to state that the New Deal was a revolution or at least a departure from the American tradition, today most historians accept Henry Steele Commager's judgment that the New Deal "was no revolution, but rather the culmination of half a century of historical development." On one occasion, Commager even asserted that Franklin Roosevelt "was the greatest conservative since Alexander Hamilton."

At the same time that the distinctions between periods have disappeared, historians have also played down the distinctions between groups. Undoubtedly, this has been a reaction on the part of the historian to the increasing homogeneity of American society. Though one can find such writing in almost any aspect of American history, the consensus thesis has been particularly important in reinterpreting regional, social, and intellectual history.

In a recent collection of essays, *The Southerner as American,* some of the nation's best historians of the South contend that the traditional emphasis on the South's distinctiveness and on the conflicts between the South and the rest of the nation is wrong historically. Attempting to minimize the distinctions between the South and other parts of the nation, these writers argue "that the most important fact about the Southerner is that he has been throughout his history an American. The conflicts that have been so much a part of the Southern experience have occurred between Southerners and within Southerners as much as between North and South." They maintain that the South's history has never properly been understood, that the South has seldom been viewed in its proper relations with the rest of the nation. Even southerners have been unable to understand themselves. As a result, the South accepted and in part created "a false history, a false image of itself, and a mythical social ideal that Southerners had not really accepted even in the heyday of secession." The writers imply that this false history cannot be corrected until the similarities between the South and the rest of the nation have been properly studied.

Impressed by the homogeneity which he found in this country as an English observer, Henry Pelling in his *American Labor* presents an interpretation typical of the consensus thesis. Unlike much of our labor history, which emphasizes the conflict between labor and management, Pelling's book minimizes the class conflict in American history. The author stresses the similarity in the economic thinking of management and labor during much of the American past, and points out that both held views akin to a laissez-faire concept of economics. Pelling argues that "the final permanent characteristic of American labor . . . is its lack of class consciousness," its failure to develop a self-identifying stereotype, a characteristic also shared by American businessmen.

What Henry Pelling has done for labor history, Sidney E. Mead has undertaken for the history of American religion. In his writings, he plays down the issues separating the various religious groups and argues that the only things separating the various denominations have been their irrelevant characteristics—that the essentials of every sect have been held in common by all groups. Thus, he concludes that "a sense of irrelevance has always haunted" America's religious leaders.

In the area of foreign affairs, we are told that to continue thinking in terms of a conflict between isolationists and internationalists is meaningless, that the concept of isolationism must be discarded as a myth. Samuel Lubell and others now tell us that what historians have generally referred to as isolationism amounts to little more than the existence of pro-German and anti-British ethnic prejudices and the exploiting of these prejudices by an opposition political party, and yesterday's isolationists may well appear to be tomorrow's internationalists.

But in no type of historical writing are the themes of continuity and consensus so well combined as in recent American literary scholarship. The fashion is to discover in American literature a stable, unchanging tradition. Over and over again, writers analyze James Fenimore Cooper, Ralph Waldo Emerson, Nathaniel Hawthorne, Herman Melville, Walt Whitman, Henry James, Mark Twain, Scott Fitzgerald, Thomas Wolfe, and William Faulkner. The result has become a unified literary past. For example, Richard Lewis in his *The American Adam* describes the hero of Faulkner's "The Bear" as Cooper's Natty Bumppo "recreated by the dark energies of a Hawthorne." In discussing *The Great Gatsby,* Richard Chase suggests that Scott Fitzgerald's hero is in the tradition not only of Benjamin Franklin but also of Natty Bumppo, Melville's Ishmael, and Huck Finn. "He shares their ideal of innocence, escape, and the purely personal code of conduct. Like them he derives his values not from the way of the world, but from an earlier pastoral ideal."

Despite the popularity of these conservative interpretations, the themes of consensus and continuity were certainly not the only ones which have been stressed since 1945. Some of our best histories in recent years have emphasized the conflict in the American past. Nowhere has this been more evident than in the brilliant writing by Allan Nevins and Bruce Catton on the Civil War or Arthur Schlesinger, Jr.'s colorful accounts of Franklin D. Roosevelt. Nevertheless, the themes of consensus and continuity have been more widespread than any other and have had a considerable impact on the writing of American history.

Though such interpretations may have distorted certain aspects of the American past, these themes have served a very useful purpose. In a period when the American people have had an insatiable desire to develop an image of themselves and to explain their institutions to people of other nations, the consensus and continuity themes have helped to point out the distinctiveness of American history—thus permitting the American people better to understand what it means to be an American.

The consensus thesis has taught us that American society has operated within a much narrower framework than societies whose histories have been the stories of conflict between extreme ideological positions. But despite the narrow ideological framework within which American history has occurred, there has been much conflict in the American past. Though the French and Russian revolutions were much more radical than the American, the Americans did have a revolution of considerable proportions which swept away many Old World legal, political, economic, and social vestiges. In subsequent periods of American history, the struggles to free the slaves, to abolish imprisonment for debt, to enfranchise the propertyless, to organize labor unions, or to guarantee the civil rights of all Americans were not created by the imaginations of ambitious historians any more than the conflicts between Hamilton and Jefferson, McKinley and Bryan, agrarianism and industrialism, management and labor. For the participants of these struggles, the battles were no less real than conflict in any other society. Without conflict, disillusionment, and tragedy, American development could not have taken the course which it has. These factors are as indispensable for understanding our nations' past as America's optimistic, democratic tradition.

As American historians continue to reflect the values and sentiments of their contemporary society, the themes of conflict and diversity will probably receive greater emphasis in historical writing during the sixties. Already, there is evidence that the tone of the 1960's will be substantially different from that of the Age of Eisenhower. Significant is the election of John F. Kennedy as president, following his campaign promising basic changes in domestic and foreign policies. After almost a decade of silence, college students throughout America have once again made the nation's headlines. They are fighting the loyalty oath provisions of the National Defense Education Act, supporting Negro sit-in demonstrations, urging nuclear disarmament, participating in freedom rides, assisting the establishment of a peace corps, and rioting against the House Un-American Activities Committee. While critics such as C. Wright Mills, David Riesman, and William H. Whyte, Jr., protested against the middle-class conformity of the 1950's, sociologists are again emphasizing the variety which still exists in American society. Though few observers will deny that ethnic and regional distinctions are disappearing in America, writers are beginning to stress class differences as an important source of diversity in American life. Perhaps it will not be long before historians respond to this new temper and again stress the variety, change, and conflict which have made American history so rich in human experience.

Part Three

A Dissenting Neo-Progressivism in the 1960s: The New Left Historians

9

The Historian as Participant

STAUGHTON LYND (1967)

The 1960s crystallized a dissenting mood within the larger post-war climate of opinion. It would not be accurate to say that the dominant temper of the 1940s and 1950s was dissipated, for in fact it remained supreme, at least among older age groups. However, particularly among the younger generations, there emerged a significant echo of the early twentieth-century social protest and sympathy for reform.

Even public events during the late 1950s and the 1960s suggested some changes in the popular temper. Official government concern for Negro civil rights in the South was supported by thousands of young white Northerners who went South to help in voter registration and to agitate with Negroes on behalf of equal treatment. Republican control of the White House was after eight years interrupted by John F. Kennedy's call to the New Frontier and a war, or a skirmish at any rate, with domestic poverty. Despite the gradual involvement of the United States in a Vietnamese war during the 1960s, public opinion clearly did not support this war as it had the Korean War in the early 1950s, and anti-war sentiment mounted to heights unequalled since the early and middle 1930s.

As sometimes has been the case with conflicting climates of opinion in a given society at a particular time, correlations could be made in the United States during the 1960s between attitudes and age groups. Daniel Boorstin and Richard Hofstadter, for example, were born during World War I and achieved intellectual and scholarly maturity during the 'thirties and 'forties. The development of their thought was crucially related to the socialist and reformist dreams of the 1930s, the consequent disillusionment of many radicals in the late 1930s and the 1940s, and the celebration of traditional America during the Cold War of the late 1940s and the 1950s. The

Reprinted by permission from Staughton Lynd, "A Profession of History," *The New Journal,* I, November 12, 1967, pp. 10-12. Reprinted, with slight alterations, in *New American Review #2,* The New American Library, New York, 1968, pp. 192-205, from which the present text is taken.

confrontation of their youthful hopes with European totalitarianism, from which resulted their rejection of progressive or radical social thought, comprised the major intellectual event for the generation represented by Boorstin and Hofstadter. By contrast, those younger Americans born during or after the Great Depression grew to maturity during the Cold War. The existence of totalitarianism constituted for many of them either, on the one hand, something taken for granted and of little interest or, on the other, a starting point rather than a conclusion, as it had been for the older generation. Many of the younger Americans saw the Cold War against Communism to lack moral sanction even before the Vietnam situation reached its climax, especially in view of the unfair treatment of Negroes at home and the inability to end poverty in what was the world's richest country. By the 1960s these younger Americans had created among themselves the greatest predisposition for change and the most intense criticism of domestic and foreign policy since the 1930s.

The unusually frank autobiographical essay reprinted below by Staughton Lynd (b. 1929), a young professor of history who has taught at Spelman College and at Yale and Roosevelt Universities, clearly revealed the relationship between his reformist sympathies and his historical scholarship. Lynd has been one of the leaders during the 1960s both in the civil rights movement and in the protest against American foreign policy in Vietnam. He was director of the Mississippi Freedom Schools in the summer of 1964, and he visited North Vietnam and reported the trip in *The Other Side,* published in 1966, where he criticized the role of the United States in the war.

Lynd's essay in 1967 was reminiscent of Charles Beard's "Written History as an Act of Faith" more than 30 years before. Also an activist, Beard dismissed historical determinism in his presidential address in 1933; he also dismissed the possibility of historical objectivity, and asserted that each historian had to select his own interpretative scheme in which to arrange his data. Furthermore, Beard accented the importance of having an awareness of the various possibilities for change and of developing an ability to predict the future. Beard went on to declare that the wisdom of a historian was in part dependent upon whether the future validated his views. Finally, Beard accepted as legitimate the fact that personal social preferences formed a part of each historian's interpretative scheme, and indicated that his own preference—also his prediction—was that modern man was moving in the direction of a collectivist democracy.

Lynd, a greater activist than Beard and even more critical of the United States, found himself confronted by many of the same questions. Convinced that an economic interpretation of history was fundamental, Lynd's first research project was an examination of Beard's thesis that the conflict over ratification of the Constitution was a conflict among certain economic groups. In retrospect, Lynd admitted that the particular area he chose for his test case could have been predicted to reveal confirmation of Beard's hypothesis, as Lynd had hoped it would. Lynd was aware that his own work thus exemplified Beard's statement about the influence of a historian's bias and the arbitrary selection of research topics but, like Beard, he saw no escape from it. Further, since Lynd had taught in a Southern Negro college during the civil rights movement, he felt increasingly drawn to research topics of great contemporary consequence. After having reviewed the question of whether it was possible for a historian to carry out his scholarship with complete objectivity and having concluded that this was not possible, Lynd faced the question of historical determinism, in its Marxist form. Here Lynd's greater activism made him approach the problem not so much from Beard's perspective—of the past as being inevitably determined to the historian in retrospect—but from the angle of the historical participant himself at the time of his participation. To the participant, Lynd argued, the world was and had to be open to many possibilities; given that fact, it would not do for the historian retrospectively to assert that what was chosen necessarily had to be chosen. The extent of Lynd's commitment to active participation can be perceived by realizing that this shift in viewpoint from the retrospective historian to the active contemporary participant led him to establish the criterion for judging why things happened as they did. Consistent with his emphasis upon history as a contemporary event, Lynd suggested that it is by focusing upon the recent past, the present, and the future that historians capture the fresh recollections of participants and influence current affairs. Like Beard, Lynd concluded with the hope that historians could create a past usable for reform of the present and the hope that history was moving in the direction of a collectivist democracy.

A profession, according to Webster's International Dictionary, is an "open declaration" or "public avowal" as well as "the occupation, if not purely commercial, mechanical, agricultural, or the like, to which one devotes oneself." The word itself suggests that a profession is not just something a person does but something he believes in doing. Those who profess a religious faith recognize that their profession becomes dead unless it is renewed by frequent rediscovery of its reason for being. Accordingly, the religious professor may quest from a first to a second, from a second to a third profession of religious faith during a lifetime's experience of ultimate things. The man committed to a craft should ask no less of himself. He should frequently inquire what task it was that he chose this particular set of tools to perform, and be prepared to change tools if the task's requirements have come to seem different to him.

I

I decided to become a historian when I was twenty-nine. I had "taken" (an odd word) no more than two or three semesters of history as an undergraduate. But during a checkered, prolonged adolescence in which I did graduate work in city planning, served as a non-combatant conscientious objector in the United States Army, milked cows and made children's toys in a utopian community, and organized site tenants on New York's Lower East Side, I carried about with me two books on history: *The Historian's Craft* by Marc Bloch and *The Idea of History* by R. G. Collingwood.

I liked these books. Bloch's appealed to me because he wrote it as a member of the French Resistance, without the aid of books and papers, shortly before his death at the hands of the Nazis, and because he conveyed a sense of history as a craft: something that had its own tools, which demanded (so to speak) a feel for cloth and leather before one could do it well, a discipline to which a man might apprentice himself.

History as described by Bloch appeared to be controlled by the opaque, objective events with which it was concerned, and thus to be less prone to arbitrary manipulation and subjective whim than other social science disciplines.

The Idea of History was attractive for the opposite reason. It demythologized the aura surrounding the historical profession by insisting that all that a man could know of the past was the minds of other men, so that "history" in fact amounted to rethinking a portion of what human beings had thought before. "Progress," then, was defined by Collingwood as action proceeding from thought that had experienced the best of previous thought before deciding how to act. Taken together, the two books seemed to me the embodiment of intellectual elegance; the intellectual activity they analyzed appeared solid, and serviceable to strivings toward a better world, which mattered very much to me.

When I "went in" to history I began with Charles Beard's interpretation of the United States Constitution. I think now that there were two reasons for this choice, again somewhat in tension with each other.

At the time I explained my choice of subject matter on the ground that Beard's was the most important attempt to date at an economic interpretation of American history, and that I was enough of a Marxist to find this a logical point of departure. If that *was* the reason why I began my work as a historian by seeking a local microcosm in which to test the thesis of Beard's *Economic Interpretation of the Constitution of the United States,* I have mixed feelings about it now. On the one hand it still makes sense to me that, like any other scientist, the historian should formulate hypotheses and then test them against a restricted range of data, such as what happened in one area, or in one man's life. On the other hand I am now more conscious that I selected a range of data that I could be relatively certain would substantiate a thesis I hoped was true. I studied opposition to the United States Constitution in Dutchess County, New York, because Dutchess County had a history of landlord-tenant conflict very likely to be connected with how groups aligned themselves for or against ratification of the Constitution. The bias involved in my selection of Dutchess County did not necessarily invalidate my findings, but it raised serious question as to their generalizability. I believe this is how bias characteristically operates in the work of other historians, too: not in deliberate mishandling of evidence, but in selection of research design.

The second reason I began with Beard became clear to me only gradually. Beard's work dealt with the American Revolution and its overall meaning. Implicitly, and to a certain extent explicitly, Beard raised the question of whether the Founding Fathers were motivated not only by abstract ideas and a devotion to public welfare, but also by personal economic interests. If the latter alternative was overstated, might it not still be true (as Beard sometimes more sophisticatedly put it) that their view of the public welfare was conditioned by the experience of a governing class in which individual Fathers participated by virtue of their birth and/or wealth? These questions were important to me because, as one considerably alienated from America's present, I wanted to know if there were men in the American past in whom I could believe.

This is the kind of feeling historians are not supposed to have. Not only did I have it, but, as time went on, it increasingly seemed to me more honest to confront my feeling squarely for what it was rather than pursue it in the guise of research about, say, the curious discrepancy between the portraits of the revolutionary artisan in the books of Carl Becker and Charles Beard. What "really interests me," I found myself saying, is not whether or not the United States Constitution was a reactionary coup d'etat, but whether anyone at that time "really believed" what the Declaration of Independence said.

After graduate school I taught for three years in a Negro women's college in Atlanta, Georgia. Historians are not supposed to be influenced by their personal experiences, but I was, profoundly. Here were students with a greater stake than mine in knowing—not just entertaining an interpretation, but knowing—whether the signers of the Declaration of Independence were idealists who failed to carry out their full program, or hypocritical racists who killed Indians and bred Negroes while declaring that all men are equal. No doubt both answers were "too simple" and the truth was a more complicated third thing. But what *was* the truth? I did not know because I had not examined that question with sufficient seriousness to let it guide my own research. Incredibly, my research like that of Beard, Becker, and other Progressive historians, had tacitly assumed that white artisans and tenant farmers were the most exploited Americans of the late eighteenth century, overlooking the one-fifth of the nation that was in chains.

For my Negro students it was almost as important to know the true character of their collective past as to be at ease with their personal histories. One brilliant girl described to me the moment when, looking at the photographs in a collection of slave narratives, she realized, "These were my forefathers." After I conventionally began a survey course in American history with the Pilgrims, another excellent student, who had the courage to express her personal past by inviting my family to her sharecropper father's home at Christmas, was also brave enough to ask me, "Why do you teach about your ancestors and not mine?" Next year, I began the course with the slave ships, only to hear from a third student, "You are teaching me a special history rather than treating me like everybody else." Willy-nilly I was functioning as therapist in addition to historian; in reporting the past I turned it, whether I wished to or not, into a medium for the discovery of personal identity.

At issue was not whether history, like a lump of dough, can be made into any shape one pleases. The question was rather that if history, like a mountain, can be viewed from many different standpoints all equally "objective," perhaps it makes sense to approach it from the direction that has most personal meaning to the observer.

Meantime, I was beginning to chafe at the role of observer, no matter how defined. Teaching in the midst of the civil rights movement brought home the aphorism (here slightly rephrased) of Marx's *Theses on Feuerbach:* "The historians have interpreted the world; the thing, however, is to change it."

II

By these stages I arrived at a conception of history that has much in common with that of the eighteenth century. Just as Jefferson found virtues to emulate in Plutarch and mistakes to be avoided in the story of republican Rome's decline, so I would have the young person of our own time (supposing history to interest him at all) encounter Jefferson (or Malcolm X) with the question, What can I learn about how to live?

In the nineteenth century this approach to history came to be condemned as moralistic. History, Ranke and his followers maintained, was not a lamp of experience to light the path ahead but a simple record of "how it really happened." Professional historians accepted Ranke's attitude as the definition of objectivity.

But as Carl Becker demonstrated in his *Declaration of Independence,* Ranke's creed of "wie es eigentlich gewesen" presupposed a belief that history "just as it happened" and "the existing social order" were "the progressive realization of God's purpose." The Rankian historian had no need to moralize because what history had achieved already was satisfactory to him. In Becker's paraphrase: "history is God's work, which we must submit to, but which we may seek to understand in order that we may submit to it intelligently." This was objectivity only in the sense that it made man an object of history rather than a maker of it.

It would oversimplify, of course, to suggest that radicals draw lessons from history whereas conservatives are content to narrate it. Among the lessons drawn from history by the Founding Fathers were that economic equality was impossible in a populous society, that democracy was weakened by the growth of commerce, and that, because power followed property, it would be chimerical to attempt to destroy chattel slavery by political means. These were conservative lessons inasmuch as they inclined the leaders of the Revolution to live with inequities they might otherwise have protested.

Moreover, the most influential Rankian of the nineteenth century was none other than Karl Marx. He too, like Hegel and Ranke, believed that ethical goals need not be imposed on history because they were inherent in it. He too, despite a youthful emphasis on man as historical protagonist and creator, believed that "freedom is the recognition of necessity."

Accordingly, for someone like myself who was more and more committed to the thesis that the professor of history should also be a historical protagonist, a complex confrontation with Marxist economic determinism was inevitable. I do not pretend to be on the other side of this problem, certainly one of the major intellectual challenges of our time. But I have a few tentative conclusions.

Two recent neo-Marxist statements on the problems of historical determinism and man's freedom to choose are *What Is History?* by E. H. Carr and *Search for a Method* by Jean-Paul Sartre. Let us attempt to close in on this problem by following the logic of these two authors.

Carr has been much influenced by Collingwood, whom he describes as "the only British thinker in the present century who has made a serious contribution to the philosophy of history." Carr's book includes such Collingwood-like observations as the following:

The nineteenth century was, for the intellectuals of Western Europe, a comfortable period exuding confidence and optimism. The facts were on the whole satisfactory; and the inclination to ask and answer awkward questions about them was correspondingly weak. Ranke piously believed that divine providence would take care of the meaning of history if he took care of the facts . . . .

And again:

The nineteenth-century fetishism of facts was completed and justified by a fetishism of documents . . . . But . . . no document can tell us more than what the author of the document thought—what he thought had happened, what he thought ought to happen or would happen, or perhaps only what he wanted others to think he thought, or even only what he himself thought he thought.

Nevertheless, Carr finds his way back from these iconoclasms not only to a rather conventional view of the historian's craft but also to an orthodox Rankian-Marxist position that ethical judgments of historical events are irrelevant because the events themselves are determined. He does so by means of a most unsatisfactory argument. In the present moment, Carr appears to concede, real choice exists and ethical criteria are therefore pertinent. However, once an event has occurred it should be considered inevitably determined, and one who fails so to consider it must be suspected of wishing it had happened otherwise. As Carr puts the matter:

. . . plenty of people, who have suffered directly or vicariously from the results of the Bolshevik victory, or still fear its remoter consequences, desire to register their protest against it; and this takes the form, when they read history, of letting their imagination run riot on all the more agreeable things that might have happened, and of being indignant with the historian who goes on quietly with his job of explaining what did happen and why their agreeable wish-dreams remain unfulfilled. The trouble about contemporary history is that people remember *the time when all the options were still open* [my italics], and find it difficult to adopt the attitude of the historian, for whom they have been closed by the *fait accompli.*

With this comment Carr seeks to dispose of what he calls the "red herring" problem of historical inevitability. But if in fact I have the freedom to act one way or another, how can I turn around and assert, the moment after I have acted, that I had to act the way I did? To borrow for a moment Carr's own *ad hominem* approach, I am inclined to think that his position is that of the perennial observer, who has never devoted his energies to making his "wish-dreams" real. It cannot be a resting-place for someone called to making history as well as writing it.

Sartre's argument, if I understand it correctly, is similar. Beginning with the assertion that the abstract and schematic character of twentieth-century Marxism made necessary the creation of existentialism if real human experiences were to be grasped in its concreteness. Yet Sartre concludes that as a richer Marxism, faithful to Marx's own complexity, develops, existentialism will wither away.

The logic of a Carr or a Sartre appears to me to disintegrate in the face of the twentieth century practice of revolutionary Marxists themselves. Every successful Marxist revolutionary has made his bid for power in defiance of what passed in his day for the "laws of historical development." The Russian Mensheviks were right in contending that decades of industrial development were necessary before the Russian proletariat would be large enough to make such a revolution as Marx predicted; but Lenin led the Russian Revolution regardless. The supremacy of will-power and endurance–the so-called subjective factor–to all environmental obstacles was so obviously the key factor in the Chinese Revolution that it has become the defining characteristic of "the thought of Mao Tse-tung." And would any one seriously argue that Fidel Castro's defiant handful in a fishing-boat was the inevitable outcome of inexorable historical forces?

The conception of historical causation by Marx (or at least by the later Marx) followed closely Adam Smith's model of the working of the capitalist market. Like the laissez-faire entrepreneur, so the actor in the Marxist historical drama could not correctly anticipate the outcome of his actions, for that outcome was the unplanned result of each actor's false anticipations. But the act of revolution is precisely the ability to take purposeful action with confidence that intended consequences can be achieved. The revolutionary transforms not only an oppressive society but the laws of development of that oppressive society. Despite invocation of man's future passage from the realm of necessity to the realm of freedom, Marx, I think it is fair to say, assigned this happening to the period after a revolutionary seizure of power and hence did not fully appreciate the fact that any revolution–at least as it appears to those who take part in it–requires a decision by individual human beings to begin to determine their own destinies at whatever cost.

"At least as it appears to those who take part in it": here is the heart of the matter. I have been trying to show that professional historians, whether Marxist or non-Marxist, tend to view history from the sidelines, to give too little weight to that ethical dimension that is critical only for the man who must make decisions, to regard as historically determined what is merely historically past, and in sum, to do violence to the sense of reality of the historical actor in the present moment. I hope I will not be misunderstood to believe that there are no "historical forces," that historical causation does not exist, that any one can do anything he wants in history at any time. The point, rather, is that whereas to Marx or Sartre human energy and striving are, as it were, *at the service of* the movement of impersonal historical forces, for the man trying to make history such forces are merely matters he must *take into account* in attempting to achieve his self-determined goals. The psychotherapist Victor Frankl, who himself lived through the concentration camps, reminds us that in the most oppressive of situations men still retained a significant ability to decide what would happen to them. To say the same thing in another way, men can be beasts or brothers at any level of technological development.

III

How would the work of the historian be different if man's existential freedom to choose became that work's point of departure?

The following are some provisional answers.

1. Historians ordinarily assume that history can better be written about events at some distance in the past than about present happenings. No doubt this generalization holds good for certain kinds of events, such as diplomatic events, the sources for which tend to be kept secret until after the passage of many years. But does it apply for example, to the history of the common man? I think not. Anyone wishing to write the history of the post-World War II civil rights movement could undoubtedly write it better now than five years from now, and better five years from now than a quarter-century hence. The reason is that the primary sources for these events are, by and large, neither written nor secret but the memories of individual living persons, which will become less accurate and accessible as time goes on.

History in the form of chronicling of the present tends to be considered mere journalism, a debasement of what proper history should be, because the passage of time is assumed to give "perspective." Without wholly discounting this argument, it nevertheless seems to me to depend too much on the assumption that there is a single causal pattern underlying events–a skeleton beneath the living tissue–which will appear stark and clear in retrospective view.

The historian's first duty, it seems to me, is the sensitive chronicling in depth of the important events of his own lifetime.

2. Whether in writing about the recent or the distant past, the historian suggests to the protagonist of the present new alternatives for action. Just as all of us, with or without the help of therapists, occasionally look back to our individual pasts to find strength for new beginnings, so with or without the help of historians, Americans who wish to change their present society have used the past as a source for forgotten alternatives. The past serves us as a means toward that "frequent recurrence to fundamental principles" which the Virginia Bill of Rights advised.

The differences between this use of history and that which follows from a traditional emphasis on causation may be illustrated with reference to the war in Vietnam. The American intellectual community has devoted itself, to an extent that must be without precedent, to becoming amateur historians of this conflict. Nevertheless, after all the books and teach-ins the simple question, Why Vietnam?, remains almost as obscure as it was in February, 1965.

An economic explanation of American policy is difficult to demonstrate because American investment in Southeast Asia is relatively slight; but no other coherent hypothesis appears to have been offered. As to the motivation of "the other side," no doubt documents presently unavailable would help somewhat. Yet to whatever extent Wilfred G. Burchett is right in his ascription of the origins of the present war to a series of spontaneous local outbreaks in 1957-1959, one suspects that the participants themselves might be hard put to provide a definitive causal analysis of the interaction of local grievances, National Liberation Front leadership, and encouragement from Hanoi.

Does this mean that the historian has nothing to offer in Vietnam? Or even, in view of the misuse of the Munich analogy by the American government, that a solution might more readily be found if the habit of historical argument could be proscribed? I think not. Where the historian could be helpful, in my opinion, is not by deeper but still inconclusive research into the past, but by projecting alternative scenarios for the future. Considerable experience is available as to the behavior of revolutionary nationalist movements under varying environmental pressures. Without presuming to predict the future, historians might help American policymakers to be more flexible and imaginative by prophesying, so to speak, a variety of outcomes to the present bloodbath. (Howard Zinn's *Vietnam: The Logic of Withdrawal* exemplifies the use of history I have in mind.)

Thus a second, presently unfamiliar task for the historian would be the projection of alternative futures on the basis of the richness of the experience of the past.

I can delineate the tasks I am recommending to historians more sharply by exemplifying their opposites. Here again, I draw negative examples from radical historians so as to make it clear that the distinctions I propose are not those whereby radicals have traditionally defined themselves.

Some time ago a student of my acquaintance, a member of Students for a Democratic Society, asked me if I thought he should do graduate work in history. I said I did not know and suggested that he write to several of the young radical historians. John did so, mentioning in his letter to each that I had told him there were others in the field of American history who were much more optimistic than I was about "carving out a radical approach to the field that does not get lost in the usual hair-splitting and inconclusiveness to which the profession is prone."

One of John's answers was from a brilliant young scholar whose particular interest, like the work of Albert Soboul, George Rudé, and E. P. Thompson, is the history of the inarticulate.

His letter began:

> I think we know about as much about the role of the common man in American history as we would know about Watts if the McCone Commission were our only source . . . . History has been written by elitists who assumed that when the common man acted, he did so for irrational reasons, or because he was manipulated in some way. Much of the excitement of the field to me is that all kinds of good things might have happened that we don't know anything about because of the distortions of history as it has been written.

My own quarrel with this argument is not with its contention that history has been distorted but with its hope that the truth can be restored. Let the reader consider any popular movement of our own day in which he has participated. For instance, take the Mississippi Summer Project of 1964. Half a dozen good books have already been written about it, one a collection of letters by student volunteers, a second narrating in detail a single volunteer's experience, a third in large part composed of documentary appendices. In addition, the event was exhaustively "covered" by press and television. But do any of us who took part in that adventure seriously imagine that anything more than fragments of it will ever be set down in communicable form? Less than three years after the event, who now knows where the idea for a Freedom Democratic Party came from or what really happened at the Democratic Party convention at Atlantic City?

Considerations such as these as to the inevitable inadequacies of contemporary chronicling suggest skepticism about the possibility of recovering "the history" of popular movements in the past. A few handbills, if fortunate, perhaps some police records, notices of meetings from contemporary newspapers, the gossip of upper-class letter-writers, very likely fragmentary tax and election records: isn't this more or less what we rely on to reconstruct what happened, and is it not infinitely less adequate than the documentary record, which itself is so inadequate, in the case of more recent movements? I know from experience the temptation to fill in the gaps with personal "wish-dreams," and to present the result with a spurious air of finality.

John received a second letter from another outstanding young radical scholar, who said in part:

> I probably disagree with Lynd as to what we can do. Politically, neither love nor violence will help us much, because we are beyond politics in the sense that this is a functionally totalitarian country with a liberal rhetoric, and reason and exemplary Christian behavior will not alter the politics of those in power. [But] in purely intellectual terms, radicals have much to do and it seems to me that they can define and analyze the nature of the beast we confront on a much higher level of sophistication and precision than we have up to now.

Is this not quibbling while Rome burns? Can it satisfactorily define the scholar's task to be able to say "I told you so" amid the ruins? Should we be content with measuring the dimensions of our prison instead of chipping, however inadequately, against the bars?

IV

What, then, should be the historian's craft and the idea of history?

I believe that what distinguishes the historian from other social scientists is not that he writes about the past, but that he considers things in process of development. History and sociology are not concerned with different objects; they are different ways of looking at the same object. Hence the historian need not be embarrassed if he concerns himself more with the present and future than with the past.

I also believe that the historian's concern with the future is not to predict but to envision, to say (as Howard Zinn has put it) not what *will* be but what *can* be. The past is ransacked not for its own sake, but as a source of alternative models of what the future might become.

Implicit in my discussion has been a third idea, that "writing history" does not necessarily involve "being an historian": in other words, that chronicling and envisioning are functions that might be as well or better done by many persons with part of their time rather than full-time by a few. He who acts as well as watches may acquire kinds of knowledge unavailable to him who watches only. (That the converse is also true is, of course, a commonplace.)

To these fundamental delimitations of the historian's role I should like to add two major qualifications.

Human beings, at least those born into Judaeo-Christian cultures, appear to need to formulate a collective past. Presumably, it will always be mainly the job of the historian to respond to this need responsibly, that is, in a way that does not do violence either to the facts of the past or to the human beings of the present. Despite the alleged anti-historicism of the New Left, the need for a collective past is felt with particular keenness today by young people. Many rebellious young Americans have profoundly mixed feelings when they confront our country's history. On the one hand, they feel shame and distrust toward the Founding Fathers who tolerated slavery, exterminated Indians, and in all their proceedings were disturbingly insensitive to values and life-styles other than their own. On the other hand, there is a diffuse sense that the rhetoric of the Revolution and the Civil War spoke then and speaks now to hopes widespread among mankind. Thus in November, 1965, Carl Oglesby, then president of Students for Democratic Society, asked an antiwar demonstration gathered at the Washington Monument what Thomas Jefferson or Thomas Paine would say to President Johnson and McGeorge Bundy about the war in Vietnam. Thus in August, 1966, when the House Un-American Activities Committee subpoenaed antiwar activists, the head of the Free University of New York issued a statement invoking the Green Mountain Boys, and the chairman of the Berkeley Vietnam Day Committee appeared in the hearing chamber in the uniform of an officer of George Washington's Army.

The professor of history is among other things the custodian of such memories and dreams.

My second qualification is that in a macrocosmic sense I believe Marxism is correct in its understanding of where humanity has been and is going. Think of it as a backdrop to the stage on which historical protagonists play their self-determined parts. It is nonetheless an essential element in the drama. The historian who does not grasp the fact that mankind, whatever else it is doing, is making an agonized transition from societies based on private property to societies that are not, is in my view out of touch with what is happening in the second half of the twentieth century. I hasten to add that these new societies may not be more humane than those they replace. Still, the interesting question of our time will appear to future historians as that one—namely, Is a humane socialism possible?—rather than the one that presently preoccupies the American psyche, Will capitalism or socialism prevail? And from where I stand, this is a ground for hope.

10

Populism, Authoritarianism, and the Historian

NORMAN POLLACK (1964)

Admiration for the Populists had been commonplace among progressive historians as they traced the roots of modern American reform to the late-nineteenth-century agrarian protest. Consequently when criticisms by Richard Hofstadter and others were made during the 1950s alleging that the Populists possessed limited understanding of their times, that they expressed irrational conspiracy views of history, and that they nursed the seeds of anti-Semitism, one part of the reformer's usable American past was seriously challenged. The significance of the following essay by Norman Pollack (b. 1933), professor of history at Michigan State University, rested not only in his affirmation of Populism as a model for humane reform, but mostly in the sweeping indictment of American historians during the post-war years who, like Richard Hofstadter, located authoritarian tendencies in Populist reformers as a part of their reaction to European totalitarianism. Pollack, a participant in the civil rights movement and a severe critic of United States policy in Vietnam, also argued that interpretations which emphasized the element of consensus in American history wrongly minimized the extent of political dissent at the same time, and hence deprived today's would-be reformers of examples and lessons from the past.

Pollack's essay opened with a summary of Populism as a progressive, socialistic reform ideology, which was, in his own view, a more radical and theoretical ideology than even the older and equally sympathetic progressive historians had said. The question Pollack posed was why Populism had been criticized by historians in the years after World War II. On his assumption that neither Hofstadter nor anyone else had uncovered evidence to justify criticism of the Populists, Pollack's question was a valid one and suggested

---

Reprinted by permission from Norman Pollack, "Fear of Man: Populism, Authoritarianism, and the Historian," *Agricultural History,* 39, April, 1965, pp. 59-67. The essay was originally read at a meeting of the Southern Historical Association, November, 1964.

that the answer was to be found in the post-war climate of opinion, since it could not be found in the documents of the past. His argument was that the disillusionment of post-war historians over the rise of totalitarianism in Europe had not merely made them sensitive to authoritarian characteristics in American history, as they themselves admitted, but had made them so disillusioned that they could no longer see any good in men generally nor specifically in those who professed humanitarian reform ideals. Thus, according to Pollack, post-war historians such as Hofstadter were not only reacting to McCarthy when they searched for authoritarian traits in the past, but were becoming like McCarthy in trying to purge the past of radical idealism. Pollack agreed that there were indeed sources of authoritarianism in American culture, but he denied that Populism was one of them. When he went on to discuss what he thought the center of authoritarianism was in urban, bureaucratic, routinized, impersonal middle- and lower-class life, Pollack made an indictment of American society which revealed the critical mood of the younger generation in the 1960s. It is possible to see the connection between the hostility of the nonpolitical "hippies" toward the meaninglessness of contemporary life, and the radical political protest of the New Left, in Pollack's highly political critique of organizational society. If government, business, labor, professional, and university life dehumanizes, trivializes, and renders the individual schizophrenic, either "hippy" withdrawal or radical social reform is clearly imperative. Populism, according to Pollack, represented radical reform as a way out of the dehumanization of modern America. The rejection by critics of Populism and of its reform idealism suggested to Pollack that the critics themselves had accepted the authoritarianism of organizational society and that they felt themselves threatened by the moral presence of the Populist protest. It became necessary to purge the threat, which they attempted to do by making a scapegoat of Populism just as the anti-Semite has traditionally done with the Jew. Populism was the conscience of America, Pollack concluded, and needed to be heard.

Populists sought the establishment of a just social order founded on a democratized industrial system and a transformation of social values, each reinforcing the other in the direction of greater concern for the welfare of all. They rejected unbridled individualism and the competitive mentality, maintaining instead that neither a few nor a class should enjoy the benefits of civilization. The quality of life of the masses was the index by which to measure social improvement. There was little of the self-conscious in the Populist enshrinement of the common man: Society must be attuned to *his* needs, or it ceases to be democratic. Yet in place of a society suffused with an equalitarian spirit, a society which is responsive to the growth of all and oppresses none, Populists pointed to the mortgage-ridden farmer, the unemployed worker, and the so-called "tramp" moving from one town to the next in search of work. In place of the free citizen, deriving benefit from his labor on the farm or in the factory, determining the policies under which he is to be governed, and enjoying a sense of dignity in his daily life, Populists found man to be impoverished, voiceless and degraded. Thus their critique of existing arrangements went beyond economic conditions to embrace the question of the individual's plight, his de-humanization, his loss of autonomy in a society which rapidly reduced him to a dependent state.

Their protest was a consequence of the times, not only of the 1890s but of the preceding two decades, where the rule was all-pervasive hardship: declining crop prices; increased tenantry and share-cropping; an appreciating dollar; the ever-present mortgage in the West, and even more pressing, the crop-lien in the South; business combinations, tariffs and artificially high prices in the manufacturing sector; a railroad system which practiced discrimination against the farmer, gave preferential treatment to favored shippers, dominated state legislatures, blackmailed towns into issuing bonds, held large tracts of land off the market, refused to assume a proper share of the tax burden, and contributed to the creation of a closed system for the distribution of goods. Populists recognized that the industrial worker confronted similar conditions: subsistence wages, company towns, frequent unemployment, and the use of coercion in the form of Pinkertons, militias and imported strikebreakers to prevent him from rectifying the situation by forming unions. Finally, Populists confronted a political framework where grievances were never aired, and if anything, were obscured by the raising of all manner of diversions from the "bloody shirt" to the cry of tariff. Populists addressed themselves to each of these issues, as well as to others of a like character. Theirs was indeed a response to the times, but it was also something more; it was an attempt to transcend those times, and in the act of transcending the existing social context, to pose an alternative conception for the development of America.

Populism was not a retrogressive social force. It did not seek to restore a lost world of yeomen farmers and village artisans. The reverse was true. Of course Populists borrowed from the past, but they borrowed selectively. What they took was not a petrified pre-industrialism but a set of political principles, principles which they believed could be applied at any point, present and future as well as past. From Jefferson and Jackson came the recurring theme of "equal rights to all, and special privileges to none," from these and other sources came the labor theory of value, and from the Constitution came the commerce clause and other passages sanctioning government regulation in the general interest. Beyond this Populists did not go, for their gaze was directed to what lay ahead rather than to what lay behind.

In seeking to democratize rather than abolish industrialism, Populism was a progressive social force. Yet its orientation was progressive not only because it based its remedies on an accommodation to social change, but also because in pursuing these policies it adopted a highly affirmative stance. The two are difficult to separate. For to be forward-looking while not at the same time possessing confidence that men do have the power to remake their institutions and values is to be as helpless, as escapist, as the one who rests content with a restoration of the past. To acquiesce in social change does not, by itself, insure a progressive outlook. A more positive frame of mind is required, and this Populists had. Woven into the texture of their thought was the insistence that men *could* consciously make their future. Populists contended that there is nothing inevitable about misery and squalor, nothing irreversible about the tendencies toward the concentration of wealth and the legitimation of corporate power. Not the impersonal tendency but men themselves are responsible for the contemporary society, and for this reason men can—according to Populists, must—alter the course of that society in a humanistic direction. What stands out, then, about the Populist mind is an affirmation of man, a faith in man's capability to shape his own history.

This positive aspect of Populist thought is not exhausted by the fact that numerous concrete proposals were offered to attack existing problems. More important was the attitude behind their formulation, and ultimately, the attitude toward the relation between the individual and his government. In keeping with the emphasis on men as the wielders of power and the source of legislation, Populists held that there was nothing sacred about the status quo, or for that matter, about the institutions which safeguarded that status quo. They did not repudiate the notion of law and order, but they did assert that *existing* law was class law, intended to protect the rich at the expense of the poor, and that order meant in the contemporary context the imposition of legalized repression to prevent the broadening of that law. Thus Populist reforms stemmed from an attitude of healthy skepticism concerning the sacrosanct nature of government. Since government was no more than an instrument to be used for good or ill by the groups which controlled it, then let the farmers and workers organize to secure that control, and prevent further encroachments on the general welfare.

Yet Populists found even this to be entirely too negative. Government should be more than a neutral observer. It was created to *serve* man, and must be a dynamic force in bringing about equality. Thus, Populists contended, government must be a responsive tool, one which can actively intervene in the economy to regulate matters affecting the public interest, and when necessary own outright monopolies of this character, and can just as actively aid the underprivileged and work for a more equitable distribution of wealth.

From this brief overview of Populist thought, with the emphasis on its rational, humane and affirmative qualities, it is clear the speaker dissents from the recent interpretation of Populism as the source of American anti-Semitism and proto-fascistic behavior. He does not find the movement xenophobic, irrational, opportunistic and in search of a scapegoat, and he does not transform its social protest into status striving, its discontent into the addiction to conspiratorial delusions, its attempts at farmer-labor alliances into retrogressive utopianism. In sum, he does not conceive Populism as an authoritarian social force. It is not necessary to review the critical literature here. Who the writers are and what they have said is by now common knowledge, as perhaps are my views on Professor Hofstadter's work,[1] on the incidence of anti-Semitism in the movement,[2] and my positive statement on the nature of midwestern Populism.[3] There will appear very soon an assessment of Professor Handlin's contributions to the dialogue,[4] and my documentary history of Populism which will run to 500 pages.[5]

I did not come here today to rehash the controversies of the past, but to look to the future. I submit that the time for bickering is over, and that the following should be conceded by all, so that we can go on to more pressing problems as historians: one, the past decade and a half has witnessed the unwarranted denigration of Populism, and because Populism has served as the type-form for radicalism, we have also seen the unwarranted denigration of the reform tradition in America as well; two, the critics not only have not worked in the primary materials, but have ignored an impressive array of books, monographs and articles which flatly contradict their case; three, that whatever their motives, and I should like to think these centered upon a commendable endeavor, to ascertain the roots of authoritarianism in American life, they have not only failed to explain the rise of proto-fascism—and have so obscured the picture that we know less today than we did at the start of the 1950's—but historians have turned against the very currents of democracy and humanism resisting its rise. Opposed to scapegoating, these historians have nonetheless, and with no evidence, found their own scapegoat, the Populist movement.

I take these three considerations as no longer open to doubt, and will not stop to offer point-by-point refutations of the critical literature, or summarize the writings of Professors Hicks, Woodward, Destler, Arnett, and a host of others to show the humane character of Populism, or the fact that times *were* hard, and hence that Populists did not respond to nonexistent grievances. Therefore, the question must now be asked, why–despite overwhelming evidence to the contrary–did historians embark on the denigration of Populism, and why did the recent interpretation gain such widespread acceptance? Given the facts that critics neither refuted earlier scholarly works nor presented new evidence, given the facts that these earlier works saw not irrationality but the concern for human dignity, and not one pointed to anti-Semitism, given the facts that Populism expressed compassion for the under-privileged, both Negro and white, and that historians had agreed in viewing the movement as the summation of a whole century of American radical thought, where Man, written large, was at the center of the political universe, given this and more, much more, I think it can be said that the justification for the reinterpretation lies not in history but in the mind of the historian, and more specifically, the historian who feels compelled to rewrite the past with a vengeance.

When Professor Woodward suggests in "The Populist Heritage and the Intellectual" that critical currents in historical writing were a response to McCarthyism in the early 1950's, I think his explanation for what has happened is too charitable. I submit that there is a world of difference between standing up against McCarthyism and seeking to understand its roots unencumbered by predispositions as to where to look, on one hand; and not only capitulating but then turning on one's own philosophic heritage by identifying with the hated object, McCarthyism, on the other. Yet, the latter is precisely what happened. Since there was no objective basis for singling out Populism, one can only conclude that the ultimate destructive force of McCarthyism was not to keep men silent, but to make them purge the very tradition of humanitarianism and radicalism for which the Populist movement stood as a notable example in the American experience. It is no coincidence that Professor Hofstadter's archetypal radical turns out to be not the man who protests against social injustice or economic inequality, but one who wants only a larger share of the pie, who wants to scramble up the ladder, who is governed in short by the capitalist-on-the-make mentality. The judgment is revealing. I see here not only a pre-occupation with present-day values, and the attempt to read them back into the past, but also the rock-bottom of cynicism and disillusionment over man.

Now, I do not deny that the historian is influenced by the present when writing about the past. Whether Professor Carr in *What Is History?* specified the interaction between present and past to everyone's satisfaction is less important than his insight on how the historian must be aware of the dominant trends of his age when exploring the past. Still, by no stretch of the imagination does this reciprocal relation permit one cavalierly to disregard the past and write solely from the present, which I feel the critics of Populism have done.

Clearly, there is nothing wrong with revisionism as such; this is the dynamic force in the writing of history. Nor should historians avoid the questions which the present generation wants to ask of the past. On the contrary, I must state again that the search for the origins of authoritarianism is a significant endeavor. With this said, however, the overall point remains: one cannot use a legitimate topic, a topic in which all of us are interested, as a shield to hide behind while reading current biases into the past.

I have left the original question hanging, of why the denigration of Populism. Let me relate it to a further line of inquiry: say we did not get off to a false start in the early 1950's, is it probable that historians would look automatically to agrarianism as the source of authoritarian behavior? Would they have maintained at the outset that one can speak of an agrarian life-style which is intrinsically proto-fascistic? If their work were infused with a guiding assumption as to where to start, is it clear they would begin with non-urban instead of urban sources of the problem? I think not.

The standard literature on the middle classes provides ample testimony that the strains of modern society are not confined to the agrarian sector. The writings of Max Weber, Hans Speier, Franz Neumann, Robert K. Merton and C. Wright Mills, just to name a few, are too substantial and too familiar to have been overlooked by students of authoritarianism. Likewise, it seems highly unlikely that a post-World War II scholar could be unaware of the historical and sociological trends contributing to the breakdown of Weimar Germany and the rise of Nazism. The point is that in both cases—the corpus of writings on the nature of industrial society; and the principal example where proto-fascism erupted into its fully matured form—the signs lead directly to the middle and lower middle classes as the most volatile and unstable stratum in modern times.

The next step, it appears to me, one naturally evolving out of the discussion of the topic, would be to follow through on these insights. Yet, despite such obvious signs of non-agrarian authoritarianism, historians resolutely refused to investigate these other social forces. I think the gap reflects a blind-spot; a blind-spot made all the more significant because of the simultaneous willingness to place sole responsibility on agrarianism.

That the blind-spot relates to the larger question of why the denigration of Populism occurred in the first place will be noted momentarily. That it is due in part to the sociological backgrounds of historians themselves can, however, be mentioned at this time. This is by no means the key to the problem, but it is important. If in fact there are distinctly urban and middle class sources of proto-fascism in the United States, as *is* the case in Western European societies, then historians whose roots are urban and middle class would find it difficult, indeed distasteful, to contemplate such a possibility. And it would be equally painful for American society as a whole to question its foundations. The temptation is very great to look elsewhere for an explanation—to the non-urban, non-middle-class movements in American history. In a word, the shortcomings lie outside the prevailing patterns in present-day society; they are products, instead, of the very forces which challenged these patterns.

My point, then, is that while there may be rural sources of authoritarianism, one cannot ignore the urban sources as well. I cannot possibly go into a full-scale examination of these urban sources in a paper of this size. Let me merely indicate that of the writers referred to earlier, I find Max Weber's *Theory of Social and Economic Organization* extremely valuable in pointing to the essential instability of bureaucratic society, an instability he located at the very core of modern industrialism. For Weber, the process of rationalization—the drive for predictability, calculability and efficiency permeating all realms of existence—leads to instability because it generates a sense of depersonalization in the individual, and psychological insecurities in the society at large. As will become clear, it is this instability which serves as an ideal breeding ground for proto-fascism.

Rationalization is a highly dynamic force. Once it begins, no sector of the society can be exempted, whether work processes, distribution procedures, or legal system. It spreads from the assembly line of the factory, to the assembly line of the white collar world, even to the assembly line of the individual's thought processes. In the quest for stabilization and efficiency, society cannot permit uneven or chaotic development. Spontaneity becomes suspect; it upsets calculations.

As Weber pointed out, rational society can be summarized by two overriding factors: bureaucratic organization and the routinization of tasks. The former, with its rigidity and its pecking order in the chain of command, has received widespread commentary, from Kafka and earlier, down to the trivialized accounts of today about the organization man, I say trivialized because what recent writers fail to comprehend, in their desire to obfuscate the stultifying effects of bureaucratic forms, is Weber's point on the built-in schizophrenia in the society geared to these forms.

But why this built-in schizophrenia in the structure of society? For Weber, the concept of "office" (which is the basic unit in the bureaucratic form of social organization) requires a strict separation of one's public and private lives. The occupant of the office becomes, as it were, divided into two compartments. On the job, his functions are severely circumscribed; he has a narrow sphere of competence, and cannot go outside that sphere. Again a premium is placed on calculability. He is bound by generalized rules. Initiative and creativity are discouraged. Indeed, all personal reactions must be eliminated. This means not only that human problems are treated in terms of categories, itself a sign of the objectification of social relationships; but also, that the bureaucrat must stifle hostility and resentment against the bureaucracy itself.

What are the consequences of these bureaucratic traits (and by bureaucracy I mean of course the dominant pattern of rational society, and do not confine the term to such examples as government) for the rise of authoritarianism? First, the repressed feelings, precisely because they have no outlet within the generalized norms of the bureaucratic structure, will break through in some manner. This institutionalized repression, for that indeed is the dominant feature of the structure, is further compounded by the boredom and sterility of the work itself. The result is that a great deal of tension, with no possibility for release, has been built up. Or, if there is release within the structure, it takes the form of even more slavish devotion to the rules, which in turn only intensifies the repression. This is where Weber's insight into the compulsory separation of roles becomes significant. What is pent-up in one realm of existence, will then be expressed in another. That this condition has meaning for the development of proto-fascism should be sufficiently clear, but I will expand this point shortly.

The second general consequence of these bureaucratic traits is more readily detectable. Every aspect of bureaucratic organization points to one underlying response: the uncritical and in time mechanical submission to authority. The command structure serves as an impersonal conveyor belt. One obeys orders from above, and transmits them to those below. The orders themselves are not questioned. Further, one arrives at decisions not on the basis of individual discretion but according to stipulated rules, once more reinforcing the submission to authority. Mutual expectations, the cement of bureaucracy, are established through conformity—conformity to commands, conformity to rules, conformity to bureaucratic patterns of thought.

Combining these two results—the high degree of repression with no effective channels of expression and the proneness to submission—one can see why I am led to the conclusion that rational society, however indispensable to modern industrialism, rests on a precarious foundation.

Turning now to the second major feature of rational society, the routinization of the work process, one finds that this too generates psychological insecurities which lead to authoritarian behavior. In the drive to rationalize, to make the productive system more efficient and predictable, it becomes necessary to alter the relationship between man and the machine. As tasks are reduced to a smaller and smaller number of standardized operations, the individual himself no longer holds his job on the basis of skill and insight. Instead he is transformed into one more interchangeable part in the larger machinery. The culmination of rationality is not only to make man subordinate to the machine, but to make him into a machine. Thus, when these simplified procedures have been introduced, it becomes literally possible to bring in anyone off the street, and teach him to perform the tasks.

As in the case of bureaucracy, the consequences of routinization are also significant. First, the individual, far from deriving intrinsic gratification from his work, experiences utter boredom, or more likely, frustration. Performing a minute segment of a vast operation, he does not even see his contribution to the final result. Not only are tasks reduced to simpler operations, but the individual is reduced to a condition of all-pervasive malaise. Productive forces become impersonal; work becomes impersonal; society itself becomes impersonal. Man is a helpless subject, searching for meaning in a world of objects. And in time, he too begins to feel like an object, which merely serves to intensify his helplessness, and makes his search for meaning all the more frantic.

Second, in a situation where work has been so thoroughly simplified, where skill based on accumulated learning counts for nothing, where one individual can readily be substituted for another, men regard themselves as dispensable and replaceable. Self-respect is destroyed, only to be supplanted by fear. One constantly asks, especially during hard times: when will my turn come—when will I be cast out and replaced by someone else?

Regrettably, there is insufficient time to illustrate the foregoing remarks by looking at specific historical situations, but I submit that the case of the German salaried employee would be instructive. Let me simply state that as the white collar sector expanded, its social level went down. This in turn meant that the social distance, so crucial to the psychological security of the middle classes, was also breaking down. And the result was panic.

Thwarted in his public role, the individual will vent his aggression in his private life. Bewildered, helpless, insecure, he will be ripe for all manner of promises to restore meaning to his life. Trapped in the morass of routinized procedures, he will personalize an impersonal world through the search for a scapegoat. Faced with submergence into the working class, and hence with the destruction of his whole way of life, he will turn on bended knee to The Leader for a solution. Predisposed to authoritarianism from the very workings of bureaucracy, he will be vulnerable to anyone who claims to have the answers. The "salariat," as Sigmund Neumann aptly termed this class, was indeed a source of proto-fascism. The story is a familiar one, and since many of the factors relate not merely to Germany but to bureaucratic society itself, not without meaning elsewhere as well.

The phenomenon I have been discussing is distinctly urban and middle class in character; hence, there is reason to conclude that the strains accompanying the industrial transformation are by no means confined to agrarian sources. Yet, can we face up to this, can we drop our guard long enough to consider the possibility that the traits noted here *might* contribute to American authoritarian behavior, or the further possibility that authoritarianism has become incorporated into the social matrix of our times? Intuitively the historian and the society at large draw back from rigorously looking inward. That is understandable, for we live in an age of uncertainty; we seek reassurance, and not self-knowledge.

This brings me to the main point of the paper. Historians currently engaged in re-writing the past, I suggest, are torn within themselves on viewing the post-war world as both distasteful and pleasant, and in this, they mirror a larger ambivalence in the American mind itself. Our society too is torn. As I see it, the essence of the Enlightenment heritage, the affirmation of the rationality of man and the confidence in his ability to make the world over, is being dessicated under the glaring sun of Cold War stresses. Torn between fear on one hand, and self-glorification on the other, the chief casualty in this ambivalent process has been our faith in human potentiality.

Herein lies the meaning of the denigration of Populism. Why have historians been so quick to strike down the Populist movement, and why have the allegations, although without foundation, enjoyed such widespread acceptance? The question can no longer be evaded. Specifically, I submit that Populism represents all that we are not; it stands for the very affirmation we no longer feel; and because we do not find within ourselves the internal sources of strength to face the modern world, we have turned swiftly and relentlessly on the movement for possessing the courage and other qualities which we today lack. Critics of Populism write from a clearer present-day perspective than they realize. For what we project onto Populism is no more than our own times.

At the risk of repeating myself, let me state again that there was no earthly reason, either in the form of new evidence or in the alleged similarities between Populism and McCarthyism, to account for the denigration of the Populist movement. The heritage was, and is today more than ever, rich in meaning. Its philosophic core was so imbedded in American ideals that even opponents in the following half-century could charge no more than that Populists were misguided, in their eyes, for veering so far to the left. But the ideals themselves were not questioned.

Turning to the present, one would have thought it was the ideal creed in opposing McCarthyism. In Populism, intellectuals had ready at hand ample precedent in the American past for standing their ground against allegations that social welfare thinking and regard for human rights was un-American. Likewise, foreign policy considerations cannot explain the decline of the Populist image. In the 1950's America sought to appeal, and still does, to the underdeveloped nations. Here, above all, the image should have been nurtured. As a tradition of agrarian radicalism, it offered a meaningful appeal to these people. Few experiences in the American past could better promote the sense of common ties based on having gone through the experience of rapid industrialization. So, once more I state that the explanation for the denigration of Populism lies deeper.

In taking stock, I think we can dismiss the critics as being of little importance. Just as there would have been McCarthyism (under whatever label) had the junior senator from Wisconsin not been on the scene, there would also have been an attempt to purge the American past of dissident elements had several scholars not made their respective contributions. The ground swell was too overwhelming to be the work of any one man or group of men. To blame a handful provides too simplistic a solution, for the problem touches on the nature of society and not on the activities of a few historians.

The reasons underlying the denigration of Populism are complex, and cannot be more than tentatively blocked out in this paper. My remark a moment ago that historians are purging the past of dissident elements—a point I made four years ago in connection with *The Age of Reform*—can serve as a point of departure. We have witnessed over the last dozen years a trend in historical writing which superimposes a straitjacket of consensus on the American past. By that I meant in 1960, and still mean, that all traces of social protest are being eradicated in favor of a model which characterizes the historical development of the United States as no more than a euphonious assertion of capitalist-on-the-make values. There was no conflict, only harmony; and certainly not the existence of hard times which might give rise to genuine grievances. In sum, our society exhibits a pattern of splendid equilibrium.

Four years ago, I could not see beyond this point. Today, I should like to ask, what are the larger implications of the consensus framework? Is it a temporary response to Cold War conditions? If so, how does one account for our excessive fear over admitting that social protest existed in the past, or our zeal in superimposing a pattern of equilibrium on that past, or finally our alacrity in accepting the charges against Populism? In a word, does not the quest for consensus reflect a deeper anxiety than that stemming from a concern over McCarthyism at home and tensions on the international scene?

Perhaps the clue to the disease lies in its symptoms. Consensus tells us a great deal about the society receptive to its message. First, it is an unmistakable sign of stereotypic thinking. There is not only the tendency rigidly to categorize data, as a substitute for the analysis of specific evidence in a unique historical situation, but also the endeavor to categorize the entire span of our history in the same mold. We now know that stereotypy is a dangerous trait, and not just the mark of intellectual carelessness. Stereotypy signifies that the capacity for individuated experience is absent; facts are not treated in their own right, but only in terms of pre-arranged categories. In a nutshell, the significance of this pattern of thinking is that it represents the desire to eliminate uncertainty from one's existence. Rigid ego-defenses are erected as a barrier against seeing what one does not want to see. Conflict cannot be tolerated. Contrary ideas cannot be admitted, for fear that they will threaten one's very identity.

Second, consensus militates against adopting an intraceptive outlook. We are afraid to look inward, afraid to confront our past in all of its intricacies—in all of its blemishes as well as strong points. Anti-intraception betrays an attitude which places a premium on process and form, rather than on what is human in history. Fearing what we might find in ourselves, we regard the problems of man as an unsafe subject of discussion. The same barrenness of ego comes through as in the case of stereotypic thinking. All men, the noble and the base alike, are reduced to a common formula, and made over into the image of ourselves. Populists and Jacksonians are capitalists-on-the-make because we are capitalists-on-the-make. For them to be different, to have dreams and aspirations which differ from our own, might serve as a reproach to our own values. Whether this represents self-glorification of present-day America, or self-loathing, or both, is less important than the larger picture which anti-intraception suggests. American society lacks the confidence in itself to take a close hard look at its past, both the best as well as the worst in that past.

Finally, consensus reveals an even more disturbing trait. By characterizing the American past in terms of a homogeneity in values, experiences, and goals, we have promoted the myth of national purity. This is different from the chosen-people strain in our history, for the emphasis has shifted. We are no longer John Winthrop's city upon the hill for all to see and take heart in, nor even the turn of the century expansionists who want to civilize the little brown brother to the South and across the Pacific, although no doubt each of these sentiments persists down into our own times. Rather, the stress is upon uniformity for its own sake. The impulse is entirely negative. For it serves to bring cohesion out of chaos, a sense of belonging where that sense is not felt, in sum, a belief in homogeneity which provides the feeling of self-identification with the ingroup as opposed to the other, the stranger, all those who lie outside the national experience.

Hence, consensus contributes directly to ethnocentric patterns of thought. Through the assertion of purity comes the erection of mental walls, with the rigid ingroup-outgroup dichotomy defining who shall be on either side of the barriers. In such a situation, with stereotypic thinking and anti-intraception as derivative responses, further impetus is given to maintaining homogeneity, past as well as present, at all costs. This uniformity of outlook becomes a crutch: our past stands for fundamental agreement, marking the progressive realization of the expectant capitalist. We now have a sense of continuity between present and past, and the added reassurance that present-day institutions and values are the product of universal approval on this side of the wall, that is, among the ingroup. From here it is but a short step to maintaining that social protest upsets the equilibrium, threatens the consensus, denies the homogeneity of the nation, and thus is a form of treasonable conduct.

It is difficult to escape the conclusion that the critics of Populism and the society which finds the charges so congenial to its temperament exhibit the very traits of authoritarianism they impute to others. Not willing to admit the existence of authoritarian currents in ourselves and in our society, we project them onto others–the outgroup, the Populists, indeed the reform tradition in America.

Thus, Populism becomes for the historian and the larger society what the Jew is for the anti-Semite. Both historian and anti-Semite require a scapegoat, and the character of that scapegoat is incidental. For each hates not Populists or Jews but himself. Each cannot affirm man, each has little faith in human potentiality or confidence in man's ability to shape the future and rationally control society, each cannot confront the possibilities of self-fulfillment in humanity–and frightened by these thoughts, each turns blindly to dependence on the homogeneous folk or the static past. In the final analysis, the denigration of Populism signifies the fear of man.

When I suggest that the consensus framework and McCarthyism are, far from being at opposite poles, actually one and the same underlying trend, I am of course not directing these remarks so much to the critics of Populism as to the society they faithfully mirror. Populism stands as the conscience of modern America. It means frank and full discussion over essentials, and not blind submission to the status quo; it means the people, indeed the much maligned common man, can take the future in hand and make a better world, and not elitist despair over human nature and contempt for popular movements as being degenerate mobs; it means taking the earlier democratic values of American society at face value and trying to implement them, and not the cynical, amoral pragmatism of today which finds the very notion of ideological commitment to be a sign of the crackpot. Populism is our conscience, and we cannot face it.

When I point to similarities of response in the critic and the anti-Semite, I do not mean the former (and society at large) is necessarily anti-Semite. One need not be an overt anti-Semite to reflect the authoritarian thought patterns outlined here. To call the critic an anti-Semite misses the point, for both share in common a deeper negation of man. We have only begun, since World War II, to appreciate fully that anti-Semitism itself is more basically dehumanizing than an attack solely on Jews. Simply put, we know from psychoanalytic studies that ethnocentrism, stereotypy and anti-intraception, found in critic and anti-Semite alike, constitute the core of the authoritarian personality.

In the comparison I am drawing between the critic (and the society he reflects) and the anti-Semite, I know of no more penetrating analysis of this underlying authoritarianism than that presented by Jean-Paul Sartre in "The Portrait of the Anti-Semite." It is this statement of the problem which best explains what is happening in American society, why so much stress is placed on consensus, and why at bottom we have witnessed the denigration of Populism. When Sartre speaks of the anti-Semite, we could just as readily insert the critic of Populism, or better yet, the form such criticism takes.

For both critic and anti-Semite share in the search for uniformity. And both deny the efficacy and wisdom of social protest, not only out of cynicism of man's desire for human betterment and his ability to achieve improvement (utopian is a term of reproach for both), but also out of the fear that protest leads to change and change means the end to stability and certainty in one's life. Thus both cling to present-day values because they cannot plan for the future. They enshrine the status quo as a means of escaping from the responsibilities of living. Sartre describes this defeatist outlook as the product of men "who are attracted by the durability of stone."

What is consensus but this state of mind? The static equilibrium, the ahistorical consensus, these alone provide reassurance. We see an orientation here, to quote Sartre, "in which one never seeks but that which one has already found, in which one never becomes other than what one already was." And to insure this equilibrium, I might add, both must have a scapegoat. Balance is attained by eradicating the evil one. Then all is well again.

Sartre's portrait of the anti-Semite is summed up in these words: "He is a man who is afraid. Not of the Jews of course, but of himself, of his conscience, his freedom, of his instincts, of his responsibilities, of solitude, of change, of society and the world; of everything except the Jews." This too captures the significance of our own attack on the Populist movement as an escape from ourselves and the challenges of our age. Sartre concludes on a note which reaches to the innermost recesses of the authoritarian mind. "Anti-Semitism, in a word, is fear of man's fate. The anti-Semite is the man who wants to be a pitiless stone, furious torrent, devastating lightning: in short, everything but a man."

Indeed if Populism is the conscience of modern America, I submit we should look to that heritage and take pride in what we see. The Cassandras of despair have had their day. The time has come to call a halt to the erosion of human values, and to the denigration not only of Populism but of man himself. Why fear today and tomorrow when we as a nation have had our share of splendid yesterdays? America has in Populism a rich tradition for moving in the direction of the affirmation of man.

FOOTNOTES

[1] Norman Pollack, "Hofstadter on Populism: A Critique of 'The Age of Reform,' " *The Journal of Southern History,* XXVII, November, 1960, pp. 478-500.

[2] Norman Pollack, "The Myth of Populist Anti-Semitism," *American Historical Review,* LXVIII, October, 1962, pp. 76-80.

[3] Norman Pollack, *The Populist Response to Industrial America,* Harvard, Cambridge, 1962, available in paperback.

[4] Norman Pollack, "Handlin on Anti-Semitism: A Critique of 'American Views of the Jew,' " *Journal of American History,* LI, December, 1964, pp. 391-403.

[5] Norman Pollack, ed., *The Populist Mind,* Bobbs-Merrill, Indianapolis and New York, 1967.

11

Commentary on the New Left Historians

IRWIN UNGER (1967)

The following selection by Irwin Unger (b. 1927), professor of history at Washington Square College, New York University, was the first essay written on the young neo-progressive historians born during the Great Depression who published their first scholarship in the 1960s. Unger provided a comprehensive survey of their work, which he related to the emergence of a younger generation's protest against the status quo.

The young historians have objected to the post-war interpretations which minimized conflict and which celebrated mainstream America to the exclusion or minimization of reformers, radicals, as well as possibilities of genuine change. In the cases where New Left historians have accented consensus, it has been coupled with condemnation of that consensus. Unger's evaluation of the neo-progressive scholars was that they deserved credit for the instigation of a dialogue with the post-war historians who by the 1960s were most numerous and influential, but he was critical of their exploitation of the past for purposes of present reform.

It is impossible not to notice that there is a new political Left in America. The struggle for civil rights, while endorsed by liberals and "moderates," is largely led by young people of radical commitment. The student protests on university campuses derive their fire from young men and women who reject much of American life in the 1960's. Rent strikers, peace marchers, and Vietnam protestors–all are deeply skeptical of the affluent society. Almost everywhere throughout the country, but especially where masses of young people are thrown together–most notably, of course, at the universities–new organizations, new journals, new movements are emerging, dedicated to restoring a radical voice to the contention of ideas in the United States.[1]

The average newspaper reader knows the New Left for its activism. But it is not surprising that a movement that enlists so many college students, and particularly graduate students in the humanities and social sciences, should also have a reflective side. While consistently pragmatic in their day-to-day activities, the various New Left groups have begun to feel the

---

Reprinted by permission from Irwin Unger, "The 'New Left' and American History: Some Recent Trends in United States Historiography," *American Historical Review*, LXXII, July 1967, pp. 1237-1263.

need for theory and analysis. Their experience has already given birth to a New Left sociology, economics, and political science.[2] They are now beginning to create a new, radical history, particularly a new radical American history.

To understand this development, one must recall what has happened in American historical writing in the last two decades. As described by John Higham in his important article, "The Cult of the 'American Consensus,'" which appeared in 1959,[3] certain trends were already clear. Since the 1940's something striking and significant had happened to the intellectual climate that surrounded the historians of America. They had abandoned the notion of struggle as the central theme of our past. Until the postwar years historians had acknowledged and indeed had emphasized the existence of social ills and social strife in the United States. The American past, like the past of other nations, seemed a series of confrontations between antagonistic and competing economic and class interest groups. American colonial history disclosed a sharp battle of yeoman and provincial nabob. The Revolution was both a struggle over "home rule" and over "who should rule at home." The Constitution was a class document. Battles between Hamiltonians and Jeffersonians, Whigs and Jacksonians, were struggles between the privileged orders and the commonalty. The Civil War was a collision of an industrial North and an agrarian South. And so it went: through the age of the robber barons, the war with Spain, Progressivism, the Great Depression, the New Deal. The binding theme of our history was class conflict, or at least an American version of it.[4] The United States, then, was not "exceptional." The fine details of our history were different, perhaps, but at heart the American past was similar to the European past. The one plausible alternative to the class conflict view of American history—Frederick Jackson Turner's frontier thesis—by the 1930's had been thoroughly demolished, it seemed, by the combined attack of Marxists and "Progressives."[5]

As described by Higham, the new history of Louis Hartz, Richard Hofstadter, Samuel Hays, David Potter, and Daniel Boorstin seemed to assert either that there had been no struggle in our past or that the struggle had been generated not by some real but by some imagined injustice. Rather than cataclysmic change, abrupt, angry, cacophonous, American history had been almost sedate. Americans had disagreed with one another, of course, but not irreconcilably or over the basic issues of property and political democracy. The experience of transplanted Europeans with a "new country" of abundant, unexploited resources had been fused with Lockean liberalism, engendering a mood of pragmatic moderation in all but a few American souls. The postwar generation of American historians had concluded, Higham wrote, that continuity, contentment, and "consensus" characterized the history of the nation; all else was either the illusion of the historian or that of his protagonists.[6]

Since 1959 the list of "consensus" historians has lengthened considerably. For the colonial era one might cite Clarence Ver Steeg's *The Formative Years.* For the period of the Confederation we not only have Robert E. Brown's *Middle-Class Democracy and the Revolution in Massachusetts* and *Charles Beard and the Constitution* but also Forrest McDonald's *We the People* and *E Pluribus Unum.* For the early national period there are the books of Paul Goodman and Noble Cunningham. For the Jackson era we have had, since 1959, the work of Lee Benson, Bray Hammond, Walter E. Hugins. For the Civil War period there are David Donald, Eric McKitrick, Stanley Elkins, and Stanley Coben. For the late nineteenth and early twentieth centuries we have Robert Wiebe's *Businessmen and Reform,* and, most recently, David J. Rothman's *Politics and Power.*[7]

Such an assemblage of authors immediately suggests the inadequacy of Higham's description. With a larger sample before us, we can now see that while the new postwar historians include consensusites pure and simple, they also include those, who in rejecting the dualisms of their predecessors, prefer to replace them with a pluralistic view of the American past. Instead of a simple dialogue the historical stage presents a complex and tumultous crowd scene. It is also clearer now that social psychology and the other social sciences have profoundly influenced this complex view of the past. Higham believed in 1959 that the behavioral approach enabled the new generation of historians to obscure conflict in America by "psychologizing" it. Men thought they were exploited and victimized when they really were just emotionally disturbed. While it is true, as Higham noted, that the postwar historians are impressed by the stability of American society and by our broad agreement over fundamentals, we now know that many of them take social conflict quite seriously. But they define conflict more broadly than did the "progressive" historians of the previous generation. Besides the traditional haves versus have-nots in their many separate guises, we now have Catholic versus Protestant, dry versus wet, rural versus urban, white versus black, old versus young, ins versus outs. These are real conflicts, but they are psychologically or socially defined and open to the imputation that they are merely sick phantoms in the mind. We take seriously the man who finds himself in an economic vise; we tend to despise or pity the man who suffers from status anxieties. Somehow *Angst* seems less real than hunger.

It is easy to see why this shift in the analysis of conflict reduces the emotional charge of past historical movements. Not only does it suggest that all the discontented are mere malingerers, but it is also difficult to identify heroes and villains. If nothing else, both the guilty and the injured in a pluralistic society often turn out to be but a small part of some larger group. Businessmen can no longer be condemned as a whole. They disagree among themselves and can scarcely be held responsible for anything collectively. Farmers are no longer just farmers. They are northeastern truck gardeners, or Wisconsin dairy farmers, or Kansas wheat-growers, or southern cotton planters, and they do not all suffer the same fate at the same time.

These ambiguities inevitably encourage a kind of neutrality and detachment that are congenial to the use of new statistical techniques borrowed from the sister social sciences. No longer intent on proving a case for "the people," historians can subject all the old conclusions to the dispassionate test of social statistics. There is no inherent reason why radicals cannot employ the same tools, but so far, with an occasional exception, the fascination with numbers has been the province of the postwar, "middle generation." Perhaps the young men of the Left fear that the figures will not bear them out. Certainly in American economic history the work of the new "cliometricians" has given comfort to "conservative" interpretations of such diverse issues as the origins of the American Revolution, the plight of the late nineteenth-century farmer, and the culpability of the robber barons.[8]

It would be a serious mistake to insist that there is absolute unanimity in either approach or conclusions among the postwar generation of historians. To some degree they are all "post-Beardians" since they are all trying to escape the Beardian matrix which imprisoned American history in the first four decades of this century. But they go beyond Beard in a number of distinct ways, and the label is at best only moderately useful as a descriptive term. Nevertheless, despite the difficulties of definition, Higham in 1959 clearly detected the beginnings of an important and substantial change in the writing of American history, and it is this change that is now beginning to generate a reaction among the young men of the Left.

It may now seem clearer what there is about the postwar history that antagonizes the new radicals. They are not primarily offended by the rejection of "historical materialism," the keystone of traditional Marxist historiography. A few Marxian "Old Leftists" like Herbert Aptheker, Philip Foner, and Harvey O'Connor are still writing history. But the New Left historians are not the captives of an official ideology.[9] We must "*Americanize the radical program* by bringing historically native radicalism up to date," writes Harold Cruse in *Studies on the Left,* a major forum of the New Left history.

We do this by accepting what we need from the "Marxist method" insofar as the method applies to American social history. . . . While we allow that historical laws are universally applicable, these laws operate according to the dictates of different social ingredients in different places. We accept the fact that the Marxian revolution *could have happened* at a certain time given the proper leadership and impetus.[10]

When, as in the case of William Appleman Williams, the New Left historians make much of Marx, it is more often the early "soft" Marx, who speaks of "alienation," than the "hard" Marx of *Das Kapital,* with its class struggle and progressive "immiserization of the proletariat."[11]

Beard is a different case. The New Left has joined an older group of historians to perpetuate the Beardian vision.[12] In direct proportion as he has become a false prophet of the new postwar history, Beard has become the Moses of the New Left.[13] Williams, a man who actually owes little to Beard—except, perhaps, on recent American foreign policy—feels compelled to announce in his bellicose style, "it . . . seems appropriate, in view of all the bigoted and career building attacks, acts of purification in the form of misrepresentation, and even smart-alec criticism by supposed aristocrats, to acknowledge formally my respect for and debt to Charles Austin Beard."[14] Yet much of the homage is ceremonial. At their best, the New Left historians feel free to diverge from both masters. When they do, the results are often interesting.

It is not, then, uncritical loyalty to a particular master that makes the New Left bridle at the postwar history. It is rather what they perceive as the tone, commitment, and power of the post-Beardian historians that annoys and angers the young radicals. The most obvious of these characteristics is, of course, the imputed political conservatism of their elders. The new history is, so it seems to the young Leftists, history at the service of an elitist and aristocratic definition of society, and the "American Celebration." Until recently, notes Arnold Rogow, the American intellectual's "view of the common man was essentially Jeffersonian." Now the common man is being "muckraked," and the older liberal tradition is being repudiated as the intellectuals adopt the New Conservatism.[15] To Norman Pollack the new history represents the "treason of the intellectuals." Frightened by Joseph McCarthy's witch-hunts, they cravenly retreated from the exposed Left to a safe Right.[16]

Equally irritating to the New Left, though less widely advertised, are the supposed institutional power and influence of the post-Beardians. Intellectually complacent, often supercilious, they are, we are told, firmly implanted in the prestigious eastern private universities, where they form an academic establishment capable of using its professional power to proscribe dissent and encourage conformity.[17] Indeed, there is among the young radical academicians a sense of persecution that, since it is largely anticipatory, seems excessive. Convinced that they are struggling against a pernicious power elite, they see in their professional lives what they are convinced obtains in the flow of American history itself. The conspiracies against the people by the interests find a parallel in the efforts of the historical establishment to suppress the radical voice.

But perhaps the worst offense of the postwar history is its failure to provide the New Left with a "usable past." The charge like the term is ambiguous. "Usable past" implies in the first place a concern for historical guidelines, an interest that the New Left surely shares with much of mankind. At this point it would be well to recall that the New Left is programmatic and activist; it is the product not of a great book or a great prophet but of the social maladjustments of our day. Many of the young scholars who have joined the recent attack against the historiographic trends of the past decade have been men living and working very much in a radical and dissenting present. As historians and radicals it is natural that they should seek wisdom in the past. Staughton Lynd, a talented New Left historian, has been quite explicit about the need for a usable radical past to provide direction for the new radical community, which otherwise appears doomed, he declares, to rehash problems its predecessors have already settled.[18]

But the concept of a usable past also suggests that history may serve as a political weapon. To the young Leftists the most obvious partisan use of history is to domesticate radicalism in America. In all fairness, it must be said that this is largely a counterattack. The Right has always insisted that radicalism is un-American, a foreign import embraced only by those who have no roots in the native culture or who have lost contact with those roots. But until quite recently the conservative claim has not been academically respectable, for from about 1910 until the late 1940's the giants of the profession devoted their scholarly energies to exhibiting the long and honorable record of insurgency and dissent on the frontier, on the farms, in the mining camps and factory towns. Now, some of the leading scholars of the nation have apparently given the old charge intellectual sanction of an impressive order. There is no native American radicalism, they say—not one that any balanced man would wish to acknowledge. Radicalism has always been an exotic import, ill-suited to American circumstances, and hence deserving of the isolation and failure it has always suffered. The challenge is clearly fundamental. If there has been no true dissent in America; if a general consensus over capitalism, race relations, and expansionism has prevailed in the United States; if such dissent as has existed has been crankish and sour, the product not of a maladjusted society but of maladjusted men—then American history may well be monumentally irrelevant for contemporary radicalism. As scholars and social critics, simultaneously, the young New Left historians of course find this conclusion impossible to accept.

Having dismissed the new postwar history, what do the young men of the Left hope to put in its place? It is not possible to say in a simple, categorical way. The young radicals know what they reject, and in fact their dislikes are often what most satisfactorily defines them.[19] They are not, however, as clear about what they accept. Dissensions within the New Left history are as general and intense as disagreements among the socialists, anarchists, pacifists, existentialists, and Neo-Populists who compose the New Left movement. It is a panorama as complex as the pluralistic history the young radicals would refute.

There is indeed an ambitious attempt at a general synthesis of America's past by a New Left historian of good credentials,[20] *The Contours of American History* by Professor William A. Williams of the University of Wisconsin, but unfortunately this interesting book fails as a chart to the emerging radical history. The major theme of *The Contours* is the persistent tension in America between the two world views of commonwealth and individualism. The first, identified with "mercantilism," is the very womb out of which the American nation emerged. As used by Williams, "mercantilism" must not be confused with the selfish, retrograde economic doctrine of the standard textbook discussions. It means a benevolent paternalism displayed by an enlightened class of gentlemen—the "gentry"—who placed the interest of the whole community above that of any single group including themselves. While not without its serious limitations, most notably its recourse to foreign expansion to solve domestic problems, mercantilism represents the benign side of the American tradition. Opposing it, and virtually without redeeming qualities, is "laissez-nous faire," and, what is its essential synonym, "individualism." To Williams this world view is socially corrosive, fostering competition rather than cooperation, anomie rather than community, profits rather than justice.

This may seem to be a predictable Leftist dualism and may suggest at first glance the basis for a reconstructed radical history. Actually it gives aid and comfort to the enemy. Williams offers little to the New Left. It is quite clear from *The Contours* that few Americans ever questioned the sacrosanct nature of private property or ever could see much beyond more property or more geographic expansion as the solution for internal problems. Elements of American society did indeed differ in the depth of their social insight and the degree of their humane sympathies, but except for the small and impotent groups of socialists at the end of the nineteenth century, they all suffered from the same fatal weakness of social imagination. In a word, though Williams can scarcely intend it, we are back at consensus![21]

In fact *The Contours* proves a constant embarrassment to the younger radical scholars. Williams not only accepts the broad theme of an American consensus; he also accepts a surprising number of the specific judgments of the post-Beardian history. He agrees with Brown and McDonald that support for the Revolution and the Constitution transcended class lines.[22] He accepts the thesis of Hammond and Hofstadter that the Jacksonians were aggressive capitalist enterprisers.[23] He agrees that the abolitionists were often difficult and unreasonable men who failed to understand the complexities of race adjustment.[24] He acknowledges the dark side of Populism, although he is critical of what he considers the supercilious tone of its recent detractors.[25] To Williams, Franklin Roosevelt is a man who cherished power for its own sake; Hoover, a true progressive in the mercantile tradition.[26] The book, moreover, is saturated with old-fashioned philosophical idealism. Ideas, not interests, are what count in history, for mercantilism, at least, is no mere rationalization of individual or class advantage. Derived from Biblical moralism, it is tough and autonomous with the power to blunt and tame the acquisitive instincts.[27] This is scarcely the stuff out of which to construct a new radical history, and with regret several of the young Leftist historians have conceded as much.[28]

If we stopped at this point, it would be difficult to see in what way it is possible to consider Williams a radical historian at all. His credentials derive, I think, from two major themes of *The Contours.* The first is his radical indictment of individualism and his extravagant praise of the proto-collectivism of the "gentry." In the absence of a viable socialist tradition the "mercantilism" of the gentry must satisfy Williams' yearning to discover virtue in the American past. The second is Williams' treatment of American foreign policy. Here the young Leftists find strong support for their conviction of America's total depravity. From the very outset, according to Williams, the United States has been an expansionist nation, preying on its weaker neighbors, whether the precivilized Indian tribes or the weaker national states and decrepit empires on its borders. This expansionism is a strangely persuasive mirror image of Turner's frontier thesis. Rather than a succession of new opportunities, each American frontier was a new evasion.

It was not democracy that renewed itself in each new "West"; it was capitalism, and American foreign policy was merely the instrument of this evasive westward thrust.[29]

But neither mercantilism nor expansionism provides a historical framework for the New Left equal to class struggle for the old. In the end *The Contours* is too personal and idiosyncratic. Williams is an angry dissenter who, despite his announced faith in a cooperative society, is beholden to no man for his historical vision, or, one is sometimes tempted to say, for his historical facts. But still the radical scholars listen to Williams. He may supply little they can use for understanding America's domestic affairs, but he most emphatically speaks to them on the history of American foreign policy. *The Contours* and Williams' specific works in diplomatic history[30] have had a powerful impact on a group of young diplomatic historians, many of whom have worked with him or under him at the University of Wisconsin.

The most successful of these younger scholars is Walter LaFeber,[31] whose book, *The New Empire,* won the Albert J. Beveridge Award in 1962.[32] LaFeber is a sophisticated and urbane historian. Yet he is willing to make his radical philosophical stand quite explicit. In a 1962 book review he praises the tradition of Beard and Arthur B. Darling in American diplomatic history and assails those historians who "since 1945 . . . have been preoccupied with knifing Beard with one hand and using the other hand to pen caricatures of a unique unblemished Republic which became a world empire with little conscious human intervention."[33] The thesis of *The New Empire* is that America's venture into imperialism in the 1890's was neither a historical accident nor a new departure. It was the culmination of a process dating at least to the 1850's or 1860's, the roots of which were primarily economic. Post-Civil War American imperialism sprang from the need of manufacturers for raw materials and markets. It was not absent-mindedness that led to the war with Spain and the annexation of Hawaii, the Philippines, and Puerto Rico; it was the demands of businessmen.

LaFeber does not approve of American expansionism, but he is not a crude polemicist. His imperialist businessmen and policy makers are "responsible, conscientious men who accepted the economic and social realities of their day . . . and . . . were unafraid to strike out on new and uncharted paths in order to create what they sincerely hoped would be a better nation and a better world."[34] Several other members of the Wisconsin school of diplomatic history are both less temperate and less convincing than LaFeber. John W. Rollins, in an essay on the anti-imperialists and American foreign policy in the twentieth century, reaches the tortured conclusion that even most of those who balked at overt American colonialism in the years since the Spanish-American War have been expansionists and imperialists. They may not have endorsed American occupation and control, but they have endorsed American economic penetration, and this is the same thing. Free trade, foreign investment, Point Four aid–all, presumably, have been tools of American hegemony.[35] Lloyd Gardner examines the foreign policy of the New Deal and concludes that following the disastrous economic setback of 1937-1938, "the New Deal forsook viable domestic remedies and readied itself for the pursuit of . . . world frontiers . . . as its solution to the crisis of the 1930's." In the end Gardner comes very close to attributing America's entrance into World War II, once cheered by the Left as the defense of democracy and freedom, to the reluctance of the Axis Powers to accept American demands for "liberal trade and the Open Door."[36] New Left revisionism could not be better designed to antagonize the generation that waged the crusade against fascism!

There is, in the New Left diplomatic history, an interesting rehabilitation, explicit or implied of isolationism. Williams himself seems to be its source. By denying the serious practice of isolation by the United States he makes the few sincere advocates of minding our own business into rare, heroic souls.[37] Beard's obscure 1934 attack on American intervention in European affairs, *The Open Door at Home,* has become an object of veneration among the Wisconsin school.[38] They give isolationist Progressives like William Borah credit for rare prescience in foretelling the dangers of the "garrison state, the weight of military costs, the penetration of American economic power into almost every sphere upon the globe, and the loss of liberty at home and abroad."[39]

The message in all this is clear. America's recent aggressive and provocative foreign policy is not the response of the moment; our reaction to world problems after 1945 was merely the latest term of an American tradition of aggrandizement that commenced with John Smith. From first to last, cupidity has been the governing principle of our relations with strangers, and we must not expect more of our acquisitive, capitalist society.

In its strictures on America's earlier foreign affairs the New Left is obviously projecting onto history its present cold war fears and frustrations. The pattern of present-mindedness persists in its view of America's domestic past. Just as they would transform the country's relations to the non-Western world, the young radicals are committed to reorienting American society itself, and nothing fascinates them more than their radical predecessors and the movements they inspired and led.[40]

As we have seen, the radical attempt to recover America's "progressive" past seems to serve a number of purposes simultaneously. It satisfies a natural curiosity about radical antecedents and represents an understandable quest for direction. But more important, and less disinterested, the New Left's concern with the nation's reformist past is an attempt to establish its own legitimacy.

This search for a historical sanction is the main concern of Pollack, although at times it might appear that his real purpose is to dethrone the leading representatives of the "establishment." Leaving aside this strong acerbic aspect of Pollack's work, we find that his main point is that there has indeed been a viable radical tradition native to America, a tradition associated with agrarian insurgency, which reached its apogee during the Populist revolt. Far from fleeing the industrial realities of the day, as has been suggested by Oscar Handlin, Hofstadter, and others, the Populists realistically diagnosed the problems of emerging industrialism and realistically prescribed for them. Neither rural xenophobes nor ignorant paranoids but perceptive radical humanitarians, they produced a critique of capitalist society still valid today. Indeed their analysis of American industrial capitalism closely paralleled Marx's dissection of early European industrial society, which suggests to Pollack the "extremely exciting prospect" that the "Populist experience might well challenge a basic proposition in historical writing–the uniqueness of America." True, contemporary American Marxists opposed the Populists, but only because the Marxists were excessively sectarian and poorly attuned to the needs of the American environment.[41]

Pollack's defense of the Populists from some of their more intemperate critics, largely sociologists and political scientists, has been useful. He has, I think, at least made us realize that Populism had a humane and progressive side as well as a retrograde, nativist one. He has not, however, made many converts to his major thesis–the viability of the Populist tradition–even among the New Left. Despite his impassioned pleading, Populism appears too *petit bourgeois* and too intellectually ambiguous to serve as part of our radical past.[42] His chief allies appear to be men identified with the old liberal Left who have retained their sympathy for insurgent rural America.[43] More congenial as ancestors for the New Leftists than the provincial dissenters of the 1890's are the certified urban radicals, the Socialists and anarchists. Williams, after–in *The Contours*–dismissing the Socialists of this era as impotent, later converts them into seers "who made between 1890 and 1917 the most relevant and mature adaptation to the end of the frontier."[44] James Weinstein, editor of *Studies on the Left,* has made that journal virtually into an instrument for pulling Socialism into the mainstream of American history.

In this endeavor, Weinstein is battling the prevailing view that Socialism failed in the United States because of its own inner inadequacies. On the contrary, he asserts, American Socialism did not fall; it was knocked down. After riding a great popular wave during World War I, Socialism was smashed by the patriotic suppressions perpetrated by the Wilson administration.[45] Socialism is America's "hidden heritage," which has been maligned and abused as much by the historians as by the Attorney General. The historians "have provided little that is usable to the newly emerging American left." "But not all generations," he concludes in a manifesto, "have an equal stake in obscuring the past. Hopefully the new historians of American radicalism will be more disposed to learn from it, and less inclined to bend it, however subconsciously, to their more narrow and immediate purpose."[46]

Weinstein's concern is with the mainstream Socialism of Eugene Debs. But part of the New Left prefers anarchism to Socialism and has sought to recover an antiauthoritarian radical past for the United States. Richard Drinnon, a self-declared radical, has written a sympathetic biography of anarchist Emma Goldman that turns that eccentric but truly interesting woman not only into a "courageous, compassionate, intelligent human being" but into a prophetess of dangerous totalitarian tendencies within the Left.[47] Henry David Thoreau is another radical who appeals to the anarchist Left. When Lynd recently questioned Thoreau's pacifist and anarchist credentials, the resulting furor amply confirmed his claim that the author of *Civil Disobedience* had "become the patron saint of the new radicals and of all unadjusted Americans."[48]

The young men of the Left find it possible to identify with the political failures and outcasts. Urban middle-class reform, on the other hand, earns their contempt. Gabriel Kolko considers the progressive movement a fraud. The mass of early twentieth-century legislation ostensibly designed to regulate business in the interest of the common good was really engineered by businessmen themselves, anxious to prevent destructive competition.[49] The combination of glittering promise and empty performance in progressivism in the end headed off "the radical potential of mass grievances and aspirations of genuine progressivism," or, in other words, of true social reconstruction.[50] Martin J. Sklar tells us that Progressivism was a movement

> led by and consisting of large corporate interests and political and intellectual leaders affirming the large corporate industrial capital system, and convinced of the necessity of institutionalizing reforms, legal and otherwise, to accommodate the nation's law and habits and the people's thinking, to the new corporate business structure and its requirements, domestic and foreign.[51]

While Sklar, unlike Kolko, concedes that what emerged was reform and not mere sham, it is as difficult to recognize in his Progressivism as in Kolko's anything of the humanitarianism, the self-criticism, and the social imagination that historians have generally found in the liberal political movements of the early twentieth century.

The New Left treatment of the New Deal so far has been skimpy. But it is fairly clear, from some interesting fragments, what it will look like when it fully emerges. In a sharply critical review of Arthur Schlesinger, Jr.'s, *The Age of Roosevelt,* Jacob Cohen declares the "New Deal marks the last act . . . by which American politics accommodated itself to the problems of economic justice raised by the system of countervailing powers." He denies to Roosevelt and his associates the honorable label of "pragmatists." Pragmatism possesses a vision of society out of which true social experimentalism can emerge. The New Deal was goalless and aimless, without either moral or practical purposes.[52] "In the long run what *did* the New Deal do?" asks Marc Schleifer.

Are there other, more flourishing offspring of the corporate and progressive income tax than Madison Avenue expense-account culture, and the Pentagon? With the exception of Jimmy Hoffa and a few remnant leftist unions, what significance and militant honor is there now in a "strong" trade union movement? Who can better remember Pearl Harbor than the hundreds of thousands of dead Chinese, Koreans, Vietnamese, Laotians, Filipinos, etc., we have killed since the end of the Second World War?[53]

The New Left's harsh judgment of twentieth-century reform is not, I suggest, the inevitable conclusion imposed by the facts. It is dictated, in the first place, by ideological predispositions. Young Left historians like Kolko cannot endorse any political movement that did not aim at a cooperative society. Progressivism also gets bad marks, one suspects, because it was so eminently respectable. Kolko characteristically attacks the muckrakers as men "with commonplace talents and middle class values."[54] The assault on the New Deal, on the other hand, is a more complex matter. For some of the New Leftists it is an adolescent blow for independence. The New Deal was the political faith of their parents in a quite literal way. In rejecting it they are rejecting their fathers and their fathers' faith.[55] For others, as Schleifer's polemic suggests, the New Deal is the immediate source of the liberal welfare state, and they despise it as much as they do the flaccid, self-satisfied society that they hold as its direct descendant.

Each of these reform movements poses a problem of identification for the New Left. Whether they pass muster is not self-evident. To each must first be put a series of questions: Was it truly radical? Was it proletarian? What were its relations to the existing establishment? Each of the young men is asking himself: would I have supported it? For past reform movements there is, then, as yet no prescribed New Left canon of historical virtue, and the young Leftists are at this point groping for appropriate attitudes and responses. There is one exception to this uncertainty. There is no doubt how the young radicals would have responded to the movement for racial equality in America, and there is no ambiguity in their attitudes toward the historical champions of the Negro.

Without a doubt the struggle for Negro equality during the last century and a half has received more attention from the New Left than any other single "progressive" movement of our past. There is no need to belabor the present-mindedness of this concern. It flows from the intense immersion of the Left today in the problems of civil rights. What could be more obvious to even the most superficial student of history than that the battles of Little Rock, Selma, and Birmingham are the lineal descendants of those fought by the abolitionists and later by the Radical Republicans? To the New Left the label "New Abolitionists" for modern civil rights militants is more than a metaphor.[56]

In some sense, of course, the New Left history of abolitionism writes itself. There is no question about when to cheer and when to hiss; the problem is in identifying the historiographic, not the historical, heroes and villains. Up to this point, as we have seen, the New Left historians have been able to write history as rebuttal–rebuttal of some position of their professional elders. With the history of the American Negro, and the struggle over his lot and future, difficulties arise. The trouble is that the academic establishment already occupies the high ground. Even in the bad old days of the 1940's and 1950's the historiography of the race question in America was becoming radicalized. Paradoxically, at the very moment American historians were allegedly turning to the Right, they had adopted an egalitarian view of the Negro, and to a lesser extent were becoming more sympathetic to his friends. It was not Williams or Lynd who rehabilitated the abolitionists; it was Dwight Dumond and Gilbert Hobbs Barnes. It was not W. E. B. DuBois or James Allen alone who were re-evaluating the accomplishments of black Reconstruction; Francis B. Simkins, Robert Woody, and Vernon Wharton were doing it equally well.[57] As far back as 1949 Arthur Schlesinger, Jr., who epitomizes for the New Left the academic as well as the political establishment, was insisting that the Civil War, however deplorable and destructive, did justify itself by destroying slavery.[58]

The New Left has compensated for this lack of a historiographic enemy, I believe, by singling out one of the few prominent middle generation historians who appears to be critical of the abolitionists. There may be legitimate grounds on which to quarrel with David Donald's work, but the Left, I believe, chiefly dislikes his reluctance to accept the abolitionists at their own estimate. When, in 1956, in a composite social portrait of the abolitionists, and later in his *Charles Sumner and the Coming of the Civil War,* Donald suggested that antislavery men were not exempt from the ego drives, the neurotic compulsions, the personal failings, and the capacity for self-deception that afflict other men, he called down on his head the wrath of the neoabolitionists. Louis Ruchames charges Donald with "insensitivity to the evils of slavery." His biography of Sumner is "the subversion of the character of a founding father of American civil equality. . . ."[59] Fawn Brodie accuses Donald of performing a deft "surgical operation" on Sumner, not for the purpose of analyzing the man but to malign and discredit the cause he fought for.[60] Aileen Kraditor detects in Donald's essay, "Toward a Reconsideration of Abolitionists," as well as in Hofstadter's portrait of Wendell Phillips in *The American Political Tradition,* a "contempt for reform movements in general."[61]

It is not enough, I submit, for the New Left to make sentimental gestures. It is too bad that in their defense of the abolitionists they have not tackled the hard question Donald raises: why did so few out of so many Americans respond to the evil of slavery in such a way as to risk wealth, reputation, and even personal safety? A truly radical answer might be that America was so thoroughly and universally corrupt in its racial attitudes that only men who were virtually at war with their environment could really appreciate the evil of slavery and take an active and risky part in its destruction. Indeed, at least in part, this seems to be the implication of one New Left author, Leon Litwack, who notes that racist bigotry in ante bellum America pervaded every sector of society, including abolitionism itself.[62] Instead of such a bold assault on American values, however, the New Left seldom does more than reiterate the evil of slavery—a fact no one seriously disputes—as sufficient explanation for the abolitionist impulse. In their anxiety to protect the civil rights movement, they have failed to face the obvious historical problem.

The abolitionists are a New Left "hero class."[63] To Pollack, at least, the Populists are another. Strangely, the wage earners of America do not seem to constitute a third. As a group, the "common people" receive little attention from the young radicals. Kolko and Michael Harrington, both young men of the Left, have "rediscovered" poverty in the United States after the liberals declared it extinct.[64] But although the continued presence of the poor in an ostensibly rich nation suggests still larger contrasts of wealth, and condition in the past, neither work is, properly speaking, historical.

More satisfactory is Stephen Thernstrom's *Poverty and Progress,* a work that suggests how truly useful it can be to examine American mythology with the skeptical eye of the Left. Basically Thernstrom seeks to discover whether nineteenth-century America was really a land of opportunity for the laboring man. Unlike many of the new radicals, who, with Mills, confuse computers with conservatism, he is not afraid to use statistics or the insights of social psychology, and the resulting marriage of radical skepticism and post-Beardian technique produces a lively offspring.

In his study of Newburyport in the mid-nineteenth century, Thernstrom puts the notion of America as a working-class paradise to the test. Whatever may have been true of the contemporary West, wages for common labor in the Massachusetts town between 1850 and 1880 were not high, he says, and the ubiquity of child and female labor demonstrates the inability of workingmen to support their families unaided. The community was not classless. Industrialism heightened social antagonism and aroused serious fears among the middle class, which sought to smother social unrest under the rhetoric of "the self-made man." The function, or at least the result, of this mythologizing was to turn class frustration into class guilt and reduce the danger of social upheaval by directing working-class discontent inward against the discontented themselves.[65]

Thus far it is easy to recognize the New Left tone. But the rest of the study is a first-rate piece of social analysis that transcends any special ideology. Was the myth of the self-made man valid, Thernstrom asks. In part. Ingeniously squeezing convincing conclusions out of the manuscript census returns, Thernstrom demonstrates that while few unskilled wage earners, native or immigrant, left the blue-collar class, their sons often did move up to semiskilled status, and, more interesting, it was possible for a working-class family, by exploiting every able-bodied member, and by "ruthless under consumption" to acquire some property, usually the family home.[66] In a word, mobility did exist in America, or at least in Newburyport, but it was limited and did not preclude class antagonisms and much human misery.

Thernstrom's book clearly opens up impressive possibilities for writing working-class history. Yet he has few followers or imitators among the New Left. The fact demands an explanation, for in the 1930's and 1940's, radical historians wrote passionate, engaged studies of the labor movement.[67] The answer, of course, is that the radical intellectuals no longer regard the laboring man in the same approving way. To the old Left the workingman was an object of both solicitude and hope. Time has made a mockery of both these sentiments. Industrial unionism has triumphed, but it is clear to the Left that it has only succeeded in creating another self-centered privileged class. As a social being the American wage earner has succumbed to the mindless distractions of consumerism; as a political being he and his leaders are among the chief supporters of the "Warfare State." The disillusion is profound, and, among some of the New Leftists, the working class has been replaced by the radical students and intellectuals themselves as the anticipated agents of progressive change.

If the New Left refuses to worship the wage earner, it more unexpectedly refuses to curse the businessman. Kolko, at least obliquely, attacks the "revisionist" business historians for their uncritical appraisal of the robber barons,[68] and, in his studies of the progressive era and of railroad regulation, he pictures businessmen as operating covertly off stage in a way scarcely designed to win our approval.[69] Allen Solganick explicitly calls his recent article in *Science and Society* a "rebuttal" of the entrepreneurial school of business history.[70] But these two essays do not amount to much of an indictment, and we must place alongside such mild strictures of businessmen and their academic champions the rather favorable press provided by scholars like Williams, LaFeber, and Lynd.

While the New Left may not exalt workers at the expense of businessmen, surely, one assumes, they must reject a major premise of the new postwar history: the relative classlessness of America and the absence here of serious class conflict. No one really insists that revolution was endemic in the United States, but in at least two instances, surely in the 1770's and again in the 1860's, Americans killed one another on American soil for reasons that appeared to them fundamental. Until recently most American historians–both Marxists and liberal progressives–were prepared to agree that on these two occasions something like a class conflict did occur in the United States. Then came the challenge. To the post-World War II historians the American Revolution was not a social cataclysm; it was a nationalist struggle for independence. Its sequel, the Constitution, was not a Thermidorian reaction but a popular document supported by all classes. The Civil War was not a struggle between industrial capitalism and agrarianism. It was generated by the failure of the political system, or the growth of rival sectional ideologies and mythologies, or the weakness of institutional bonds in America, or the mistakes and misdeeds of leaders and followers. There is indeed conflict in all this, but it is the conflict of the post-Beardian history: it is pluralistic rather than dualistic, psychic rather than material.

Now the challengers have themselves been challenged, Staughton Lynd of Yale University, chief New Left historian of the Revolution and the

Confederation period, accepts a modified version of the class conflict motif. In an interesting brief study of Federalism in Dutchess County, New York, in the 1780's, Lynd concludes that the Beardian political dichotomy between Federalist magnates and Antifederalist yeomen is generally valid. The struggle over the Constitution, in the Hudson Valley at least, does have many of the elements of a dualistic class struggle. On the other hand he acknowledges serious flaws in the Beard-Becker interpretation. The adoption struggle was not one between former Tory Federalists and former patriot Antifederalists but between large magnates and landlords on one side and the yeomanry led by the lesser gentry on the other.[71] In an article in the Marxist journal *Science and Society,* Lynd gives us a still more muted Beardianism. If the New York experience is any guide, he tells us, the Constitution in its genesis was neither an antidemocratic weapon of an elite, nor a timeless, neutral distillation of political wisdom. Admittedly the Federalist leaders in New York were social conservatives. Yet they were also "deeply public-spirited men, critical of any tendency in each other to put private concerns before devotion to country and firmly committed to republican government." As for the party rank and file, they were often the city artisans who feared the foreign manufactures that the weak government under the Articles of Confederation could not exclude. Together these groups, the one fearful of the leveling spirit that had arisen during the war among the yeomanry and their leaders, the other anxious to protect its livelihood, succeeded in getting adopted a document that "established the most democratic government in any major nation of the world at that day."[72] This may be Beardian, but it is Beard in a highly sophisticated version and without the intrusive polemical tone.

Lynd's work on the Confederation period like Thernstrom's in social history reveals some of the possibilities of the New Left history. When used with imagination and flexibility it can tell us important things about complex historical events. In any case the questions the Left asks are still apt to be the interesting ones. Unfortunately that second great national crisis, the Civil War, has not received an equally perceptive treatment, although the work of Beard, Howard K. Beale, William B. Hesseltine, Du Bois, and others suggests the plausibility of a class conflict analysis.

The relative poverty of results arises, I think, from an intellectual and emotional dilemma that confronts the New Left historians when they contemplate the Civil War. On the one hand the war was a heroic battle for freedom, as the successful abolition of slavery attests. Was it also, as Beard and the Marxists would insist, a sectionalized struggle of classes with the North representing middle-class industrialism and the South aristocratic feudalism? If the latter, the New Left, with their jaundiced view of middle-class capitalist America, can at best be ambivalent about Union victory. If the former, where is class struggle? If both, how does one account for the selfish ruling class performing an act of such colossal generosity as emancipating the slaves? The old Left handled the problem in either of two ways. For Beard it scarcely existed; *The Rise of American Civilization* reveals him as relatively insensitive to the evils of slavery and harshly critical of the abolitionists.[73] There is, then, no crusade for freedom to embarrass him in his belief that the war was at heart an act of aggression by capitalists against agrarians.[74] A Marxist like James Allen, a man obviously alive to the moral issue of slavery, solves the problem by supposing the Radical Republicans, the agents of emancipation, to be also the political wing of a *progressive* industrial capitalist class. The war that freed the slaves also established the social preconditions for the eventual revolution. Both events, in a word, were historically necessary and historically progressive.[75]

Neither of these solutions would seem possible for the New Left. One way to solve the difficulty is by acknowledging a sort of ambiguity in human affairs, which, in the last analysis, is fundamentally uncongenial to the New Left style. Irving Howe, who represents a bridge between the old and the New Left, notes that the war contained "a double truth." The conflict, he writes in a review of Edmund Wilson's *Patriotic Gore,* "did mark the victory of modern capitalism and did let loose those tendencies toward a centralized state which Wilson deplores, but also the Civil War brought to an end the system by which one man could own another and therefore . . . it represents a major turning in the moral development of the United States."[76] Similarly Howard Zinn, attempting to absolve the abolitionists from the grave charge of starting a bloody conflict, believes that, while the war was fought over slavery, it was not the result of the antislavery agitation. Paralleling the antipathy between abolitionist and slaveholder was a more potent conflict between "antitariff, antibank, anticapitalist [and] antinationalist" southern agrarians on the one side and the "natural political leaders and controllers of the national economy" on the other. It was the second group of antagonists who caused the war, for only they possessed sufficient power. But once the war had started, these powerless abolitionists transformed it into an irresistible attack on slavery![77]

The other escape from the dilemma is to ignore, like Beard, the whole moral side of the great conflict. This is the course of Eugene Genovese of Sir George Williams University, one of the few confirmed Marxists among the young radical historians. Genovese redraws the economic lines between North and South and restores the struggle of material interests to the center of the stage. Slavery, at least by implication, caused the war, not because it aroused the moral indignation of the Western world, but because it isolated the South from the progressive economic currents of the day. Wedded to its slave system the South became increasingly feudal and backward. Ultimately "the South's slave civilization could not . . . coexist with an increasingly hostile, powerful and aggressive Northern Capitalism."[78]

The New Left counterattack on the historiographic trends of the last twenty years is still in its early stages. We see at present only the tip of the iceberg. Beneath the surface still lies the main mass of young radical scholars just now completing their training at the major cosmopolitan graduate schools. In the next few years these young men will be joining in the attempt to reconstruct a coherent Leftist view of the American past,[79] and in a period when the American intelligentsia has become fascinated by the radical student movement, these young historians will receive, I predict, an unusual amount of attention and display.[80] If for no other reason, then, than their impact on the literate public, they will have to be reckoned with by their professional elders. But they must also be listened to for the health of the historical profession. No discipline should be without a dialogue, least of all one that represents a difficult and problematical marriage of the humanities and the social sciences. Unanimity is fine in science, unanimity over the nature of man's past suggests either an official line or a disturbing poverty of imagination. Neither circumstance can be applauded by an honest scholar no matter what his ideological allegiance.

But prudential motives aside, does the New Left history deserve the attention of the senior men? I think it does. True, there has yet been no young radical scholar of arresting style or impressive technique. But, of course, great historians, unlike great mathematicians, are made, not born. For a group composed almost entirely of men and women in their thirties, the young radicals have done work that deserves respect. They cannot compete in craftsmanship with the men they have chosen to oppose, but surely we ought to extend to them the same courtesy of judging them against their peers that we extend to the more conventional younger scholars.

Ultimately, of course, their reception must depend not on their craft but on their content. Do they have anything to say that is worth listening to for its own sake? At their best I believe they do. As a historian personally convinced that Americans encountered a narrower range of cultural and political experience than did Europeans, I do not take seriously the reassertion of class war of some of the more militant radical scholars. But the work of Thernstrom, LaFeber, and even Williams is a useful antidote to the self-congratulatory note that may be found among some of the post-World War II historians. America may not exhibit as grim a record of exploitation and brutality as Romanov Russia or Bourbon Spain or Regency England, but it had its agonies and its injustices. More important, it had its evasions and its "unfinished revolutions." American "exceptionalism" did not include total exemption from the ills that societies are heir to; it most emphatically did not exclude failure.

But there is also a debit side of the ledger. The New Left has frequently confused intellectual disagreement with the battle of generations and has often failed to play the scholarly game by the most elementary rules of fair play. The young radicals are often bad tempered. In their civic concerns they are angry dissenters from the nation's current foreign and domestic policies, and they sometimes allow the tone and rhetoric of the picket line and the handbill to invade their professional work. The historical "establishment" is not the political establishment in Washington, and the young men of the Left must not treat scholarship as an opportunity for a political harangue.

But beyond these matters of taste there are weaknesses in the emerging class conflict history that threaten to stultify the whole New Left historical enterprise. The young radicals' rejection of the historical currents since 1945 has all too often implied a denial not only of "consensus" conclusions but also of the social sciences and the new statistical methodology. Admittedly both of these new methods can be abused, but by rejecting these analytical tools the young radical historians are, in effect, disarming themselves and perhaps, ultimately, are consigning their efforts to sterility. Their response is all the more surprising when we recall the old Left's respect for science and for "scientific" history.

But most disturbing of all is the New Left's exaggerated present-mindedness. It suggests a contempt for pure history, history that has not enlisted in the good fight. The young radicals' efforts are generally governed not by the natural dialogue of the discipline but by the concerns of the outside cultural and political world. Clio at their behest has conned a uniform and does battle for social virtue. It is true that a number of the middle generation have themselves been influenced by a conservative political bias; more common among them, as we have seen, is a political neutrality which, however inadequate for citizenship, is surely useful for scholarship.

It would be a pity if their social consciousness uncritically committed the emerging generation of American scholars to any prescribed reading of the American past. It would mean the loss of much youthful talent for history. It would also be a loss for the American political Left. If history has any programmatic value, surely it must be history that is allowed to speak for itself. Let the New Left ask its own questions of the past, but let the past then say its piece. America may well be "exceptional." Knowing it may be ultimately more useful for the Left than denying it. And in the end there is no need to confuse the truths of the past with the needs of the present and future. The complexities and perplexities of the next few decades may well justify the cooperative commonwealth without the need to play tricks on the dead.

FOOTNOTES

1. By now descriptions of the New Left have become so numerous that it would be a formidable task to supply a reasonably complete list. The following, however, are among the best: Richard Armstrong, "The Explosive Revival of the Far Left," *Saturday Evening Post,* May 8, 1965, 27-39; various authors, *Partisan Review,* XXXII (Spring, Summer, Fall, 1965), 183-205, 341-72, 526-42; *Dissent,* IX (Spring 1962), 129 ff.; Irving Howe, "New Styles in 'Leftism,' " *ibid.,* XII (Summer 1965), 295-323; Staughton Lynd, "The New Radicals and 'Participatory Democracy,' " *ibid.,* 324-33. The recent book by Philip A. Luce, as the author admits, is not a discussion of the broad spectrum New Left but rather of its Trotskyite and Communist extreme as represented by such groups as the Progressive Labor party and the DuBois Clubs. (See Luce, *The New Left* [New York, 1966].) A recent anthology of New Left writings, Paul Jacobs and Saul Landau, *The New Radicals: A Report with Documents* (New York, 1966), begins with a long and useful introduction by the editors. Finally, see Jack Newfield, *A Prophetic Minority* (New York, 1966).

2. The outstanding New Left sociologist is, of course, C. Wright Mills. Robert Theobald and Ben Seligman may be said to represent a New Left mood in economics. For a sign of a New Left political science highly critical of the predominant "abstracted empiricists" or "behavioralists" of the discipline, see the review by Walter Batya of Frederick Barghoorn's *The Soviet Cultural Offensive* in *Studies on the Left,* II (1961), 90 ff.; and the article by James Peters, "Ideology and United States Political Scientists," *Science and Society,* XXIX (Spring 1965), 192-216.

3. John Higham, "The Cult of the 'American Consensus,' " *Commentary,* XXVII (Feb. 1959), 93-100.

4. For the best brief description of the "progressive" school of American historical writing that flourished from about 1910 to shortly after World War II, see John Higham *et al., History* (Englewood Cliffs, N. J., 1965), pt. III, Chap. III.

5. For the attack of the Marxists, who preferred a class struggle interpretation of the American past, see Louis Hacker, "Sections or Classes," *Nation,* CXXXVII (July 26, 1933). For a parallel assault by old-line progressives who, like the Marxists, found a class conflict view of our history congenial, see Fred A. Shannon, "The Homestead Act and the Labor Surplus," *American Historical Review,* XLI (July 1936), 637-51; Charles A. Beard, "The Frontier in American History," *New Republic,* XCVII (Feb. 1939), 359-62; Carter Goodrich and Sol Davidson, "The Wage-Earner and the Westward Movement," *Political Science Quarterly,* L (June 1935), 161-85, LI (Mar. 1936), 61-116. For a good brief review of the changing fortunes of the Turner thesis, see Gene M. Gressley, "The Turner Thesis: A Problem in Historiography," *Agricultural History,* XXXII (Oct. 1958), 227-49. For the attack of the 1930's, see esp. 232 ff.

6. Higham, "Cult of the 'American Consensus,' " *passim.* See Also Robin Brooks, "Class Distinction, Then and Now," a review of Staughton Lynd's *Anti-Federalism in*

Dutchess County, New York, in *Studies on the Left,* IV (Winter 1964), 74-75. Higham does not mention Oscar Handlin who, it is now clear, has been immensely influential, both through his own work and his students', in developing the post-Beardian canon. For a mature expression of Handlin's views, see his volume *The Americans: A New History of the People of the United States* (Boston, 1963).

7. The full citations for these works are as follows: Clarence Ver Steeg, *The Formative Years, 1607-1763* (New York, 1964); Robert E. Brown, *Middle-Class Democracy and the Revolution in Massachusetts 1691-1780* (Ithaca, N. Y., 1955), and *Charles Beard and the Constitution: A Critical Analysis of "An Economic Interpretation of the Constitution"* (Princeton, N. J., 1956); Forrest McDonald, *We the People: The Economic Origins of the Constitution* (Chicago, 1958), and *E Pluribus Unum: The Formation of the American Republic, 1776-1790* (Boston, 1965); Paul Goodman, *The Democratic-Republicans of Massachusetts: Politics in a Young Republic* (Cambridge, Mass., 1964); Noble Cunningham, *The Jeffersonian Republicans: The Formation of Party Organization, 1789-1801* (Chapel Hill, N. C., 1957); Lee Benson, *The Concept of Jacksonian Democracy: New York as a Test Case* (Princeton, N. J., 1961); Bray Hammond, *Banks and Politics in America from the Revolution to the Civil War* (Princeton, N. J., 1957); Walter E. Hugins, *Jacksonian Democracy and the Working Class: A Study of the New York Workingmen's Movement, 1829-1837* (Stanford, Calif., 1960); David Donald, *Charles Sumner and the Coming of the Civil War* (New York, 1960); Eric McKitrick, *Andrew Johnson and Reconstruction* (Chicago, 1960); Stanley Elkins, *Slavery: A Problem in American Institutional and Intellectual Life* (Chicago, 1959); Stanley Coben, "Northeastern Business and Radical Reconstruction: A Re-examination," *Mississippi Valley Historical Review,* XLVI (June 1959); Robert H. Wiebe, *Businessmen and Reform: A Study of the Progressive Movement* (Cambridge, Mass., 1962); and David J. Rothman, *Politics and Power: The United States Senate, 1869-1901* (Cambridge, Mass., 1966). Needless to say, this list is not complete.

8. On the Revolution, see Robert P. Thomas, "A Quantitative Approach to the Study of the Effects of British Imperial Policy upon Colonial Welfare: Some Preliminary Findings," *Journal of Economic History,* XXV (Dec. 1965), 615-38; on the post-Civil War farmer, see Allan Bogue, *Money at Interest: The Farm Mortgage on the Middle Border* (Ithaca, N. Y., 1955); Leslie E. Decker, *Railroad Lands and Politics: The Taxation of Railroad Land Grants, 1865-1897* (Providence, R. I., 1964); on at least one group of robber barons, see Robert W. Fogel, *The Union Pacific Railroad: A Case Study in Premature Enterprise* (Baltimore, Md., 1960); for an overview of the whole "cliometric" literature, see Douglass North, *Growth and Welfare in the American Past: A New Economic History* (Englewood Cliffs, N. J., 1966).

9. Indeed, they are sometimes embarrassed by the excesses of doctrinaire party-liners like Aptheker. See, e.g., Joseph A. Ernst, "Historians and the Colonial Era," *Studies on the Left,* I (Winter, 1960), 79-84.

10. Harold Cruse, "Americanizing the Radical Program," *ibid.,* III (Winter 1963), 69.

11. Cf. Eugene Genovese, "William Appleman Williams on Marx and America," *ibid.,* VI (Jan.-Feb. 1966), 76.

12. As, e.g., C. Vann Woodward, Matthew Josephson, and Jackson T. Main.

13. Other gurus of the New Left include Paul Goodman, the social thinker and novelist, Herbert Marcuse, and Barrington Moore, Jr. All these men have helped form the New Left's vision of recent America, but none—except perhaps Moore—seem as yet to have had much effect on the way the New Left writes history.

14. William Appleman Williams, *The Contours of American History* (Cleveland, 1961), 490.

15. Arnold A. Rogow, "The Revolt against Social Equality," *Dissent,* IV (Autumn 1957) 369-70. For a complaint from an older Populistic liberal and Beardian, see C. Vann Woodward, "The Populist Heritage and the Intellectuals," *American Scholar,* XXIX (Winter 1959-60), 55-72.

16. Norman Pollack, "Fear of Man: Populism, Authoritarianism and the Historian," *Agricultural History,* XXXIX (Apr. 1965), 59-67.

17. See the remarks of Richard Drinnon in an interview by Peter Loewenberg in *Studies on the Left,* II (No. 1, 1961), 79 ff. For an attack on the academic "establishment" which transcends the discipline of history, see the prospectus, "The Radicalism of Disclosure," *ibid.,* I (Fall 1959), 2-4.

18. Staughton Lynd, "Socialism, the Forbidden Word," *ibid.,* III (Summer 1963), 14 ff. At the same time, however, Lynd was agreeing with N. Gordon Levin, Jr., that there was little if any native American radicalism. See Lynd's reply to Levin's letter in *Commentary,* XXXV (Jan. 1963), 74-75. For what Lynd does see as radical in the American past, see below, pp. 221-24.

19. This negative quality of almost all the New Left intellectuals has been noted by Michael Walzer, a young Leftist historian of English Puritanism. (See Walzer, "The Young Radicals: A Symposium," *Dissent,* IX [Spring 1962], 129 ff.)

20. What constitutes "good credentials" for the New Left is exceedingly hard to say. Members of the New Left do not carry party cards; nor do they always acknowledge their affiliations. In selecting my New Left historians I have used a combination of personal knowledge, self-identification, internal evidence, and a sort of historical dead reckoning. The system, I am certain, is fallible. Some of those I have included among the Left will, perhaps, object to being so labeled. On the other hand others, surely, will be chagrined at being left out. Nevertheless I do not believe my imperfect definitions vitiate my conclusions.

21. This implicit acceptance of consensus in *Contours* has been noticed by Higham, among others. See Higham's review of the book in *Studies on the Left,* II (No. 2, 1961), 73-76. Michael Wreszin, another young radical historian, observes the same phenomenon in Richard Drinnon's biography of Emma Goldman (*Rebel in Paradise: A Biography of Emma Goldman* [Chicago, 1961]). Drinnon's saving grace, Wreszin notes, is that unlike the conservative historians, while noting the consensus, he deplores it. (See Wreszin, "Heresy in Paradise: A Partisan for Emma," *Studies on the Left,* IV [Winter 1964], 80.)

22. Williams, *Contours,* 105 ff., 138 ff.

23. *Ibid.,* 222 ff. Indeed, Jackson's victory in 1828 is viewed as something of a national disaster.

24. *Ibid.,* 250-55. He even defends the Old South from abolitionist attack! (*Ibid.,* 281-82.)

25. *Ibid.,* 333-38.

26. *Ibid.,* 440, 445.

27. *Ibid.,* 32 ff.

28. See, e.g., Staughton Lynd's review of Williams' *Contours* in *Science and Society,* XXVII (Spring 1963), 227 ff.

29. This point, implied in *Contours,* is made explicitly in Williams' latest book, *The Great Evasion: An Essay on the Contemporary Relevance of Karl Marx and on the Wisdom of Admitting the Heretic into the Dialogue about America's Future* (Chicago, 1964), esp. the introduction.

30. E.g., William Appleman Williams, *American-Russian Relations, 1781-1947* (New York, 1952), *The Tragedy of American Diplomacy* (Cleveland, 1959), *The United States, Cuba and Castro* (New York, 1962).

31. LaFeber was actually a student of Professor Fred Harvey Harrington at Wisconsin, although he acknowledges that he is deeply indebted to Williams for instruction. (See Walter LaFeber, *The New Empire: An Interpretation of American Expansion, 1860-1898* [Ithaca, N. Y., 1963], 428.)

32. That it should win this prestigious award casts some doubt either on the hostility of the establishment toward the New Left or on their academic influence.

33. Walter LaFeber, "The Conscious Creation of a 'World Wide Empire,' " a review of Richard Warner Van Alstyne's *The Rising American Empire,* in *Studies on the Left,* II (No. 3, 1962), 103 ff.

34. LaFeber, *New Empire,* ix.

35. John W. Rollins, "The Anti-Imperialists and Twentieth Century American Foreign Policy," *Studies on the Left,* III (No. 1, 1962), 9 ff. This paper was the subject of a symposium and is followed by comments by Harold Baron and Thomas J. McCormick, who seem to function as a cheering section rather than as critics.

36. It is obvious that part of the New Left attack on Roosevelt's foreign policy derives from Charles Beard's influential work, *President Roosevelt and the Coming of the War, 1941: A Study in Appearances and Realities* (New York, 1948). Gardner refuses, however, to accept the most extreme of Beard's charges, that Roosevelt engineered United States entrance into World War II for party purposes. (See Lloyd Gardner, "From New Deal to New Frontier, 1937-1941," *Studies on the Left,* I [Fall 1959], 29 ff.) In Gardner's recent book, *Economic Aspects of New Deal Diplomacy* (Madison, Wis., 1964), the polemical tone is still more muted.

37. Williams, *Tragedy of American Diplomacy,* esp. Chap. IV.

38. See, e.g., Gardner, "From New Deal to New Frontier," 30.

39. Orde S. Pinckney, "William E. Borah: Critic of American Foreign Policy," *Studies on the Left,* I (No. 3, 1960), 48 ff., esp. 61.

40. Only this intense preoccupation will explain the recent publication of Sidney Lens's *Radicalism in America* (New York, 1966). This book is an unimaginative narration of liberal-radical activities in America by an editor of the New Left journal *Liberation.* It might have been written by Vernon Parrington in the 1920's, though it is endorsed by Lynd and is clearly intended to teach the young Left something of their predecessors.

41. Pollack's major statement of his position will be found in *The Populist Response to Industrial America* (Cambridge, Mass., 1962), but see also the following articles: "Hofstadter on Populism: A Critique of 'The Age of Reform,' " *Journal of Southern History,* XXVI (Nov. 1960), 478-500, "The Myth of Populist Anti-Semitism," *American Historical Review,* LXVIII (Oct. 1962), 76-80, "Handlin on Anti-Semitism: A Critique of 'American Views of the Jew,' " *Journal of American History,* LI (Dec. 1964), 391-403; and "Fear of Man." The words quoted are from *Populist Response,* 82-83.

42. Pollack has not been totally rejected by the New Left, but it seems to me that, if only by their silence, they suggest that they find his work unconvincing. For an outright attack on Pollack by a member of the Left, see Ann Lane's review of *Populist Response* in *Science and Society,* XXVIII (Summer 1964), 326 ff. It is interesting that the plausible forerunners of the Populists, the Jeffersonians and Jacksonians, have been virtually ignored by the New Left, Williams again excepted. The only suggestion of a

new radical position on either of these movements that I have found is contained in two reviews of Benson's *Concept of Jacksonian Democracy.* In both cases the reviewers disapproved of Benson's attempt to place Jacksonian Democracy within the broad consensus framework. (See Lynd's review in *Commentary,* XXXIII [Apr. 1962], 366-68; Michael Lebowitz, "The Significance of Claptrap in American History," *Studies on the Left,* III [Winter 1963], 79 ff.)

43. Writers like Walter T. K. Nugent, Robert F. Durden, Paul Holbo, and C. Vann Woodward, who have recently championed the agrarian insurgency of the 1890's, are in the last analysis to be seen rather as men of rural background defending a rural Neo-Populist tradition against an urban attack than as members of the New Left seeking to legitimate radicalism in America. (See Irwin Unger, "Critique of Norman Pollack," *Agricultural History,* XXXIX [Apr. 1965], 75-80.)

44. In a symposium on Socialism published in *New Politics,* I (Spring 1962), 40.

45. See James Weinstein, "Anti-War Sentiment and the Socialist Party, 1917-1918," *Political Science Quarterly,* LXXIV (June 1959), *passim,* and "Socialism's Hidden Heritage: Scholarship Reinforces Political Mythology," *Studies on the Left,* III (Fall 1963), *passim,* see also Weinstein's exchange with Gerald Friedberg, *ibid.,* IV (Summer 1964), 79-97.

46. Weinstein, "Socialism's Hidden Heritage," 108. Weinstein is not an unbalanced doctrinaire. In defending American Socialism against Friedberg's charge of inner failure he concedes that "a tradition of political democracy, relative social mobility, and a generally increasing standard of living made possible by the expansion of American capitalism from the end of the Civil War to the middle 1920's" kept Socialism in America from becoming "a majority political movement." (See the exchange with Friedberg [p. 90], cited in note 45 above.)

47. Drinnon, *Rebel in Paradise,* vii *et passim.*

48. Staughton Lynd, "Henry Thoreau: The Admirable Radical," *Liberation,* VII (Feb. 1963), 21 ff.; for the response to Lynd's article, see *ibid.,* VIII (Apr. 1963), 22 ff.

49. In this insistence on the competitive nature of late nineteenth- and early twentieth-century business enterprise, Kolko is at serious odds with the old Left and the traditional Marxist thesis of the growing monopolization of the American economy. He also disagrees, of course, with the Populist-progressive view of economic trends during the period.

50. Gabriel Kolko, *The Triumph of Conservatism: A Reinterpretation of American History, 1900-1916* (New York, 1963), *passim,* esp. 285. The same theme in a narrower compass may be found in Kolko's volume on railroad legislation during the progressive period. (See *id., Railroads and Regulation, 1877-1916* [Princeton, N. J., 1965].)

51. Martin J. Sklar, "Woodrow Wilson and the Political Economy of Modern United States Liberalism," *Studies on the Left,* I (No. 3, 1960), 17 ff., esp. 40.

52. Jacob Cohen, "Schlesinger and the New Deal," *Dissent,* VII (Autumn 1961), 461 ff. It is interesting to compare this long review of *The Age of Roosevelt* with another by an orthodox Marxist. The latter, written under the pseudonym "George Brand," is far more sympathetic. (See George Brand, "Toward a History of the New Deal," *Monthly Review,* XII [May 1960], 28 ff.)

53. Marc Schleifer, "A Socialist Plea for Black Nationalism," *ibid.,* XV (Sept. 1963), 225 ff.

54. Kolko, *Triumph of Conservatism,* 161.

55. What else can we make of the following: "The more I came to think of it the more I came to hate my brainwashed childhood's beloved memory of Franklin Delano

Roosevelt. Everybody's liberal Jewish middle-class parents will cry like mine if they ever read this. ('After all, didn't he save the Jews and take us out of the depression?') Because I am a Socialist, and not a liberal, I know the answer." (Schleifer, "Socialist Plea," 225-26.)

56. Howard Zinn, *SNCC: The New Abolitionists* (Boston, 1964); see also Lynd's assertion that "the search for an American radical tradition should begin with the Abolitionists," since only they "punctured with the contempt it deserves, the white liberal hypocrisy that America is and has always been a democratic country without a feudal past. . . ." (Letter in *Commentary,* XXXV [Jan. 1963], 74.)

57. The works referred to are: Dwight L. Dumond, *Antislavery Origins of the Civil War in the United States* (Ann Arbor, Mich., 1939); Gilbert Hobbs Barnes, *The Anti-Slavery Impulse, 1830-1844* (New York, 1933); W. E. B. Du Bois, *Black Reconstruction in America, 1860-1880* (New York, 1935); James Allen, *Reconstruction, Battle for Democracy, 1865-1876* (New York, 1937); Francis B. Simkins and Robert Woody, *South Carolina during Reconstruction* (Chapel Hill, N. C., 1932); Vernon Wharton, *The Negro in Mississippi, 1865-1890* (Chapel Hill, N. C., 1947). It would of course be a mistake to equate these older "liberals" with the New Left radicals. Their sympathies for the Negro and his friends did not run as deep, nor were they as unequivocal, as those of the young Leftists of today. Still, the advent of the Whartons and the Dumonds in the 1930's and 1940's represents a distinctly liberal shift in the historical treatment of race in America.

58. Arthur Schlesinger, Jr., "The Causes of the Civil War: A Note on Historical Sentimentalism," *Partisan Review,* XVI (Oct. 1949), 969-81.

59. Louis Ruchames, "The Pulitzer Prize Treatment of Charles Sumner," *Massachusetts Review,* II (Summer 1961), 761, 749.

60. Fawn Brodie, "Who Defends the Abolitionist?" in *The Antislavery Vanguard: New Essays on the Abolitionists,* ed. Martin Duberman (Princeton, N. J., 1965), 52-67. This essay has been reprinted in *Dissent,* XII (Summer 1965), 348-59. The Duberman volume is a mine of New Left opinion on the antislavery movement. See particularly the essays by Lynd, Howard Zinn, and Duberman himself, in addition to Brodie's article. The essay by Silvan Tomkins, "The Psychology of Commitment: The Constructive Role of Violence and Suffering for the Individual and for His Society," suggests that the New Left has not been entirely willing to abandon social psychology to the older generation. The attempt to utilize psychology to reveal new things about the abolitionists, while at the same time avoiding the pitfall of behavioralism, is not successful, however. Tomkins merely clothes in psychological jargon the position of the Left that the evil of slavery was enough by itself to explain the abolitionist reaction to it.

61. See Aileen Kraditor's review article, "The Abolitionist Rehabilitated," *Studies on the Left,* V (Spring 1965), 101. Actually the most "conservative of Donald's writings is his essay, "An Excess of Democracy," reprinted in the paperback version of *Lincoln Reconsidered: Essays on the Civil War Era* (2d ed., New York, 1956), 208-35. This piece has not yet been noticed by the New Left, however.

62. Leon Litwack, *North of Slavery: The Negro in the Free States, 1790-1860* (Chicago, 1961).

63. The term is Rogow's in "Revolt against Social Equality," 370.

64. Gabriel Kolko, *Wealth and Power in America: An Analysis of Social Class and Income Distribution* (New York, 1962); Michael Harrington, *The Other America: Poverty in the United States* (New York, 1964).

65. Stephan Thernstrom, *Poverty and Progress: Social Mobility in a Nineteenth Century City* (Cambridge, Mass., 1964), Chaps. I-III.

66. *Ibid.*, 80-137.

67. E.g., Philip Foner, *History of the Labor Movement in the United States* (2 vols., New York, 1947-65); Leo Huberman, *The Labor Spy Racket* (New York, 1937).

68. Gabriel Kolko, "The Premises of Business Revisionism," *Business History Review,* XXXIII (Autumn 1959), 335 ff.

69. See esp. Kolko's *Railroads and Regulations, passim.*

70. Allen Solganick, "The Robber Baron Concept and Its Revisionists," *Science and Society,* XXIX (Summer 1965), 257-69.

71. Staughton Lynd, *Anti-Federalism in Dutchess County, New York* (Chicago, 1962), *passim.* A more emphatic assertion of the theme of class struggle may be found in Lynd's article, "Who Should Rule at Home? Dutchess County, New York, in the American Revolution," *William and Mary Quarterly,* XVIII (July 1961), esp. 330-32.

72. *Id.*, "Capitalism, Democracy and the United States Constitution: The Case of New York," *Science and Society,* XXVII (Fall 1963), 385-413.

73. At least for the period before the rise of the Cotton Kingdom, Beard treats slavery as a benevolent institution, while he attacks the abolitionists for the "depths of their abuse and scurrility." As for the Radical Republicans, the particular postwar friends of the Negro, they are largely driven by a simple craving for power. (See Charles and Mary Beard, *The Rise of American Civilization* [2 vols., New York, 1933], I, 655, 698; II, 116.)

74. Socialists like Irving Howe misread Beard, I think, when they claim him for the North in the Civil War. Unlike the Marxists, Beard never approved of the victory for industrial America, remaining sympathetic to the end to the agrarian society that the war presumably overthrew.

75. Allen, *Reconstruction,* 17-28.

76. Irving Howe, "Edmund Wilson and the Sea Slugs," *Dissent,* X (Winter 1963), 70 ff.

77. Howard Zinn, "The Tactics of Agitation," in *Antislavery Vanguard,* ed. Duberman, 445.

78. Eugene Genovese, "The Slave South: An Interpretation," *Science and Society,* XXV (Dec. 1961), 320 ff. I do not mean to say that Genovese is a crude economic determinist: quite the contrary. In arguing, as he does, that slavery was an economic blight on the South, he introduces, quite properly, I believe, considerations of social values, the South's self-image, and other factors not usually encountered in a strict Marxist interpretation. For an extended treatment of his view on slavery, see his book, *The Political Economy of Slavery* (New York, 1965). Another example of a relatively "hard line" class conflict analysis of the Civil War is the chapter, "The American Civil War: The Last Capitalist Revolution," in Barrington Moore, Jr.'s, recent book, *Social Origins of Dictatorship and Democracy: Lord and Peasant in the Making of the Modern World* (Boston, 1966), 111-55. Moore's estimate of the war, "reached after much uncertainty," is that the struggle "was the last revolutionary offensive on the part of what one may legitimately call urban or bourgeois capitalism." (See page 112.) Moore is not, of course, of the same generation as the New Leftists, but as noted above (note 13) the young radicals turn to him for inspiration.

79. By now it is clear that this is becoming a conscious and organized goal of the Students for a Democratic Society, the largest of the New Left groups. The SDS has established within the last year the Radical Education Project, which has assumed as one of its tasks the writing of "radical history," for the purpose, as one REP letter puts it, of equipping "outrage with precision." The REP has already published its first Occasional Paper on American History, "Towards a Democratic History," by Professor

Jesse Lemisch of the University of Chicago. This is both a brief review of what has been done and a call to further effort. For additional details, see "American Radical History: A Progress Report," *New Left Notes,* Jan. 13, 1967, 2. Mr. John Roberts of NYU called the REP and its plans to my attention.

80. This fascination has already been exhibited in the extraordinary attention given Christopher Lasch's book, *The New Radicalism in America, 1889-1963: The Intellectual as a Social Type* (New York, 1965). This work, a series of lively and perceptive vignettes of various cultural radicals, is held together by an opaque and confusing thesis that actually defies all categories of Left or Right. Despite the ambiguities, Lasch has been lionized by the intellectual community, less I believe for his very real merits than for the fact that he writes in a literate way about two subjects irresistible to the intellectuals: the Left and themselves.

Part Four

The Historian and the Climate of Opinion: An Obstacle or an Opportunity?

12

The Attempt to Write a More Scientific History

ALLAN BOGUE (1967)

The preceding selections by progressive historians of the early twentieth century, post-war critics of the progressives, and the young New Left scholars of the 1960s, suggest that historical interpretations change in accordance with changes in the climate of opinion. But should this influence be applauded or deprecated? Is it good that today's histories reflect current affairs and modern thought in order that historical scholarship be vital, relevant, controversial, and interesting to contemporary readers? Or does the climate of opinion constitute an obstacle to the fullest possible understanding of the past? Is it unfortunate that over the years interpretations tend frequently to seem almost cyclical rather than cumulative as in the case of the sciences? If it is regrettable that historical knowledge does not merely grow through decades of research, but actually changes dramatically in conjunction with alterations in dominant social thought, what can be done about it?

In recent years those historians who have been most critical of the differences of interpretation that exist among their fellow scholars, and most emphatic in alleging that scholarship often reflects climates of opinion more than it reflects the historical evidence, have attempted to devise what may be called more "scientific" methods of studying and writing history.

It is difficult to describe briefly the "scientific" or "behavioral science" movement that has been developed by American historians during the 1950s and 1960s. Practitioners of the new "scientific" or "behavioral" approach to history have not agreed on a detailed program nor on a theory of history. A few behavioral historians, for example, emphasize the connections between their "scientific" approach and the "scientific" method used in the histories of the late 1800s, but most do not. Those earlier "scientific histories" represented an attempt either to apply general laws to explain the

---

Reprinted by permission, with omission of the first paragraph, from Allan Bogue, "United States: The 'New' Political History," pp. 185-207, in Walter Laqueur and George Mosse, eds., *The New History*, Vol. 4 of *The Journal of Contemporary History*, Harper and Row Torchbook, N.Y., 1967.

development of the past, or else simply to accumulate mountains of data from the past on the assumption that some later historian would be able to interpret the data. Since most contemporary behavioral historians are neither searchers for general laws nor exclusively compilers of data, they do not generally see themselves as returning to the old "scientific history." What the new behavioral historians do agree on is that most history, as it has been traditionally written, lacks both precision and utilization of rigorous methods. They argue that, because historians have not devised techniques to satisfactorily answer the questions they ask and because the questions they do ask are the wrong ones, the vague impressions and guess-work to which the historians resort, and the changing climate of opinion, all obstruct cumulative historical understanding.

Certain more specific characterizations of the behavioral movement can be made. First, the movement has been marked by attempts to systematically quantify or measure data rather than to make assessments of quantity on the basis of common sense observations. Most energy to date has been expended upon systematic voting analyses of legislative bodies and of the general population. Second, the movement has been characterized by its attempts to study all levels of the population rather than to focus upon "elite" individuals or groups as historians have traditionally done. Behavioral historians have assumed that wider coverage of the population offers an advantage in discovering underlying social processes, and the methods of quantification they employ are of course suited to mass data. Third, the movement has consciously eschewed the historian's traditional concern for moral judgment and has protested that such explicit judgments are, strictly speaking, as irrelevant to scholarship in history as to that in the sciences. This last characteristic is the least basic and least related to matters of method, but it is the most obvious to a reader of the behavioral scholarship and suggests the scientific aspirations of the behavioral movement.

Allan Bogue (b. 1921), professor of history at the University of Wisconsin and one of the leaders of the new scientific or behavioral history movement, surveyed its impact upon the study of political history in the essay which is reprinted below. Bogue emphasized that although only a minority of American political historians were behaviorists, it was a growing and increasingly influential minority. Because he forecast that the ultimate success of the behaviorists would depend upon the interest in and usefulness of their published work, Bogue reviewed their scholarship to date which consisted mainly of various types of voting analyses and comparative collective biographies of politicians. Bogue interpreted the substantive conclusions which have emerged from these quantitative studies as significant, even though not yet definitive. For instance, the influence of economic class as a single causal factor in voting has been minimized, and ethno-cultural factors have been maximized. And studies of political reform leaders have failed to substantiate the hypothesis that they came from backgrounds and groups significantly different from those of leading opponents of reform. Bogue noted that such conclusions as these might at first appear to support "consensus" rather than "conflict" interpretations of America's past, but that in fact the only casualty to result from these conclusions was an exclusively economic conflict interpretation. By closer and more systematic analysis, Bogue argued, the behavioral historians allowed room for the expression of ethnic, religious, intellectual, and economic factors either in conflict or consensus. In conclusion, Bogue summarized the objections of historians to the movement for systematic quantifications, and then made a plea for the use of new "scientific" approaches to political history along with the more traditional ones.

American historians experimented with quantification in earlier years. Frederick Jackson Turner and some of his Wisconsin students, most notably Orin G. Libby, were industriously mapping election returns and analyzing legislative roll calls at the turn of the century. Libby's plea for the systematic study of congressional roll calls appeared in the Annual Report of the American Historical Association in 1896.[1] Turner never lost his enthusiasm for such methods and the imprint of his influence shows in the major publications of a number of scholars. Work in this tradition appeared as late as 1941, but the early interest in quantification and political ecology among historians subsided, perhaps because of the inadequate statistical methods of the pioneers.

At present a small number of historians are trying to apply social-science methods and theory in American political history with varying degrees of rigor. The nine men who were early members of the American Historical Association's ad hoc committee for the collection of the basic quantitative data of American political history, and others who have since become associated with the committee's work in one way or another, are at the center of the movement. Their seminars are producing recruits for the cause, as are the seminars of some other historians who allow their graduate students to apply methods learned in satisfying the requirements of minor or related fields. During the summer of 1965, thirty-five historians gathered at Ann Arbor for a three-week seminar on voting and legislative behavior under the auspices of the Inter-University consortium for political research.[2] This group certainly did not include all the professional historians who are interested in such matters and only representative doctoral candidates were invited. Not all those in attendance, however, were deeply dedicated to a quantitative approach. It was an assembly composed in undetermined proportions of prophets, converts, neophytes, seekers, and scoffers. In the argot of the political scientist, slightly corrupted, political historians today number an overwhelming majority of standpatters, a small group of dedicated switchers, and a growing number of their new votaries. Some believe that the members of the last two categories are sufficiently different from the majority of American political historians to justify calling them behavioral historians–understanding behavioral to connote, in this instance, a strong interest in the methods, results, and implications of measurement, combined with some desire to produce research that is respectable by social-science criteria.[3] I realize that the term raises problems, but for our purposes it is a convenient label.

The behavioral historians have not yet produced an impressive body of literature bearing upon American politics. There are in print various voting studies using ecological correlations, most of them quite simple in method;[4] two books and a number of articles in which scaling techniques or simpler methods of roll-call analysis are used;[5] a number of collective biographies of political elites;[6] a couple of articles dealing with the characteristics of the national electorate between 1800 and 1840 and another surveying voting trends in presidential elections;[7] a path-breaking monograph on the importance of the time dimension in evaluating election returns, as well as a major reassessment of the political ideology and voting behavior of the Jacksonian period;[8] and several contributions concerned with the methods, problems, and promises of quantitative history.[9] This is the type of work which the behavioralists have published so far.

What kind of findings are emerging from their endeavors? In two important articles Richard P. McCormick has shown that the Jackson elections did not represent the revolution in popular voting behavior that historians have so confidently assumed for so many years, and that economic class affiliation apparently had little influence in affecting the party choice of voters during the early national period.[10] Lee Benson carried reassessment of Jacksonian democracy still further when he found that content analysis revealed basic ideological differences between Whigs and Democrats, and particularly when he discovered that the multi-variate analysis of election returns in indicator precincts in New York showed ethno-cultural conditioning to have been the most important variable associated with party choice in that state.

The writings of McCormick and Benson are perhaps the most impressive exhibits of the new historical persuasion, but a few other studies are representative. Using the Guttman scale as his major analytical tool, Joel Silbey assessed the significance of sectional and party ties in Congress during the 1840s and early 1850s, finding that party ties withstood the impact of the slavery expansion issue much better than some of the conventional literature leads one to expect. George Daniels probed the problem of ethno-cultural loyalties and the 1860 election, and his analysis of precinct voting returns in Iowa reinforced Joseph Schafer's rather neglected findings of a generation ago that a majority of German voters in Wisconsin and Illinois remained true to their Democratic party allegiance in the 1860 election.[11] Using multiple correlation techniques, Stanley Parsons destroyed a truism of Populist folklore by showing that Populist votes in Nebraska and mortgage interest rates were only slightly correlated, and that in so far as they were associated the correlation was negative rather than positive. In one of the better collective biographies published by a historian to date, William T. Kerr, Jr. has shown that the progressive leaders of Washington differed in various respects from their conservative counterparts, as well as in the major sources of their support. Thomas B. Alexander and his students have published the initial results of what has since become an elaborate least-squares analysis of social and economic attributes and voting preference in ante-bellum Alabama and which contradicts the old generalization that the "Democrats became the party of poverty and numbers, and the Whigs the party of property and talents."

A number of theses and dissertations dealing with similar or related problems are now complete. Samuel P. Hays drew upon some of these in suggesting that the urban reform movement of the early twentieth century was essentially upper class in origin, and also in proposing an ethno-cultural interpretation of national voting behavior in the period 1865-1929.[12] Joel Silbey found support in similar materials for his contention that sectionalism was not the only major influence shaping American politics during the 1850s.[13] Much other research with a strong quantitative element is under way. These studies include roll-call analyses of Congress in the early national period, during the 1850s, 1860s, and 1870s, and the progressive period, as well as of the Confederate Congress and midwestern state legislatures during the nineteenth century. Historians are preparing studies of the evolution of party structure during the nineteenth century, and others are studying popular voting behavior in states and regions in the nineteenth and early twentieth centuries. There has also been completed, or is under way, work which has important implications for political history even though its focus is not primarily political—most notably research in historical demography and population mobility, both spatial and social.[14]

Much of the new quantitative history is unsophisticated in social-science terms. A member of the AHA committee on quantitative data estimated recently that there were no more than several dozen members of the history profession at the faculty level who are conversant with statistics through multiple correlation and regression analysis, and if one omits the new breed of economic historian that is, I am sure, true.[15] This state of affairs is changing as history graduates attend statistics courses and social-science methodology seminars, but it will be some time before there is a sizable cadre of historians confidently aware of both the promises and the pitfalls inherent in quantification.

Social scientists find the theoretical assumptions of the behavioral historians rather elementary. They are not trying simply to describe "what happened," in the parlance of the old "scientific" historian, but their methods hardly conform to the basic rules of the behavioral approach sketched by David Easton in *A Framework for Political Analysis.*[16] Few behavioral historians are consciously looking for findings with predictive value, or purposefully giving their research a theoretical frame which the results may in part verify, modify, or contradict. Instead, most are still problem or topic-oriented, using social-science techniques or theory to refute or build on the work of past historians or to probe new areas which catch their fancy. Lee Benson is an exception. To a far greater extent than any of the other historical behavioralists, he tries to make his theoretical commitments explicit and believes that a historian can make a major contribution to the social sciences. He has for instance suggested certain basic propositions which, he argues, illuminate the behavior of the founding fathers:

(1) The behavior of men is determined more by the ends they seek than by the means they use to achieve those ends; specifically, men favored the Constitution largely because they favored a Commercial Society, they opposed the Constitution largely because they favored an Agrarian Society. (2) The ends men choose are positively related to the "modes and processes" by which they gain their livelihoods, the social environments in which they live, the social roles they occupy, the groups with whom they identify, and the groups with whom they regard themselves in conflict. (3) In certain historical situations, men who choose certain ends are more likely than their opponents to possess the qualities and resources needed for victory; specifically, in the United States during the 1780s, commercial-minded men like Hamilton possessed the qualities and resources needed to defeat agrarian-minded men like Clinton.[17]

Such behavioral models are rare indeed in the work of historians. Despite his concern for theoretical explication, Professor Benson's work sometimes falls short of the standards that many behavioral scientists consider essential. One searches the first edition of *The Concept of Jacksonian Democracy* in vain for any detailed discussion of the methods by which he selected his indicator precincts, or of the numbers of voters in his sample, or of correlations or significance tests underlying the party preference percentages which he ascribed to the various ethno-cultural groups living in New York during the 1830s and 1840s.[18]

It can indeed be argued that social scientists have written almost as much, if not more, behavioral history than have the political historians. Walter Dean Burnham, William Nesbit Chambers, Robert A. Dahl, Manning J. Dauer, V. O. Key, Theodore J. Lowi, Duncan MacRae, John Schmidhaeuser, and Ruth C. Silva, have all probed significantly beyond the contemporary scene and produced work that any political historian must use if he wishes to view the nation's political history in fullest perspective.[19]

More significant perhaps than the research achievements of behavioral historians has been their contribution to the building of the historical data archives of the Inter-University consortium for political research, made in co-operation with political scientists. As a number of historians became interested in quantification some years ago, they discovered in discussion that they were wasting their time in searching out and processing quantifiable information which others had already recorded. They agreed that historians needed an inventory of the basic quantitative data of American political history and ultimately, perhaps, a central data archives on which all interested scholars might draw. Following such discussions, Lee Benson, Charles Sellers, Samuel P. Hays, and William Riker (three historians and a political scientist) submitted a memorandum to the Social Science Research Council. In response the Council invited W. Dean Burnham to assess the problems of collecting election statistics in a number of states.

While these developments were taking place, the Inter-University consortium was also beginning to consider the establishment of a data archives, having as a nucleus the data collected by the Survey Research Center of the University of Michigan. When Professor Burnham's initial investigation was encouraging, the SSRC commissioned him to spend an additional year on the task of inventorying and undertaking an exploratory recovery of data. His labors were so successful that additional organization seemed necessary. Lee Benson organized a committee of historians to assist the consortium in developing a historical data archives, and the American Historical Association gave it status by designating it an ad hoc committee. In turn the committee organized state committees that undertook to exhume the county election returns from 1824 to the present and other materials. Under the imaginative leadership of its director, Warren Miller, the consortium obtained funds from the National Science Foundation for the development of the archives and the SSRC continued to be helpful. Dr. Miller appointed a historian, Howard W. Allen, as director of data recovery at the consortium, and it was hoped that almost all the county election and referenda returns would be available for use by the late fall of 1966. The historians and archivists engaged in this work may be helping to transform one area of history into a cumulative discipline, in which, for the first time, the careful historian need not duplicate every step of the research of predecessors who were interested in the same problem.

While the work of collecting and recording has gone forward at the consortium, planning conferences have considered the problems of adding legislative materials, primarily roll call votes, to the archives, and various types of economic and ethno-cultural materials which seem necessary for any considered analysis of the basic election data. At the Ann Arbor seminar in 1965, a number of historians expressed interest in essaying the difficult task of retrieving the election returns of the early national period and this work is now under way. The extent to which these collection and service programs can be maintained and extended will largely depend, of course, on the willingness of granting agencies to subsidize the work and this in turn must depend to a considerable extent on the interest which historians and social scientists show in using the archives.

Its concrete achievements and the ambitiousness of its program clearly mark the combined consortium-AHA committee project as the most impressive evidence of the development of a quantifying and behavioral bent in the historical profession. It is not the only organized effort in that direction, however. In 1964 the Mathematics Social Science Board, an offspring of the Social Science Research Council and the Institute for Advanced Study in the Behavioral Sciences, sponsored the organization of a history committee, headed by Robert Fogel of the University of Chicago.[20] The AHA ad hoc committee is concerned primarily with the development of a data archives and with training programs geared to its use. The history committee of the MSSB is seeking ways of encouraging the spread of mathematical and statistical expertise within the history profession.

The behavioral movement among American political historians reflects in part a recent tendency among historians to draw more heavily upon the social sciences for method and theory. In his reader, *American History and the Social Sciences,* published in 1964, Edward N. Saveth presents two dozen historians, writing on concepts which are more usually considered to be of primary interest to social scientists. A large number of other scholars could be added to Saveth's list, whose writings in some way reflect the influence of social-science thought or methods. The political behavioralists, however, are prepared to introduce considerably more quantification and rigor into their work than most such historians.

A few years ago, in a paper paying tribute to a successful revolution—the advent of behavioralism in political science—Robert Dahl devoted some attention to the causes of this development.[21] He stressed the pioneering work of Professor Merriam at Chicago, the contributions of the

European emigré scholars who came to this country during the 1930s, the practical experience of political scientists in government and military service during the Second World War, the empirical promise of survey research techniques, the leadership of the SSRC, and the helping hand of the foundations. No doubt he would agree that the recent tremendous advances in computer technology have helped to confirm the trend.

There are both similarities and differences between the early developments in political science and those now occurring in history. If political science lagged behind sister fields in moving toward behavioralism, the lag in history has been greater. The commitment of historians to theory was of course typically less than that of political scientists even in the most unsystematic days of political science. There is among the behavioral historians no group analogous to the European emigrés of the 1930s, trained in a different tradition from their American colleagues. Nor can we point to any history department occupying the pre-eminent position of the political science department at the University of Chicago as a disseminating center of behavioral ideas and methods. For a time in the late 1950s three historians at the University of Iowa were stressing quantification in their seminars and sending their graduates into the methods seminars of their colleagues in political science and sociology. But this group is now dispersed.

There is no pioneer of quantifying techniques in the historical profession comparable in stature to Charles Merriam. But there were a number of historians, active during the 1930s and 1940s, whose writings or seminar offerings anticipated a quantitative approach. During the 1930s James C. Malin used manuscript census rolls to prepare demographic studies that modified conventional interpretations of frontier population movements and influenced a considerable number of other scholars either directly or indirectly. This work, plus Malin's emphasis on the intensive study of the local and regional unit, make him one of the progenitors of historical behavioralism in America, even though in his later work he specifically repudiated the aims and methods of social science.[22]

In reaction against the conventional history fare that he had suffered as a graduate student, Thomas C. Cochran immersed himself during the 1930s in social-science literature, particularly sociology. Exasperated by the traditional views of the craft which several eminent historians expressed at the meeting of the American Historical Association in 1947, he advanced his rebellious ideas in "The 'Presidential Synthesis' in American History" (*American Historical Review*, July 1948). This article was a resounding attack on the traditional method of describing American political history, presidential administration by presidential administration, and a plea for a " 'social science' synthesis of American history." Cochran argued that our political history should be viewed as an outgrowth of fundamental cultural developments, and that it could be attacked most conveniently at the state level. By the 1940s Oscar Handlin at Harvard was emphasizing ethnic group dynamics and their relationship to politics, and a number of students followed his lead, undertaking detailed studies of politics at the local level. At Cornell University, Paul Wallace Gates, although primarily interested in institutional economic history, was asking his graduate students to spend time in other social-science departments. No doubt there were others trying to direct the interests of their students into new channels.

If the writings or teachings of Malin, Handlin, Gates, Cochran and others have helped to provide a favorable climate for a more intensive approach to American political history, I must also mention an early research project that had considerable influence upon the profession. During the late 1940s, Merle Curti conceived the idea of studying a frontier county in Wisconsin intensively, and providing a rigorous test of the suggestion that the frontier was a significant factor in shaping American political institutions, the thesis stated so attractively by Frederick Jackson Turner in the 1890s. Professor Curti was a graduate student under Turner at Harvard and was familiar with his interest in systematic political analysis. One of the handful of scholars who established American intellectual history on a firm foundation, he became chairman of the committee on historiography of the SSRC, organized in 1942-43, which prepared the Council's *Bulletin 54,* entitled *Theory and Practice in Historical Study: A Report of the Committee on Historiography,* published in 1946. This report clearly brought out the concern over the problems of objectivity and relativism which had perplexed and disturbed thoughtful American historians during the previous couple of decades. Both the work of his committee and the somewhat acrimonious discussions which its report provoked, turned Professor Curti's mind to the problems of objectively validating historical fact and theory. By this time also he had concluded that study of the frontier hypothesis had reached an impasse. Margaret Curti, a psychologist with sound training in statistics, had long maintained that historians should concern themselves to a greater extent with quantitative research and with the application of statistics to historical problems. This was the background of a study of Trempealeau county in western Wisconsin, designed to exploit the quantifiable information in the county records and in the manuscript censuses; *The Making of an American Community: A Case Study of Democracy in a Frontier County,* was published in 1959.

Professor Curti's statistical methods were less rigorous than some social scientists demand today and some historians have disputed the study's conclusions, but it is a milestone in American historiography. That a man who had done so much to establish intellectual history should turn his talents to such research gave respectability to quantification, as well as testifying to the versatility and liveliness of Professor Curti's mind.

As in the field of political science, the SSRC has had considerable influence in changing the outlook of historians. It has always aided historians in projects with an inter-disciplinary character. During the last twenty years it has sponsored three monographs concerned with the problems of writing history. *Bulletin 54* looked back to the relativist controversy of the 1930s; in *Bulletin 64, The Social Sciences in Historical Study,* and in the more recent *Generalization in the Writing of History,* we find a real commitment in some of the contributors to both social-science methods and theory.[23] I am not aware that any foundation has been uniquely concerned with promoting behavioralism among historians, but the action of the Ford Foundation in supporting the Institute for Advanced Study in the Behavioral Sciences has contributed to that end. Since its establishment, the administrators have generously allocated places to historians. Many if not most of the quantifiers among American political historians today have been assisted to some degree either by the SSRC or the Stanford Institute.

There are few more difficult tasks than that of explaining why one man adopts new techniques and another does not. We can point to general conditioning factors and to encouraging elements in the intellectual milieu, and we can discern apparent pre-dispositions in the individuals who innovate, but it is hard to explain in the final analysis why some take the plunge and others do not. If the SSRC has aided many of the behavioral historians it has also assisted dozens of others in the historical profession who have shown no disposition to change their approach. But aid from that agency or from the Stanford Institute must be regarded as one of a number of predisposing or confirming factors.

To some extent the behavioral historians appear to have had a broader training than usual: one was a classics major, another majored in psychology, another had a good training in mathematics and still another a double major. The prodding of graduate directors in the direction of inter-disciplinary work is remembered by members of the group. It is probably no accident that a number of them were initially interested in economic history, which has always had a body of theory and statistical method to draw upon, and in which far-reaching developments have occurred during the last fifteen years.

One learns in discussing the origins of their interests with the behavioralists that they experienced recurrent dissatisfaction with conventional political history and searched for concepts or methods that would give them greater confidence in the results of research or provide a more satisfying framework in which to present them. A number of them were particularly impressed by the work of Lazarsfeld and Key, and probing produces the names of other social scientists who set the thinking of one or more of them on a new track–Rice, Merton, Duverger, Weber, Michels, Lubell, Hannah Arendt, and Riesman. There was some reaction, too, against the practice of borrowing concepts from the social scientists and applying them without rigorous proof. In *The Age of Reform,* for instance, Richard Hofstadter suggested that declining social status was a major motivating factor among both the Populists and the Progressives. Soon status revolution threatened to become a universal historical solvent, applied unfortunately with little resort to the careful quantification that would either corroborate or disprove the hypothesis.

The most influential of the historical behavioralists specializing in American history is Lee Benson. Having completed a doctoral dissertation on the economic and political background of the Interstate Commerce Act, he went to Harvard to study location theory; there he was greatly impressed by the rigor and precision with which Walter Isard was attacking the problems of location theory, and by the more systematic approach of social scientists in comparison to historians. Moving to Columbia, he met Paul Lazarsfeld and found him appalled both by the flaccidity of historical analysis and by the ignorance of history among social scientists. Professor Lazarsfeld provided funds and encouraged Benson to investigate more precise approaches to American political history. From Benson's work at the Columbia Bureau of Applied Social Research came his long article "Research Problems in American Historiography," which provided concrete illustrations of the way in which simple time series of election results might be used to explode generalizations long cherished by historians. A few historians were already stressing quantification in their seminars, but it is with the publication of this article that the behavioral trend becomes clearly evident in American historical writing. Other research which Lee Benson began in the 1950s matured as papers on the causation of the Civil War and *The Concept of Jacksonian Democracy: New York as a Test Case.* Benson was a committed economic determinist when he began his doctoral work but, particularly in his study of Jacksonian democracy in New York, he discovered that his formula was inadequate. Ethno-cultural conditioning seemed to explain more than did economic interest.

Stimulated by a small group of social scientists at the State University of Iowa during the late 1940s, William O. Aydelotte conceived the idea of a massive study of the Corn Laws Parliament in which biographical data were to be gathered for the 800-odd members of this assembly, and these materials related if possible to party affiliation and voting behavior. The Rockefeller Foundation launched the project with a grant and Professor

Aydelotte has pushed it steadily forward, searching first for basic biographical information both here and abroad, working out satisfactory classifications of the class and business backgrounds of the members of parliament, recording the divisions, subjecting data first to correlation analysis (with rather discouraging results), then moving to scaling techniques, and along the way teaching himself social statistics and learning the technology of data processing and computer research. Given his subject matter, one is tempted to look to Namier for Professor Aydelotte's inspiration, but he maintains that his early work owed much more to Lazarsfeld and to *The People's Choice* than to Namier's studies of the British Parliament. Aydelotte has not yet summarized his research in a book-length monograph, but he has delivered a number of important papers at historical meetings, publishing some of them as articles, and he has discussed the problems and rewards of such research in numerous informal contacts with specialists in both American and European history. Once a historian recognizes that he must explain why men behaved as they did in the past, he must turn if he is a thorough scholar to the disciplines that concentrate on the explanation of human behavior; the quantification movement in American political history is one aspect of this change of direction, but commitment to quantification is not equally strong among the members of the AHA committee; one of them wrote recently:

> . . . I am not an enthusiast for quantification. Quantifiable data make up only a portion of the evidence available to the historian. Moreover, if quantifiable data are to be used intelligently, one must have a vast knowledge of the historical context of the situation; the data are not self-interpreting. Another grave danger with quantification is that it can lead to an extremely imbalanced emphasis on those factors that can be quantified, to the exclusion of others of equal or greater significance. Quantification, in other words, is merely one tool in the historian's kit; he must not misuse it or throw the other tools away.

In a series of papers and articles, Samuel P. Hays has tried to articulate and to some extent shape the new trend in American political historiography. He has indicted "conventional political history" as "so preoccupied with the outward and formal, the episodic, the unique and the individual, that it has failed to draw attention to some of the most significant developments of our political past."[24] Historians, he urges, must study political structure in detail: the voters, their socio-economic and ethno-cultural groupings, the pressure groups, the leadership cadres and the systems of decision-making that operate at every level of the American political system, as well as the inter-relationships of these elements. By studying these components of American politics in action through time, by pushing beyond the mere description of political institutions and by penetrating the fog of rhetoric and ideology we can, he promises, reach the basic facts of political motivation, influence, and power. In particular Hays emphasizes the need for study of politics at the grass roots in contrast to the national scene, and the benefits to be gained by distinguishing between political rhetoric and political reality. Recently he has settled upon the term, "the social analysis of politics" as the most appropriate description of this approach. He emphasizes that quantitative data are important tools in this analysis and has also stressed the usefulness of drawing upon the social sciences for both method and theory. Even "conventional" historians can argue that much of this prescription describes their current operations. The procedures which Professor Hays recommends differ from normal practice in American political history mainly in the relative emphasis that is placed upon local case studies, quantification, and social science theory. His articles describe what behavioralists and their students have been doing in varying degree for some time. But if his role so far has been primarily that of publicist and synthesizer, his emphasis on the historian's obligation to set his findings within some sort of conceptual perspective has been salutary. On the other hand, his unfavorable assessment of traditional history seems unnecessary or overdrawn to some behavioralists.

We can say, quite accurately I believe, that a large proportion of our political historians expend their energies in writing the biographies of individual politicians, and that others pursue their research on political bodies, groups, and movements, almost solely in personal manuscripts, newspapers, and legislative debates. Usually American historians have studied elections as unique expressions of the popular will rather than as parts of a time series, and limited their consideration of roll calls to final votes, and perhaps those on major amendments. We have as historians frequently been more impressed by what our subjects have said than by what they have done. As a group we have been unsystematic in our generalizations and too little interested in comparisons and categorization. We often fail to make our assumptions adequately explicit, and in trying to understand human motivation we often ignore the more sophisticated theorizing of the behavioral sciences. The challenge confronting the behavioral historian is to exploit the body of hard quantitative data that exists in election returns, legislative roll calls, court archives, census data (published and unpublished), state, county, and municipal records, and the great accumulation of biographical facts available in other types of sources. This involves both learning the methods necessary to master and manipulate these intimidating sources of information, and becoming more sophisticated in the techniques of research design which are necessary to set findings in useful and defensible theoretical frameworks.

Behavioral history does not promise short cuts or easy answers. If historians have over-emphasized some types of source materials, these cannot be ignored by the historian who quantifies. The scales or other devices which reveal legislative voting patterns can be interpreted fully only if we read the preceding debates. Tables, graphs, and correlations do not explain themselves; they are the product of a particular research design and are subject to various interpretations. The politician's oratory may be designed to conceal or obfuscate his behavior no less than to explain it, and the scholar who uses the *Congressional Globe* is rather like the prospector who examines a salted claim. Manuscript collections, some will say, are more reliable; here the politician lays bare his motives. He may indeed, but again he may not, and it is shocking to discover how little some of the manuscript collections, regularly cited as major sources in historical monographs, actually reveal about the men who accumulated them. In addition, any manuscript collection is at best an accidental historical accretion, pointing perhaps to conclusions that are completely different from those we would reach if all the related manuscript collections had been preserved. It is sobering also to remember that whenever a politician evaluates his election chances correctly (few run in anticipation of defeat), there are usually one or more opponents who judge the situation incorrectly. Remembering this, we will treat the explanations of politicians with caution. But the interplay of contemporary observation and explanation with quantitative evidence should allow us to push our understanding further than either type of source can carry us by itself.

In writing of cultural sources and economic change, Thomas C. Cochran points out that no one has yet developed a model in which all the variables can be quantified. "One cannot," he writes, "speak of units or doses of personality of values."[25] We will no doubt become increasingly ingenious in developing ways to measure attitudes or values indirectly; the quantifier may build some dams and breakwaters in what Matthew Arnold unfairly termed "that huge Mississippi of falsehood called history," but there are rapids he will not tame, tributaries he cannot explore, and quicksands, he still cannot plumb by quantification. So American political historians are not all going to become quantifiers, and not only for this reason. Much biography and so-called conventional political history is useful and will continue to attract many in the profession. The fact that quantification calls for extra effort rather than a substitution of effort will discourage some from essaying it.

For those who find the fascination of political history in a smooth and colorful narrative, the injection of numbers, tables, and scales may be jarring and unpleasing. The new political history must make its way by appealing to the intellectual curiosity of the reader; its impact must flow from the ideas and the sense of understanding that it imparts rather than from the colorful incident or well-told anecdote. Even so, behavioral historians need not jettison the idea that history is a literary art. There is no reason why political history should not still employ the well-turned phrase or striking illustration, even though based on a foundation of measurement.

For a time in the testing period ahead the behavioral historians may find editors suspicious and cold; their graduate students will encounter difficulties in obtaining proper training in statistics and the use of computers; both faculty and students may find it difficult to obtain financial aid because the National Science Foundation has not officially recognized historians and granting agencies of humanistic temper are not likely to support behavioral history enthusiastically. These problems may in the end be less disturbing than the limitations of the quantitative data American history and the inadequacies of the techniques now available for analyzing them. Since the behavioral historian cannot interview the dead politician of yesteryear, he is forced to place considerable emphasis on the study of aggregate data, particularly in election analysis. Here he encounters the problem of ecological correlations which W. S. Robinson described some fifteen years ago. One cannot, on the basis of correlation analysis, deduce the behavior of an individual from the behavior of the aggregate. There is, as Austin Ranney has pointed out, a good deal to be learned from the study of aggregates as aggregates.[26] What is more, it is possible in some instances to produce refined aggregate data. In some states, for instance, poll lists of the nineteenth century and census data can be combined so that we know precisely the voters represented in precinct totals and many of their social characteristics–in contrast to situations in which we know only that voters represent a certain proportion of an electorate that has as a group certain demographic, socio-economic, or ethno-cultural characteristics. Must we stop there, or can we minimize the limits of possible error in moving from aggregate to individual, or work with probabilities rather than correlation analysis? Ferreting out virtually pure ethno-cultural or socio-economic constituencies seems offhand to be a commonsense solution, which election forecasters have used successfully on occasion; but the very purity of such units may impart bias. Assuming that we can use aggregate data in good conscience, we have fewer of them than we would like. One is hard put to find historical measures of some of the variables that survey research has found to be important. The emphasis which behavioral historians are placing on the importance of ethno-cultural groups may in part reflect the fact that the ethno-cultural reference group is the easiest to identify in historical data. Moreover, the statistics of social research are unfortunately much more useful in showing the relationships between variables at a particular moment than in demonstrating change over time. Ideally, the behavioral historian requires a statistics of time series, of lag, of transition matrixes, of growth models, and of indirect relationships where the association of two factors is measured by substituting a third for one or the other. Since most social scientists restrict their research to the findings of survey research, there are few outstanding scholars in the behavioral disciplines who are interested in developing or refining the kind of statistical methods that historians would find particularly useful.[27]

Aggregate election data provide evidence of a single act, although to some extent the preparation for this act can be deduced from examination of other variables. The modern panel survey yields information about the period of preparation and sometimes adds retrospective interpretations by the actors as well. Can content analysis of newspapers or other historical documents be refined to the point where it serves in some measure as a substitute for the questionnaire? Its advocates believe that this technique has been greatly improved during the present generation. Contingency and qualitative content analysis in particular seem to promise results that are more interesting to historians than the rather mechanical exercises that were common some years ago. The imaginative and flexible analyst can indeed deduce political values, class structure, influence and power systems, and key election issues from even the highly partisan newspapers of the nineteenth century, provided he remembers that historical evidence may come in all shapes and sizes. But it seems doubtful that content analysis will soon reach the stage where it can be used to detect the exact turning points or the precise importance of the various issues in election campaigns.[28]

If the American political historian faces problems in finding adequate quantifiable data and in discovering appropriate statistical techniques, he runs other dangers in using political theory in planning and interpreting his research. In effect he may allow such theory or its related concepts to dehumanize his work. When he writes in terms of social role or status revolution, for instance, he may produce a deterministic history in which his central characters are denied the power of choice or the freedom to make rational decisions, but seem instead the captives of forces beyond their control. The predatory railroad tycoon who bribes a legislature may appear as the guardian of his stockholders, and the representative of a peer group of railroad executives rather than as a calculating offender against the ethics or law of the community. The abolitionist or progressive leader becomes a man in unconscious revolt against the societal changes that are depriving him of the position of leadership which his father enjoyed, rather than a public-spirited reformer trying to improve society from rational and philanthropic motives. "If powerful groups are denied access to formal power in legitimate ways" writes Samuel P. Hays, "they seek access through procedures which the community considers illegitimate. Corrupt government, therefore, does not reflect the genius of evil men, but rather the lack of acceptable means for those who exercise power in the private community to wield the same influence in governmental affairs."[29] Such explanations may present old material in a new light, but in careless hands they may fit facts to theory rather than using them to test theory; and certainly such analysis gives little hint of the moral indignation that some historians have found in the progressive period. Once such pitfalls are recognized, however, they can be avoided.

Some historians may consider behavioral history to be "consensus" history. In the introduction to *The American Political Tradition,* Richard Hofstadter noted in 1948 that "the common climate of American opinion" had "been much obscured by the tendency to place political conflict in the foreground of history," and showed, in the essays that followed, the very considerable agreement that had existed among American political leaders irrespective of section or party. A few years later John Higham detected a growing "cult of 'American consensus'" in both the intellectual and political history of America, and argued that "current scholarship" was "carrying out a massive grading operation to smooth over America's social convulsions."[30] It seems inevitable that the rather precise measurements and the detailed case studies of behavioral history will qualify the bold conclusions reached in some older general studies. The result need not be homogenized history, however. To prove consensus in our political history, the historian must define politics, political ideas, and the American political system narrowly. In reality it is as much a political act to exclude a racial or an economic minority from participation in formal political institutions, or to keep a depressed sector of the population in bondage by failing to provide adequate educational and economic opportunities, as it is to share in the task of choosing a presidential candidate. With this understood, American political life becomes once more the scene of fundamental political conflict. And some of the behavioralists do bring this broad view to their study of American political history.

Critics of quantification are common in the historical profession. Some of them suspect inter-disciplinary research on general principles. Arguing by aphorism and analogy, one of my colleagues points out that the supreme achievement of hybridization in the animal world is the mule—a creature without pride of ancestry or hope of progeny. Recently Professor Aydelotte discussed quantification in history in a temperate and closely-reasoned article in the *American Historical Review* (April 1966). He divides the arguments of the most vociferous critics of quantification into four categories, questioning specifically: (1) the value of the work that has been done; (2) the feasibility of this approach in view of the admittedly limited materials available to historians; (3) the reliability of the results obtained by these techniques; and (4) the usefulness or significance of the results. There can, in the end, be only one convincing answer to such criticisms: the usefulness and intrinsic interest of the publications of the behavioral historians will determine whether quantification flourishes or withers as a historical technique.

Lee Benson was sanguine about the future of the new political history when he wrote recently, "the prediction does not seem absurd that . . . by 1984, a significant proportion of American historians will have accepted Buckle's two basic propositions: (1) past human behavior can be studied scientifically; (2) the main business of historians is to participate in the overall scholarly enterprise of discovering and developing general laws of human behavior."[31] The date is ominous and the future perhaps less assured than Benson believes. But the methods and theory of the social science disciplines seem to promise much. If the behavioralists retain the broad and critical knowledge of sources found among conventional political historians, their keen awareness of the range of cultural and socio-economic differences at different times, and their willingness to search widely for alternative hypotheses, they may indeed contribute to a richer and more vital political history of the United States.

FOOTNOTES

1. Orin Grant Libby, "A Plea for the Study of Votes in Congress," *American Historical Association Report,* 1896, I (Washington, 1897).

2. This conference is described in a report prepared by Samuel P. Hays and Murray Murphey, "Research Conference on Political Data: Historical Analysis of Quantitative Data–July 26-August 13, 1965, Ann Arbor, Michigan" (mimeographed, 1965).

3. Robert A. Dahl defines the term in political science in "The Behavioral Approach in Political Science: Epitaph for a Monument to a Successful Protest," *American Political Science Review,* December 1961, p. 767.

4. George Daniels, "Immigrant Vote in the Election of 1860: The Case of Iowa," *Mid-America,* July 1962; Robert P. Swierenga, "The Ethnic Voter and the First Lincoln Election," *Civil War History,* March 1965; Stanley Parsons, "Who Were the Nebraska Populists?" *Nebraska History,* June 1963; Howard W. Allen, "Studies of

Political Loyalties of Two Nationality Groups: Isolationism and German-Americans," *Journal of the Illinois State Historical Society,* Summer 1964; Thomas B. Alexander, Kitt C. Carter, Jack R. Lister, Jerry C. Oldshue, and Winfred G. Sandlin, "Who Were the Alabama Whigs?" *The Alabama Review,* January 1963, Thomas B. Alexander and Peggy J. Duckworth, "Alabama Black Belt Whigs During Secession: A New Viewpoint," *ibid.,* July 1964; Aida DiPace Donald, "The Decline of Whiggery and the Formation of the Republican Party in Rochester, 1848-56," *Rochester History,* July 1958.

5. Joel H. Silbey, *The Shrine of Party: Congressional Voting Behavior, 1841-1852* (Pittsburgh, 1967); David Donald, *The Politics of Reconstruction 1863-1867* (Baton Rouge, 1965); John L. Shover, "Populism in the Nineteen-Thirties: The Battle for the AAA," *Agricultural History,* January 1965; Edward L. Gambill, "Who were the Senate Radicals," *Civil War History,* September 1965; Gerald Wolff, "The Slavocracy and the Homestead Problem of 1854," *Agricultural History,* April 1966, Howard W. Allen, "Geography and Politics: Voting on Reform Issues in the United States Senate, 1911-1916," *Journal of Southern History,* May 1961; Glenn M. Linden, " 'Radicals' and Economic Policies: The Senate, 1861-1873," *ibid.,* May 1966.

6. Pioneering work of this type appeared in George Mowry, *The California Progressives* (Berkeley and Los Angeles, 1951), pp. 86-104; Alfred D. Chandler, Jr., "The Origins of Progressive Leadership," in Elting Morison *et al.* (eds.), *The Letters of Theodore Roosevelt* (Cambridge, 1951-54), VIII, App. III, pp. 1462-65, David Donald, "Toward a Reconsideration of Abolitionists," *Lincoln Reconsidered* (New York, 1961). See also Grady McWhiney, "Were the Whigs a Class Party in Alabama?" *Journal of Southern History,* November 1957, Ralph A. Wooster, "Notes on the Georgia Legislature of 1860," *Georgia Historical Quarterly,* March 1961; "Membership in Early Texas Legislatures, 1850-1860," *Southwestern Historical Quarterly,* October 1965; Gerald W. McFarland, "The New York Mugwumps of 1884: A Profile," *Political Science Quarterly,* March 1963; William T. Kerr, Jr., "The Progressives of Washington 1910-12," *Pacific Northwest Quarterly,* January 1964; E. Daniel Potts, "The Progressive Profile in Iowa," *Mid-America,* October 1965; Herbert J. Doherty, Jr., *The Whigs of Florida 1845-1854, University of Florida Monographs: Social Sciences,* I, Winter 1959, pp. 63-72. Robert A. Skotheim discusses some of the methodological problems involved in this type of study in "A Note on Historical Method: David Donald's 'Toward a Reconsideration of Abolitionists,' " *Journal of Southern History,* August 1959.

7. Richard P. McCormick, "Suffrage Classes and Party Alignments: a Study in Voter Behavior," *Mississippi Valley Historical Review,* December 1959; "New Perspectives on Jacksonian Politics," *American Historical Review,* January 1960; Charles Sellers, "The Equilibrium Cycle in Two-Party Politics," *Public Opinion Quarterly,* Spring 1965.

8. Lee Benson, "Research Problems in American Political Historiography," in Mirra Komarovsky (ed.), *Common Frontiers of the Social Sciences* (Glencoe, 1957); *The Concept of Jacksonian Democracy: New York as a Test Case* (Princeton, 1961).

9. Lee Benson, *Turner and Beard: American Historical Writing Reconsidered* (Glencoe, 1960); Samuel P. Hays, "History as Human Behavior," *Iowa Journal of History,* July 1960, "New Possibilities for American Political History: The Social Analysis of Political Life" (prepared for the American Historical Association meeting, 29 December 1964 and lithoprinted by the Inter-University Consortium for Political Research); very similar to the latter is "The Social Analysis of American Political History, 1880-1920," *Political Science Quarterly,* September 1965; "The Politics of Reform in Municipal Government in the Progressive Era," *Pacific Northwest Quarterly,* October 1964.

10. Unless otherwise stated, the contributions discussed in the next two paragraphs are those appearing under their authors' names in footnotes 4 through 9.

11. Joseph Schafer, "Who Elected Lincoln," *American Historical Review,* October 1941. Schafer was a student of Turner and much of his work exemplifies the empirical side of the Turner tradition.

12. Samuel P. Hays, "The Politics of Reform," and "Political Parties and the Local-Cosmopolitan Continuum, 1865-1929," prepared for the Conference on American Political Party Development, Washington University, 1966, and cited here by permission of Professor Hays and William Nesbit Chambers.

13. Joel H. Silbey, "The Civil War Synthesis in American Political History," *Civil War History,* June 1964.

14. Stephan Thernstrom, *Poverty and Progress: Social Mobility in a Nineteenth Century City* (Cambridge, 1964); Samuel B. Warner, *Street-Car Suburbs* (Cambridge, 1962). For those interested in the rural community the work of James C. Malin is still essential; see "The Turnover of Farm Population in Kansas," *Kansas Historical Quarterly,* November 1935, and *The Grassland of North America: Prolegomena to its History* (Lawrence, 1947), pp. 278-315. Several studies bearing on Iowa are summarized with additional data of my own in Chapter I of *From Prairie to Corn Belt: Farming on the Illinois and Iowa Prairies in the Nineteenth Century* (Chicago, 1963).

15. Samuel P. Hays speaking on "Computers and Historical Research," Purdue Conference on the Use of Computers in the Humanities, 29 October 1965.

16. David Easton, *A Framework for Political Analysis* (Englewood Cliffs, N. J., 1965), p. 7.

17. Lee Benson, *Turner and Beard,* p. 228.

18. In the introduction to the paperback edition of *The Concept of Jacksonian Democracy* (New York, 1964), Benson includes a specific description of his methodology.

19. The following list is not intended to be comprehensive: Walter D. Burnham, "The Changing Shape of the American Political Universe," *American Political Science Review,* March 1965, William N. Chambers, *Political Parties in a New Nation: The American Experience, 1776-1809* (New York, 1963); Robert A. Dahl, *Who Governs? Democracy and Power in an American City* (New Haven, 1961); Manning J. Dauer, *The Adams Federalists* (Baltimore, 1953); V. O. Key, Jr., "A Theory of Critical Elections," *Journal of Politics,* February 1955, "Secular Realignment and the Party System," *ibid.,* May 1959; with Milton C. Cummings, Jr., *The Responsible Electorate: Rationality in Presidential Voting, 1936-60* (Cambridge, 1966); Theodore J. Lowi, *At the Pleasure of the Mayor: Patronage and Power in New York City, 1898-1958* (Glencoe, 1964); Duncan MacRae, Jr. and James Meldrum, "Critical Elections in Illinois: 1888-1958," *American Political Science Review,* September 1960; John R. Schmidhaeuser, "The Justices of the Supreme Court: A Collective Portrait," *Midwest Journal of Political Science* February 1959; "Judicial Behavior and the Sectional Crisis of 1837-1850," *Journal of Politics,* November 1961; Ruth C. Silva, *Rum, Religion, and Votes: 1928 Re-Examined* (University Park, Pa., 1962).

20. The members of this committee are Robert W. Fogel, Lionel W. McKenzie, Frederick Mosteller, William O. Aydelotte, Oscar Handlin, and Allan G. Bogue.

21. Robert A. Dahl, *loc. cit.,* note 3.

22. James C. Malin, *op. cit.,* note 14. Professor Malin's position on historiographic problems is developed in *Essays on Historiography* (Lawrence, 1946), and in *On the Nature of History: Essays about History and Dissidence* (Lawrence, 1954).

23. Social Science Research Council, *Theory and Practice in Historical Study: A Report of the Committee on Historiography, Bulletin 54* (New York, 1946); *The Social Sciences in Historical Study: A Report of the Committee on Historiography, Bulletin 64* (New York, 1954); Louis Gottschalk, ed., *Generalization in the Writing of*

History: A Report of the Committee on Historical Analysis of the Social Science Research Council (Chicago, 1963).

24. Hays, "New Possibilities," *loc. cit.*

25. Thomas C. Cochran, *The Inner Revolution: Essays on the Social Sciences in History* (New York, 1964), p. 142.

26. Austin Ranney, "The Utility and Limitations of Aggregate Data in the Study of Electoral Behavior," in Austin Ranney, ed., *Essays on the Behavioral Study of Politics* (Urbana, 1962), discusses the problems inherent in the use of aggregate data.

27 Gösta Carlsson comments on the "timelessness" of much social theory in "Time and Continuity in Mass Attitude Change: The Case of Voting," *Public Opinion Quarterly*, Spring 1965.

28. Ithiel De Sola Pool, *Trends in Content Analysis: Papers, Work Conference on Content Analysis* (Urbana, 1959), is a relatively recent survey of the state of the technique.

29. Hays, "Politics of Reform," *loc. cit.*, p. 166.

30. John Higham, "The Cult of the 'American Consensus': Homogenizing Our History," *Commentary*, February 1959.

31 Lee Benson, "Quantification, Scientific History, and Scholarly Innovation," *AHA Newsletter*, June 1966, p. 12.

13

A Critique of the Scientific Hope

ARTHUR M. SCHLESINGER, JR. (1962)

All historians of course agree that their methods can and should be improved, and each historian would like his own scholarship to endure rather than to pass out of fashion with the next change in the climate of opinion. To this extent, all are sympathetic to the attempt by behavioral historians to apply techniques which would make scholarship more rigorous and more certain. But most historians consider the "scientific" claims of the behaviorists to be exaggerated. Just as Beard wrote in "Written History as an Act of Faith" that the study of science did not offer an analogy for the study of history either in its promise for the attainment of scientific objectivity or its promise for formulating scientific laws, so most historians today think that neither the complexity of human beings nor the paucity of their past records allows for the establishment of a scientific history. If the behavioral historians protest that they do not mean to adopt either

Reprinted by permission from the American Sociological Association, "The Humanist Looks at Empirical Social Research," American Sociological Review, XXVII, December 1962, pp. 768-71. The paper was originally presented to the annual American Sociological Association meeting in 1962.

complete objectivity or the deterministic laws of behavior which preclude individual free choice as the foundation for their approach, most historians reply that these tenets seem nevertheless to be implicit in the behaviorist concern with quantification and in the reliance upon social sciences. Further, most historians argue that whereas traditional scholarship concerned itself with the whole spectrum of life in the past, behaviorists have tackled only the narrow range of problems with which their methods can cope. Thus many of the most interesting and important historical questions are excluded.

In the following selection (originally presented as an address to a meeting of sociologists) Arthur M. Schlesinger, Jr. (b. 1917), professor of history at the City University of New York, expressed the view of most historians toward what he called the "mystique" of quantitative scholarship. Schlesinger focused less on the use of systematic methods of quantification, and more on the value of these methods as compared to those traditionally used by historians. He singled out public opinion polls as the kind of systematic evidence which historians have lacked and which some have assumed would have been invaluable. Schlesinger minimized the value of the polls in such a way as to suggest that, through use of improved techniques, sociological pollsters collected data which ignored the most important historical question: What did people think at the time of real decision-making, as opposed to what they thought they thought at the moment when they were approached by a pollster? Schlesinger pointed out the historical problem of determining the causes of the Civil War as an example of the type of significant question which no "scientific" method can answer any better than traditional methods. Like Beard, in "Written History as an Act of Faith," Schlesinger argued that the complex human factors which compose such an important part of the historical process cannot be scientifically dissected or quantified and that the historian is always subjectively related to what he studies. Yet, said Schlesinger, the question of determining the causes of the Civil War is typical of what historians must try to answer, however imperfectly.

Because Schlesinger, like Charles Beard and Staughton Lynd, thought a different view of scholarship would have to emerge if events were actually historically determined, he discussed the question of determinism. Schlesinger imputed an implicitly deterministic philosophy to behaviorists, and, like Beard, he insisted that the evidence was insufficient to substantiate the theory. Like Lynd, Schlesinger argued that in any case, men live and make decisions as if a comprehensive determinism did not exist.

Let me, first, express my great pleasure in being here. An historian among sociologists, I fear, is a case of an inferior Daniel cast into a den of superior lions; but my natural anxiety in facing this assemblage is outweighed tonight by the satisfaction I have in being permitted to join this tribute to your president—a tribute which the humanist claims the right to share along with the card-holding empirical social researcher. However much one may occasionally differ with Paul Lazarsfeld [president of the American Sociological Association in 1962]—and even more, on occasion, with the Lazarsfeldians—one must acknowledge both the brilliance and charm of the man and notable stimulus the sociologist has provided to all students, humane as well as behavioral, of social processes. I might add that whenever I encounter Paul Lazarsfeld, I recognize the truth of an old adage much cherished by historians; that, inside every sociologist, there is an humanist struggling to get out.

As an historian, I am naturally strongly prejudiced in favor of an empirical social research. If I understand this term correctly, it refers, I take it, to two things: first, to gaining the most complete possible factual knowledge about events which have already taken place; and, second, to devising inquiries and experiments which, by enlarging our knowledge about present and future events, may enlarge our understanding of social and human processes in general. No historian can possibly deny the value of empirical social research in both senses: such research is the stuff by which historians live—and by which, I may add, we too often live carelessly and irresponsibly. I am well aware how dismally written history lacks in rigor, how impressionistic the historian's analysis so often is, how imprecise his generation [generalization?], how loose his language, how literary his whole style of attack. Insofar as empirical social research can drive historians to criticize their assumptions, to expose their premises, to tighten their logic, to pursue and respect their facts, to restrain their rhetoric—in short, insofar as it gives them an acute sense of the extraordinary precariousness of the historical enterprise—it administers a wholly salutary shock to a somewhat uncritical and even complacent discipline.

I would wish everything else I have to say this evening about empirical social research to be construed in the light of this *cri de coeur.* But I know that you have not come tonight to hear how wonderful empirical social research is. Let me therefore conclude this part of my remarks by quickly entering these two points into the record: first, my indebtedness as an historian to the sociologists who have so vastly broadened my own intellectual horizons and refined my own conception of the historical enterprise; and, second, my own intense awareness of the shortcomings, epistemological and methodological, of the enterprise. Let me now pass on the question whether, granted all this, empirical social research in the sense used by sociologists is *the* key to social knowledge.

This question, it should now be clear, has to do, not with the value of empirical social research *per se,* but with what one must call the *mystique* of empirical social research–the notion that it is, not one of several paths to social wisdom, but the central and infallible path. And this question derives particularly from the extent to which empirical social research is taken by its practitioners to mean, above all, *quantitative* research–that is, research which deals in quantifiable problems and yields numerical or quasi-numerical conclusions.

Again I do not want to be misunderstood. No historian can deny that quantitative research, complete with IBM cards and computers, can make an important contribution to historical understanding–no historian, that is, who has examined, for example, a recent production by the historical branch of the Lazarsfeld family *Massachusetts Shipping, 1697-1714,* by the Bailyns. Yet the problem remains: does quantitative research provide the best way of solving significant historical problems?

Your president raised one aspect of this question in a stimulating article in the Winter 1950-1951 issue of the *Public Opinion Quarterly* entitled "The Obligations of the 1950 Pollster to the 1984 Historian." Paul Lazarsfeld proposed here that public opinion data can be of inestimable use to the future historian in defining the 'prevailing values' of a society and in charting the interaction between ideas and social action as well as in analyzing specific events like elections. Similarly, Hadley Cantril in his indispensable survey *Public Opinion, 1935-1946* suggests how useful historians would have found a similar compilation of public opinion polls covering such confused and turbulent epochs of history as the American or French Revolution or the Civil War.

At first, the thought of the availability of such materials is deeply attractive. Yet, on reflection, I wonder whether the existence of public opinion data would, in the end, cause us to write the history of these epochs very differently. What does a public opinion poll report? It reports essentially, I would suppose, what people think they think. It does not report what people really think, because people ordinarily don't know what they really think in advance of a situation which compels them to act on the basis of their thoughts. Public opinion polling, in short, elicits essentially an *irresponsible* expression of opinion–irresponsible because no action is intended to follow the expression. The expression of opinion is not given weight or substance by a sense of accountability for consequences; when that sense of accountability enters, then the expression may very likely be different.

Irresponsible opinion is certainly of interest. It may well tell us a great deal about the general atmosphere of a period. But it is responsible opinion–opinion when the chips are down, opinion which issues directly in decision and action—which is relevant to the historical process and of primary interest to the historian. And public opinion polls do not add greatly to our knowledge of the evolution and distribution of responsible opinion. The measure of responsible opinion is not answers, but acts. As an experienced student of these matters, Harry S Truman, once put it, "I think the best poll there is is the count after election."

Polls catch public opinion in a plastic, unfinished, and superficial state, while the historian is concerned with opinion under the stress of decision, opinion as it is crystallized by events and leadership and brought to bear at points of political and intellectual action. The difference between expression without responsibility and expression under responsibility raises problems which go to the root of the whole question of assent. Cardinal Newman's old distinction between "notional assent" and "real assent" represents one salient aspect of the problem involved in the difference between "public opinion" in the polls and "public opinion" in the historical process.

Why does a political leader make a decision? The decision is generally the result of an accommodation between his own views of what is wise and the *felt* pressures on him as to what is possible. The crux of the matter is that the pressures are felt; they are politically kinetic pressures, not inert or latent attitudes. Only a crude politician construes felt pressures in terms of lobbies and pressure groups; a statesman is attuned by his own radar to a whole turmoil of public sentiment; he knows that, by action and by leadership, he can to some degree generate the pressures which will propel him along the course he has already chosen to go. Public opinion data can no doubt provide a kind of measure of his success in marshalling opinion. But his actions and the effective response to them provide a far more reliable measure. Nor do current attempts to evaluate the intensity with which opinions are held really meet the question, since they do not abolish the essential difference between responsible and irresponsible opinion. For this reason, I doubt whether full Gallup, Roper, Michigan, and Harris dossiers on the American or French Revolutions would radically change the historian's view of these historic events. The best poll there is remains the count after election—not what people say they think, but what they do.

Polls represent only one aspect of the attempt to quantify historical data. A number of excellent historians—Sir Lewis Namier and his followers in Great Britain and certain American scholars under the spell of behavioral sciences—have mounted more general attacks on classic historical questions in a formidable effort to make them surrender to quantitative solutions. This effort has a pervading complex of assumptions—that the role of human purposes, ideas and ideals in social action is vastly overrated; that history can, in effect, be reduced to a set of social, ethnic, and economic tropisms; and that the quantitative method can transform the historian into a detached and "scientific" observer. But there seem to me two main troubles with this effort–with an effort, for example, to solve quantitatively the problem of the causes of the Civil War. One is that most of the variables in an historical equation are not susceptible to commensurable quantification; the other is that the observer is too mixed up with the phenomena observed to eliminate the subjective element.

When Sir Lewis Namier condemns the tendency to exaggerate "the importance of the conscious will and purpose in individuals," he holds forth the possibility of a form of historical certitude–but he does so by dismissing a whole range of historical issues which happen not to be susceptible to quantification. This seems to me the essential trick of the quantitative approach. That approach claims a false precision by the simple strategy of confining itself to the historical problems and materials with which quantitative techniques can deal–and ignoring all other questions as trivial. The *mystique* of empirical social research, in short, leads its acolytes to accept as significant only the questions to which the quantitative magic can provide answers. As an humanist, I am bound to reply that almost all important questions are important precisely because they are *not* susceptible to quantitative answers. The humanist, let me repeat, does not deny the value of the quantitative method. What he denies is that it can handle everything which the humanist must take into account; what he condemns is the assumption that things which quantitative methods can't handle don't matter.

I would suggest that these are the things that matter most. Nor can one accept the answer that it is all a temporary shortcoming of method–that improvements in technique will soon extend the sway of the quantitative approach until it can subdue all problems. My old friend Professor B. F. Skinner tells us that this is so–and warns us that we must face the consequences. I would not assume that Professor Skinner speaks for all behavioral scientists, but I do feel that he has pursued the logic of the behavioral approach with admirable candor to an ultimate conclusion. His conclusion is briefly that "the application of the methods of science to human affairs" is increasingly and irrevocably "at odds with the traditional democratic conception of man" and "the so-called 'democratic philosophy' of human behavior." The more we understand about human behavior, Professor Skinner tells us, the less we can credit to man himself:

as such explanations become more and more comprehensive the contribution which may be claimed by the individual himself appears to approach zero. Man's vaunted creative powers, his original accomplishments in art, science and morals, his capacity to choose and our right to hold him responsible for the consequences of his choice–none of these is conspicuous in this new self-portrait.

Where the democratic view assumes a measure, however limited, of free choice and individual responsibility, science, Professor Skinner suggests, refutes such fancies and absorbs everything in a system of comprehensive determinism.

If this is so, then it is so; but the proof does not lie in assertion–or in extrapolation. It can lie only in demonstration–and in a demonstration that has not yet been made. Until it is made, those who accept this view accept it on faith. Science in such terms ceases to be a system of provisional hypothesis and becomes instead a form of poetic myth, almost of religion.

The defenders of behavioral science are sometimes given to the doubtful practice of trying to dispose of its critics by advancing theories about the personal or status insecurities which impel them to criticism. I do not wish to emulate this form of reductionism, and I will refrain, therefore, from speculating about the impulses which divide the world into what William James called the tender-minded and the tough-minded–the impulses which make some people monists and others pluralists. The point is not the psyche of the individuals, but the merit of the arguments.

The key is the demonstration–and one is compelled to doubt whether the necessary demonstration is likely to be made in the near future. For one thing, the vision of comprehensive determinism remains a psychological impossibility in the sense that no human being could conceivably act upon it or live by it. As Sir Isaiah Berlin has put it, "If we begin to take it seriously, then, indeed, the changes in our language, or moral notions, our attitudes toward one another, our views of history, of society and of everything else will be too profound to be even adumbrated." We can no more imagine what the universe of a consistent determinist would be like than we can imagine what it would be like to live in a world without time or one with seventeen-dimensional space. And it is more than a psychological impossibility: it is also a quite illegitimate extension of existing evidence. Until the omnipotence of determinism can be demonstrated by infallibility of prediction and control, one must surely stick with the provable facts and accept the existence of intractable elements in experience which may well, in the future as in the past, continue to defy quantification.

In this belief, I am encouraged by the testimony of Dr. Norbert Wiener, who has done as much as any one to invent the devices which make modern quantitative research possible. Dr. Wiener has noted the contention of behavioral scientists that the main task of the immediate future is "to extend to the fields of anthropology, of sociology, of economics, the methods of the natural sciences, in the hope of achieving a like measure of success in the social fields. From believing this necessary, they come to believe it possible. In this, I maintain, they show an excessive optimism, and a misunderstanding of the nature of all scientific achievement." Success in exact science, Dr. Wiener points out, has come where there is a high degree of isolation of the phenomenon from the observer—as in astronomy or atomic physics. But the social sciences deal with short statistical runs, and observers are deeply, inextricably and indeterminately involved in what they observe. He concludes:

> Whether our investigations in the social sciences be statistical or dynamic . . . they can never be good to more than a very few decimal places, and, in short, can never furnish us with a quantity of verifiable, significant information which begins to compare with that which we have learned to expect in the natural sciences. . . . There is much which we must leave whether we like it or not, to the "unscientific," narrative method of the professional historian.

I would qualify Dr. Wiener's conclusion only by expanding it. There is much, I would add, which we must leave, whether we like it or not, not just to historians but to poets, novelists, painters, musicians, philosophers, theologians, even politicians, even saints—in short, to one form or another of humanist. For an indefinite future, I suspect, humanism will continue to yield truths about both individual and social experience which quantitative social research by itself could never reach. Whether these truths are inherently or merely temporarily inaccessible to the quantitative method is a question which only experience can answer.

In the meantime, this humanist is bound to say that, as an aid to the understanding of society and men, quantitative social research is admirable and indispensable. As a guide to the significance of problems, it is misleading when it exudes the assumption that only problems susceptible to quantitative solutions are important. As a means of explaining human or social behavior, it is powerful but profoundly incomplete. As the source of a theory of human nature and of the universe, it is but a new formulation of an ancient romantic myth.

14

The Historian as Moral Critic

JOHN HIGHAM (1962)

In the essay reprinted below as the final selection, John Higham (b. 1920), professor of history at the University of Michigan, reviewed twentieth-century American historical scholarship and tried to resolve the conflicting demands of the subjectivity of the historian and the objectivity of the past.

Explicitly rejecting the view that scholars could or should escape their own times, Higham stressed the vitality and relevance which contemporary involvement gave to a historian's work. At the same time, Higham emphasized the narrow partisanship which could dominate the historical studies conducted by those who were primarily interested in reforming the present. He characterized the progressive histories of the earlier 1900s as congenial to the progressive and pragmatic climate of opinion, but as unattractive to the intellectual temper of the 1940s and 1950s. The dominant post-war mood brought with it different historical interpretations, ones which were not only less explicitly partisan than had been the case formerly, but in which an explicit moral perspective was almost altogether lacking. Higham expressed concern that this moral vacuum should exist in the scholarship. He did not implicitly accept the claims of the behavioral or scientific history movement as sufficient to replace the traditional moral concerns of historians. Writing in the early 1960s, before the New Left movement among younger historians was evident, he could not see the emergent neo-progressivism as an attempt to fill a moral void. From the perspective of the end of the 1960s, it can be seen that the New Left historians have attempted to answer Higham's call. But Higham would likely question whether the young radical scholars were not too narrowly partisan to escape the criticisms he had previously made of earlier progressive historians for exploiting the past for reform purposes.

Higham proposed that the historian be a moral critic in the sense that he study the moral aspects of the life of men in past generations. By focusing upon the moral assumptions and decisions made by individuals and societies, the historian would become responsive to the ethical dimension frequently ignored in purely causal analysis of how and why events occurred. Through knowledge of the moral patterns existent in the past, combined with causal analysis of what was historically possible and what was not, Higham suggested that the historian as moral critic could reconstruct and judge moral decisions without sacrificing the integrity of the past.

Reprinted by permission from John Higham, "Beyond Consensus: The Historian as Moral Critic," *American Historical Review*, LXVII, April 1962, pp. 609-625.

A perennial dilemma of historical scholarship is its need to use the resources of the present to discover what is not present, but past. The creative historian lives a double life, responsive on one side to the questions and issues of his own age, faithful on the other side to the integrity of an age gone by. Too feeble an involvement in the life of the present makes for a slack and routine grasp of the past. But present commitments that are too parochial imprison our imagination, instead of challenging it. At one extreme, historical thought is sterile, at the other tendentious. How can historians, by the strength of their detachment, rise above a constricting present, and, by the amplitude of their commitment, enter a living past?

If this is a perennial problem, it has a special pertinence for the American historian today. He usually works in a vast educational system that rewards its employees with prestige and security for predictable quantities of passionless research. The institutional setting, therefore, encourages much routine and mechanical history. On the other hand, the ideological conflicts of the twentieth century have, until now, swept many of our best historians in the opposite direction, entangling them in rather partisan commitments.

For a long time institutional restraints and ideological pressures seemed to offset and balance one another in a fairly effective way. The pull of neutrality and the push of commitment seemed enough adjusted to serve the pursuit of truth. As long as our present concerns remained fundamentally stable, a cumulative pattern of research could be observed. Conventional monographs followed easily in paths marked out by the major interpretive studies, and confidence in the progress of knowledge kept criticism within manageable bounds. Now, however, that working balance has been upset. The old ideological positions have broken down, so that the kind of present-mindedness that seemed to illuminate American history twenty years ago has largely outlived its usefulness. Many of the values and allegiances that guided our historical writing now seem unduly restrictive. There is, consequently, a danger and an opportunity: the danger of a largely negative scholarship, revisionist in motive but routine or merely clever in result; the opportunity of discovering, with the help of our newer present, a history of unsuspected richness and power.

Until very recently, two contemporary commitments dominated the interpretation of American history. First, many of the best American historians felt a close identification with particular sections or social groups. Secondly, progressive and pragmatic ideas had an extraordinary control over historical thinking. Both of these circumstances have altered.

In an increasingly homogeneous society, historians cannot be as urgently motivated by sectional, class, and ethnic ties as they were a quarter of a century ago. Then militant southerners, confident westerners, defiant Brahmins, and the first self-conscious representatives of various ethnic minorities were turning up facets of our history reflective of their claims or grievances and championing regionalism, Puritanism, or cultural pluralism, as the case might be. There is much less of this now. Younger scholars are not impelled to vindicate their respective subjects as ardently as Samuel Eliot Morison championed the Puritans, Walter Prescott Webb, the Great Plains, Carl Wittke, the immigrants, or Ulrich B. Phillips and E. Merton Coulter, the South.[1] One wonders how these various groupings in the American past will look to a new generation of historians, which is not anchored very securely in any of them.

While social changes were eroding the group loyalties of many historians, their generally progressive assumptions about American history were also breaking down. The two trends worked together. Just as progressive assumptions encouraged scholars to emphasize the struggle of contending groups in society, so the reaction against progressive historiography has discouraged such emphasis and has undermined the intellectual foundations of a group-centered point of view. We may, therefore, get to the heart of our current problem and opportunity when we understand what has happened to the progressive school of American historians.

From the American Revolution to the Second World War the great majority of our historians assumed that the underlying movement of American history was in the direction of improvement or betterment, not only in wealth but in freedom or happiness. In this movement, setbacks and even reverses had occurred, of course, when the American people were temporarily faithless to their basic principles. Such interludes were pronounced "Repressible Conflicts," "Great Aberrations," or "Great Betrayals,"[2] to indicate that they arose from mutual misunderstandings, irrational mistakes, and moral holidays, not from any fundamental defect in American culture. Even the fashionable disillusion of the 1920's left very little impress on professional historians. A President of the American Historical Association affirmed a law of progress in history in 1923, and in 1929 a leading authority on American social history urged his colleagues to synthesize their data by asking how every event or influence had checked or accelerated social evolution.[3] Attitudes such as these meant that historians were continually asking what each period "contributed" or "added" to the world of today. History was fundamentally aggregative, and even scholars devoted to the study of lost causes and vanished frontiers refused to draw pessimistic conclusions. They felt sure that the passing experience they cherished had left a permanent heritage of fruitful values.[4]

In the twentieth century these pervasive assumptions gave a strategic importance to historians who had a hardheaded explanation of the dynamics of change—historians who rendered the progressive faith realistically by explaining how and why human effort sometimes overcame human inertia and sometimes succumbed to it. Change, these scholars said, takes place through struggle, and progress occurs when the more popular and democratic forces overcome the resistance to change offered by vested interests. And so American history became a story of epic conflict between over- and underprivileged groups. Whether this strife was chiefly between sections, as with Frederick Jackson Turner, or between opposing economic groups, as with Charles Beard, or between Hamiltonian and Jeffersonian ideologies, as with Vernon Parrington, a fundamental dualism cut through the course of American history.[5]

In polarizing history vertically, the progressive realists also secured a principal of periodization. With eyes focused on the climactic moments in the continuing struggle, they dramatized the turning points when power had presumably shifted from one side to the other. Through revolution and counterrevolution, through reform and reaction, beat the rhythm of an exciting and meaningful history. Here indeed was a grand design, flexible, capacious, immediately relevant to the present interests of the 1920's and 1930's, capable of elaboration in a multitude of researches, yet simple in outline. In 1939 Arthur Schlesinger, Sr., could compress a generation of historiography and the whole span of American political history into a single sentence: "A period of concern for the rights of the few has [regularly] been followed by one of concern for the wrongs of the many."[6]

Twenty years later, to most American historians, the grand design probably looked more like a grand illusion. Many of them in the 1950's had devoted their best energies to shattering the design. It had, without question, proved wanting. Too much of the mounting data of cultural, intellectual, and economic history overflowed the dialectical categories of liberal versus conservative. The groups to whom these labels were attached proved much less persistent and cohesive in identity and aim than the design allowed. The theory that change is effected through domestic social conflict took too little account of the role of accommodation and compromise in American political history, too little account of the kind of innovation emphasized in American business history, too little account of the international influences so important to diplomatic and intellectual history.

Yet the design might have held together after a fashion—by stretching and squeezing, it might have contained a good measure of new research—if the social attitudes that went into the design had remained intact. After World War II, however, historians found themselves in a new era, much less tractable and less responsive to progressive values. Some of those values now seemed too simple and too limited in their relevance to human experience. The vaunted realism of the progressive historians no longer seemed realistic enough.

As far as historians were concerned, one of the principle casualties of the postwar world was the faith in progress itself. Few of them became prophets of doom, but fewer still remained oracles of hope. Their disenchantment owed something to the powerful polemic of Reinhold Niebuhr but more to their own sharpened awareness of America's dependence on a precarious civilization. Walter Prescott Webb's *The Great Frontier* (Boston, 1952), although too extreme in its conclusions to win general acceptance, showed how an international perspective could cast a somber light on the epic theme of American progress: the frontier thesis became an explanation of the temporary and declining vitality of modern Western civilization. Other postprogressive scholars, such as George Kennan, studied American wars and diplomacy with an eye for the tragic and with a sense of the limits of American capacities.[7] The revisionist school of Civil War history declined when its thesis that partisan statesmen had willfully ignored constructive alternatives to a "needless" war and a "vindictive" peace began to look naively optimistic.[8]

Perhaps the most widespread effect of the sober postwar mood was to deflate progressive confidence in social change. Instead of endorsing change, or distinguishing between more and less desirable kinds of change, many historians grew cautious if not distrustful toward change as such. In the work of Ralph Gabriel, Clinton Rossiter, Louis Hartz, Daniel Boorstin, Robert E. Brown, Edmund Morgan, and others, a new appreciation of continuity in American history emerged. Neither in love with modernity nor entranced by the antique, many historians now emphasized the enduring uniformities of American life, the stability of institutions, the persistence of a national character.[9]

Thus, a conservative trend of historical interpretation set in, and as it gathered momentum it displayed other attitudes often found in conservative quarters. In contrast to the progressive historians' confidence in mass democracy, one notices among historians today a skeptical attitude toward the common man and a reluctance to give full sympathy to the underdog. Such democratic heroes as Roger Williams, Nathaniel Bacon, Andrew Jackson, and Thorstein Veblen are now portrayed as less democratic or less heroic than earlier biographers saw them.[10] On the other hand, such nondemocratic figures as John Winthrop, Alexander Hamilton, Nicholas Biddle, George Fitzhugh, and John D. Rockefeller have risen several notches in historical reputation.[11]

This shift away from democratic affirmations should not be exaggerated. It has not, among many reputable historians, made heroes of the privileged and villains of their popular opponents. Such a reversal of progressive sympathies would preserve the progressive dichotomy between the many and the few, the haves and the have-nots. The deeper tendency in contemporary thought is to dissolve the old polarities. Skeptical especially of economic and ideological antitheses, historians nowadays are blending them together. Where the terms liberal and conservative still remain in use, we are finding that liberal movements were after all conservative[12] and that almost all Americans have really been liberal.[13] Instead of the two-sided nation enshrined in progressive history—a nation eternally divided between a party of the past and a party of the future, between noble ideals and ignoble interests—recent general interpretations show us a single homogeneous culture, or perhaps a balanced interplay between three elements. The trinitarian approach lends itself neatly to a reconciliation of contrasts within a final synthesis.[14] Not conflict, therefore, but consensus is now taken as the normative reality of American life.

It is not hard to understand why this should be so. Unlike the progressive historian, his conservative successor does not feel much at odds with powerful institutions or dominant social groups. He is not even half alienated. Carried along in the general postwar reconciliation between America and its intellectuals, and wanting to identify himself with a community, he usually reads the national record for evidence of effective organization and a unifying spirit.[15]

Often the strength of this uniformitarian bent is obscured by the conservative historian's delighted attention to the abundant variety of American life. Far from professing any love of conformity, he may conceive of the American whole as an infinite number of freely related parts.[16] In his more critical moments, he may fear that the process of centralization, bureaucratization, and standardization are going too far today, and he embraces the variations and complexities in American experience all the more readily because they seem to him so innocuous and impermanent. He discovers an immense variety of economic interests represented at Philadelphia in 1787, instead of only two. In restudying the Second Bank of the United States, Reconstruction, or the progressive movement, he fragments into a welter of factions what the progressive historian had thought of as "the business community."[17] Immersed in fluid experience, he is often quite pragmatic in his antipathy to formal ideologies and clearly defined categories. His sense of the unity of America, therefore, is largely unspecific and rests on a description of its multiplicity. His motto is *e pluribus unum.*

That this general approach to American history contains a large measure of truth, few will deny. Having much in common with our national mythology, it induces sympathies that are perhaps more general and less partisan than those of the progressive school. Although suffused by present attitudes, the historian of consensus is not involved so immediately and urgently in the struggles of his own time; he may be able more easily to project himself into the past on something like its own terms. The desire to see things whole, in the sense of understanding the working relationships between groups, should prove especially useful in the study of social history, which for too long was preoccupied with reform movements and social problems.

Yet the positive achievements of the conservative school seem less impressive, to date, than its attack on the old progressive formulas. Has it produced any master works of great strength and enduring significance? Perhaps, if Allan Nevins' retelling of the Civil War belongs to this school; but it is significant that Nevins' work seems to derive from an older conservative culture and to owe little to the contemporary mood. Of the outstanding books of the last ten years some have retained a modified progressive outlook, like C. Vann Woodward's *Origins of the New South, 1877-1913* (Baton Rouge, La., 1951). Some have expressed a disillusioned liberalism, like Richard Hofstadter's *The Age of Reform: From Bryan to F.D.R.* (New York, 1955) and Henry Nash Smith's *Virgin Land: The American West as Symbol and Myth* (Cambridge, Mass., 1950). The historians of consensus, on the other hand, have scored chiefly in restricted monographs or in highly generalized interpretive essays.

All in all, recent historians have been more successful in breaking down the interpretations of their predecessors than in building anew. The emphasis on consensus and continuity has softened the outlines and flattened the crises of American history. A certain tameness and amiability have crept into our view of things; perhaps the widespread interest in myths comes partly from a feeling that the realities are simply not as interesting. The conservative frame of reference is giving us a bland history, in which conflict is muted, in which the elements of spontaneity, effervescence, and violence in American life get little sympathy or attention. Now that the progressive impulse is subsiding, scholarship is threatened with a moral vacuum.

To speak, perhaps extravagantly, of a moral vacuum is to raise afresh an old question that too many of us have regarded as long since settled. Since the rise of scientific history, the legitimacy of moral judgments in historical writing has been under official disapproval. By the end of the nineteenth century, the manuals of historical method had summarily banished moral evaluation from the proper sphere of historical science; the latest handbooks continue to ignore it.[18] But the present cultural situation has reopened this question. From English and German scholars we begin to hear warnings that academic history, by shrinking from evaluation of right and wrong, has helped to weaken the spirit of personal responsibility.[19] The warning applies with special force to the current state of American historiography. With the decline of progressive values, the principal source of moral energy on which American historians have drawn in recent decades is drying up. There is no substitute in the complacent empiricism of the conservative school. Yet the present situation offers a third alternative. We have today a major opportunity for revitalizing the moral relevance of historical scholarship.

Until history became professionalized, its practitioners felt no misgivings about teaching moral lessons. History, to them, exhibited universal laws of human nature and so comprised a vast repository of political and moral example. The nineteenth-century faith in progress put a supreme confidence into such moralizing; for the historian's assumption that he stood at the summit of history, and could therefore truly judge the actions and standards of earlier times by those of his own, expunged any doubt about his moral authority. He might exercise it with advantage in any field of history, although the study of one's own country was particularly improving. "That study," said the president of Harvard University in 1884, summing up a common conviction,

> shows the young the springs of public honor and dishonor; sets before them the national failings, weaknesses, and sins; warns them against future dangers by exhibiting the losses and sufferings of the past; enshrines in their hearts the national heroes; and strengthens in them the precious love of country.[20]

The same year in which Charles W. Eliot spoke, the American Historical Association was established by men who were retreating from moral commitment in the name of science. The scientific historian aspired to be a flawless mirror reflecting an independent, external reality. By freely pronouncing judgments he would distort the picture. Yet the scientific historians, in denying themselves a judicial function, did not intend to lessen history's didactic usefulness. Secure in their faith in progress, they commonly supposed that objective history would reveal the evolution of morality in the march of events without intrusive comment by the writer.[21] Surely, over the long run, history displayed the gradual advance of wisdom and virtue. If the historian took care of the facts, the values would take care of themselves. In practice, of course, the early professional historians could not suppress moral rhetoric completely, but they could in principle forswear it without any sense of risk or anxiety, since scientific history emerged in America in a humane milieu, unperplexed by deep frustrations.

The new style progressives of the twentieth century, rebelling against the conservative implications of scientific history, were less complacent. They were activists, whose expectations of progress depended on the use of historical knowledge in order to control history. They felt less comfortable about the present than their conservative predecessors had, and they determined to link the past to current needs for reform.[22] They recognized a legitimate place for values in historical interpretation. By renouncing an unattainable objectivity, they hoped to arrive at usable truths.

In progressive hands American history became not only a struggle between the many and the few but a realm of clashing values. Once more, the American historian consciously played the role of moral critic, now with a pragmatic emphasis on the consequences of policies and ideas, instead of the easy dogmatism of a George Bancroft or a Francis Parkman. Unfortunately, however, the restoration of moral urgency in historical scholarship occurred on too narrow a front and too precarious a basis. The same progressive spirit that stirred the heart and conscience of historians, also, in other aspects, severely limited their moral vision. For one thing, the range of moral concern contracted from the whole life of man to certain political and economic issues. The progressive historian did not ordinarily search the past for light on personal codes of behavior, the great sphere of private as opposed to public morality. Nor did he show much interest in studying the resolution of incompatible loyalties, or the nature of responsibility, greatness, initiative, and the like. His view of history remained largely impersonal: he concentrated on "social forces" as the earlier scientific historians had concentrated on "institutions." The only kind of ethics that engaged the progressive historian's interest was the ethics of democracy,[23] and even here he was pretty exclusively concerned with the actualization of democratic values rather than their relation to other good.

This tendency to dwell on means rather than ends—on the attainable results of an ideal rather than its intrinsic nature—reflected the progressive scholar's reluctance to venture much beyond the accustomed limits of scientific objectivity. He wanted his values, but he wanted them in the shape of facts. Tough-minded, realistic, disdainful of nineteenth-century pieties and platitudes, he tried to be pragmatic in his moral judgments. The practical results of any historical situation—the tangible action it produced—dominated and restricted his evaluation of it. Progressive historians ordinarily retained too much confidence in progress to doubt that the course of history would vindicate their democratic and pragmatic ethics.[24]

From these antecedents, the younger conservative historians of today have come. While reacting against a reformist bias, some of them continue to measure the past by pragmatic standards. What remains for them of the moral function of the historian now that the inspiration of social progress has dimmed, and the age of reform that lasted for half a century has passed? Now that stability rather than change has become the national objective, what values can pass the pragmatic test? Only what is snugly enmeshed in the texture of American experience has clearly proved its practical worth. Deprived of an active commitment to progress, the pragmatic approach tends to endorse sheer success and survival. Having lost its critical edge, pragmatism has tended to deteriorate into retrospective piety.

On the other hand, the present situation can give rise to a very different kind of historical scholarship, a scholarship engaged in a more widely ranging and a subtler moral criticism than American professional historians have yet undertaken. A lively critical impulse has clearly survived in many quarters. It is seeking a new field of expression now that the grand design of progressive historiography no longer contains and directs it. That impulse can draw today on a richer knowledge of human motivation than scholars have ever had at their disposal before; it can achieve a sympathetic understanding of a greater variety of human types. Having learned something of the relativity of values, today's historians can exercise a morally critical function with tentativeness and humility with a minimum of self-righteousness, and with a willingness to meet the past on equal terms.

How can this come about? Let us look first at the pitfalls to be avoided; here the record of American historiography to date can guide us. None of the formal postures that American historians have conventionally adopted seem adequate today, either morally or historically. Neither the dogmatic moralist, nor the pure scientist, nor the pragmatist offers a satisfactory model.

Surely scholars may not, without corrupting history, revert to the judicial stance of a century ago. We are now too well aware of the wide disparities between ethical systems, and too ignorant of their relation to one another, to impose our own arbitrarily on another time and place. Let us beware of the easy temptations of moral judgment in essaying the difficult adventure of moral criticism. Let us operate on any subject with a conviction of its dignity and worth. Let us grant to every actor in a moral drama the fullest measure of his particular integrity; let us not destroy the drama by hastening to condemn or to absolve. The serious historian may not wrap himself in judicial robes and pass sentence from on high; he is too much involved in both the prosecution and the defense. He is not a judge of the dead, but rather a participant in their affairs, and their only trustworthy intermediary.

For these tasks, the moral neutrality of the scientific position has likewise proved wanting. In addition to the standard complaints–that it is unattainable, that it dehumanizes history, that it encourages fatalism and gives us nothing to admire—one may suggest a further difficulty. Scientific history, so far as it achieves neutrality, leaves an unbridged gulf between the subject and the reader. The scientific historian, in liberating his readers from moral absolutism, apparently assumed that they could make their own fair and independent judgments if given an unobstructed view of the past. On principle, therefore, the scientific historian did not address himself to the sensibilities of a particular audience. He did not deliberately connect its needs and perplexities with those of another time and place. Indeed, he was scarcely conscious of having an audience. Whereas the historical judge coerced the reader, the historical scientist ignored him. To write as a critic, however, is to assume an active responsibility both to a phase of the past and to a contemporary public, and to engage one with the other.

Our third model—the historical pragmatist—more nearly approximates that kind of role. He is very much aware of present needs, and his pronouncements are tentative and undogmatic. But his sympathies are limited, and his criticism does not go deep. Criteria that rest on a program of practical action take account of a restricted present as well as a restricted past. A morality confined to social engineering emphasizes results at the expense of intentions. In a progressive age, it becomes a partisan in the struggle for results. In a conservative age, it celebrates results already largely achieved.

Once the pragmatic test is suspended, historians will still analyze the results of a situation in order to discover its causes and to learn how those particular results came to be, but a moral appraisal of the situation need not depend upon its outcome. A truly sensitive critic will go beyond the practical consequences of the process he describes. He may criticize his subject, not on the ground of its present relevance, but for its intrinsic value as a gesture of the human spirit.

One may well ask, however, for more specific directions. What strategies can the historian legitimately employ without compromising the integrity of his craft? What criteria may he apply in performing the office of moral critic? How much real change in historical scholarship is implied? These questions lead us into an aspect of historiography ignored by the standard manuals and treatises on method. Discussion has not ordinarily gone beyond the point of recognizing that the historian's own values inevitably color his writing. At best, we have acknowledged this coloring as a mark of our humanity.[25] Professional historians have hardly begun to consider moral insight as something they can gain by skilled and patient historical study, not merely as something they cannot keep out of it. Historical method acquires a new dimension when we begin to speak of the criticism of life in addition to the technical criticism of documents. Then moral evaluation becomes a professional task, not just a predilection of our unprofessional selves.

A comparison with analogous developments in literary studies during the last generation may help to clarify the present opportunity in historical scholarship. The reign of the literary historian—exclusively preoccupied with historical and biographical backgrounds to literature, with sources, influences, and social conditions—was challenged by the incursion of literary critics into academic circles.[26] Various schools of literary criticism proliferated, but all subordinated factual description and historical explanation to a close evaluation of the work of art. For a time, criticism went to absurdly antihistorical extremes; English departments split into factions—literary historians versus New Critics. But the ferment invigorated literary history enormously; in the hands of men like F. O. Matthiessen, Lionel Trilling, and Harry Levin, the study of literature profited from the interplay of critical and historical perspectives.

Possibly the professional study of history would benefit at least as much from the challenge of a similar movement, directed at the criticism of life rather than the criticism of art. On this analogy, we may look forward to something more noteworthy than the recent fruitless debate over the legitimacy of those present-centered judgments that inescapably condition all historical knowledge. Instead, we may look forward to the development of a partial distinction between the kind of historical inquiry that is familiar and traditional and a newer kind that is only beginning to appear in professional circles. The older type aims chiefly at knowledge of causal relationships in a particular phase of the past; the newer type aims chiefly at knowledge of the elements of good and evil discoverable in a particular historical setting. The former type holds moral appraisal in check in the interest of causal synthesis. The latter type, with equal propriety, subordinates causal interpretation to moral interpretation. Both endeavors will inevitably reflect the historian's own commitments. Both must accept the distinctively historical obligation to deal with a whole situation in its authentic complexity. But causal history should have a form appropriate to the actual *course* of experience; whereas moral history, proceeding with a similar drive for discovery, will take whatever shape seems best suited to elaborate the problematical *qualities* of experience.

This distinction, like any classification of historical studies, should not be pressed too far, though it can serve some useful purposes. It calls attention to the need for a thoroughgoing moral criticism, in contrast to the impressionistic moral judgments that creep into historical writing at every turn. A working distinction between causal history and moral history also guards against pragmatic confusion between facts and values. Moreover, it helps to equalize the legitimacy and importance of two great objectives: the reconstruction of history as objective reality (most appropriate to causal history), and the participation in history as subjective experience (essential to moral history).[27] Causal history and moral history at their best, however, are reciprocal modes of understanding, each of which suffers from neglect of the other. Let us distinguish between them as friendly rivals in order to overcome a destructive enmity.

A closer look at the nature of moral history will suggest how it can supplement and enrich existing scholarship. One may discern, within the wide domain of moral history, two general types. The first type deals with the whole quality of a life, a complex of lives, or an age. It enables us to grasp the moral tone of a particular time and place—to feel the involuntary drift and pressure of its values against a background of alternatives delivered in other times and places. How has the notion of honor changed since the Middle Ages? What did men mean in the nineteenth century when they spoke of "character" and put implicit confidence in leaders or associates who had it? To what sorts of people did the virtue of "character" appeal and attach? What tangled combinations of courage and weakness, or of love and hate, do we find pervading a career, a movement, or a period? Similarly, moral insight may reveal fundamental polarities in history that are more illuminating than class or sectional divisions. Is the great cleavage in American history the outward one between haves and have-nots, which twentieth-century progressives observed in society, or is it rather an inward opposition, which progressives strove to reconcile within themselves, between an ethic of communal responsibility and an ethic of unrestrained individualism?

These questions point to an extended kind of moral history that shades imperceptibly into causal history, and differs only in having somewhat more interest in the intrinsic meaning of the experience and somewhat less in explaining its development. Professional historians seem to be venturing increasingly into this genre, though more readily in casual essays than in their formal, full-dress works. Carl Becker was probably the first American professional historian to become adept at an intellectualized moral history, which may help to account for his great and continuing vogue in recent years. It remains true, however, that the major works of this kind are still written mostly by literary and cultural critics like Wilbur J. Cash, Hannah Arendt, and Lewis Mumford.[28] The amateur in history plunges instinctively and often rashly into moral criticism. A quickened interest among professional scholars would surely help academic history to find its rightful place in the republic of letters.

A second kind of moral history concentrates on particular acts of choice. Here we confront not involuntary or cumulative processes, but rather the moments of important human initiative, and we ponder the moral responsibility of the agents of decision. In the 1760's the British Parliament adopted a disastrous policy of spasmodic coercion toward the American colonies. A generation ago American scholars debated the constitutionality of that policy, and British scholars are still arguing about the exact nature of English government at the time;[29] but the momentous decision that precipitated the American Revolution has not yet had close attention as a problem in political ethics. Given the political and social institutions of the day, what real alternatives were present? Who erred most culpably? What balance of folly, insight, and constructive purpose can we discern in each of the major participants?[30] The study of moral responsibility remains crude unless each of the elements contributory to a situation fully exhibits its distinctive abilities, limitations, and dilemmas. Ideally, each element should effect a criticism of the others. As the author's design unfolds, the situation becomes luminous with unexpected contingencies.

In similar fashion it should be possible to study afresh the turning points in the lives of well-known individuals: Robert E. Lee's painful decision to cast his lot with the Confederacy in 1861, William James's famous affirmation of free will in 1870, Franklin D. Roosevelt's acceptance of a third term in 1940. Seizing upon the event, the historian can undertake to clarify the degree and quality of initiative suggested by a close comparison with other individuals similarly circumstanced (James with Henry Adams, for example), and by analyzing the other choices that might conceivably have been made.

In all such studies of an act of decision, as in larger studies of the moral climate, criticism cannot do without some causal analysis. We hold people responsible only to the degree that we think them free to choose their course. The imaginable range of choice within a particular situation guides our moral criticism, which must therefore include an appreciation of the unalterable conditions that bulk large in causal history. Yet moral criticism not only borrows from causal analysis, but also contributes to it. By enlarging our awareness of the latent possibilities of a situation, criticism will suggest new causal hypotheses. Perhaps it would be better to speak, not of causal history and moral history as separate types, but of two kinds of attention, each of which contributes to historical wisdom.

There remains the difficult question of the criteria that the critic of the past may legitimately employ. Surely one must have standards. Just as surely, the only proper standards are ones common to the historian and to the world he is studying. But to try to lay down exact criteria is, I think, to misconceive our opportunity and to narrow our prospect. The historian is not called to establish a hierarchy of values, but rather to explore a spectrum of human potentialities and achievements. While maintaining his own integrity, while preserving the detachment that time and distance afford, he must participate in variety, allowing his subjects as much as possible to criticize one another. In fact, the obligation of the historian to become a moral critic grows out of the breakdown of ethical absolutes. If no single ethical system, even a pragmatic one that trusts the piecemeal results of history, does justice to all situations, a complex awareness must take the place of systematic theory. Instead of depending on fixed canons or rules, the moral critic must learn from the great dramatists, like Shakespeare, from novelists, like Tolstoy, and from the matchless example of Thucydides.

In the simplest sense, the historian commits to moral criticism all the resources of his human condition. He derives from moral criticism an enlarged and disciplined sensitivity to what men ought to have done, what they might have done, and what they achieved. His history becomes an intensive, concrete reflection upon life, freed from academic primness, and offering itself as one of the noblest, if also one of the most difficult and imperfect, of the arts.

This discussion, instead of continuing the current argument about the interpretation of American history, has turned outward toward a wider horizon. But perhaps the original issue has undergone a partial resolution. When the historian's quest for understanding reaches beyond pragmatic and empirical concerns, he need not strain to find patterns of conflict or of consensus. He will have plenty of both. He will study, as the most meaningful kind of consensus, the moral standards of an age—what, distinctively, it assumed about the conduct of life. He will find conflict wherever those moral standards clash or break down, and so force men to make a choice. In confronting all that is unstable and precarious in human values, he can discover the profoundest struggles and conflicts that the drama of history affords.

FOOTNOTES

1. Samuel Eliot Morison, *The Puritan Pronaos: Studies in the Intellectual Life of New England in the Seventeenth Century* (New York, 1936); Walter Prescott Webb, *The Great Plains* (Boston, 1931); Carl Wittke, *We Who Built America: The Saga of the Immigrant* (New York, 1939); Ulrich B. Phillips, *Life and Labor in the Old South* (Boston, 1929); E. Merton Coulter, *The South during Reconstruction, 1865-1877*

(Baton Rouge, La., 1947). Negro historians and students of labor history seem also increasingly ironic; even business history may be losing an apologetic tone.

2. Avery Craven, *The Repressible Conflict, 1830-1861* (Baton Rouge, La., 1939); Samuel Flagg Bemis, *A Diplomatic History of the United States* (New York, 1950), 463-75; Thomas A. Bailey, *Woodrow Wilson and the Great Betrayal* (New York, 1945).

3. Edward P. Cheyney, *Law in History and Other Essays* (New York, 1927), 22-24; Dixon Ryan Fox, "A Synthetic Principle in American Social History," *American Historical Review,* XXXV (Jan., 1930), 256-66.

4. Frederick Paxson, *When the West Is Gone* (Boston, 1930).

5. The economic interpretation of history, Charles A. Beard wrote in 1913, "rests upon the concept that social progress in general is the result of contending interests in society–some favorable, others opposed to change." (*An Economic Interpretation of the Constitution,* rev. ed., New York, 1935, 19.)

6. Arthur Schlesinger, Sr., "Tides of American Politics," *Yale Review,* XXIX (Dec. 1939), 220.

7. George F. Kennan, *American Diplomacy, 1900-1950* (Chicago, 1951).

8. The gradual revision, since World War II, of Avery Craven's revisionism has often been remarked upon. See T. N. Bonner, "Civil War Historians and the Needless War Doctrine," *Journal of the History of Ideas,* XVII (Apr. 1956), 193-216.

9. Ralph Gabriel's *The Course of American Democratic Thought: An Intellectual History Since 1815* (New York, 1940) anticipated a point of view that has become much more common since World War II in books such as Clinton Rossiter's *Seedtime of the Republic: The Origin of The American Tradition of Political Liberty* (New York, 1953), Louis Hartz's *The Liberal Tradition in America: An Interpretation of American Political Thought Since the Revolution* (New York, 1955), Robert E. Brown's *Middle-Class Democracy and the Revolution in Massachusetts, 1691-1780* (Ithaca, N. Y., 1955), and Edmund S. and Helen M. Morgan's *The Stamp Act Crisis: Prologue to Revolution* (Chapel Hill, N. C., 1953). Perhaps the most provocative analysis of the "togetherness" of American society and the continuity of American history is Daniel J. Boorstin's *The Americans: The Colonial Experience* (New York, 1958). See also David Potter's interpretation of the unifying influence of economic abundance in American history, *People of Plenty: Economic Abundance and the American Character* (Chicago, 1954). I have criticized this trend at greater length in "The Cult of the 'American Consensus': Homogenizing Our History," Commentary, XXVII (Feb. 1959), 93-100, an article from which some of the remarks in the next few paragraphs are drawn.

10. Alan Simpson, "How Democratic Was Roger Williams?" *William and Mary Quarterly,* XIII (Jan. 1956), 53-67; Wilcomb E. Washburn, *The Governor and the Rebel: A History of Bacon's Rebellion in Virginia* (Chapel Hill, N. C., 1957); Bray Hammond, *Banks and Politics in America from the Revolution to the Civil War* (Princeton, N. J., 1957); David Riesman, *Thorstein Veblen: A Critical Interpretation* (New York, 1953).

11. Edmund S. Morgan, *The Puritan Dilemma: The Story of John Winthrop* (Boston, 1958); Broadus Mitchell, *Alexander Hamilton, Youth to Maturity, 1755-1788* (New York, 1957); Thomas P. Govan. *Nicholas Biddle, Nationalist and Public Banker* (Chicago, 1959); C. Vann Woodward, "George Fitzhugh, *Sui Generis,*" in *Cannibals All!* by George Fitzhugh (Cambridge, Mass., 1960), vii-xxxix; Allan Nevins, *Study in Power: John D. Rockefeller* (2 vols., New York, 1953).

12. Richard Hofstadter, *The Age of Reform: From Bryan to F.D.R.* (New York, 1955); Marvin Meyers, *The Jacksonian Persuasion* (Stanford, Calif., 1957); Cecelia Kenyon, "Men of Little Faith: The Anti-Federalists on the Nature of Representative Government," *William and Mary Quarterly,* XII (Jan. 1955), 3-43.

13. Hartz, *Liberal Tradition.*

14. For example: Will Herberg, *Protestant-Catholic-Jew: An Essay in American Religious Sociology* (New York, 1955); R. W. B. Lewis, *The American Adam: Innocence, Tragedy, and Tradition in the Nineteenth Century* (Chicago, 1955); Gabriel, *Course of American Democratic Thought.* In sketching another version of the unity of American history, William B. Hesseltine has adopted a quadruple rather than a triple calculus. See his presidential address, "Four American Traditions," *Journal of Southern History,* XXVII (Feb. 1961), 3-32.

15. Allan Nevins, *The War for the Union,* (2 vols., New York, 1959), I, v; Rowland Berthoff, "The American Social Order: A Conservative Hypothesis," *American Historical Review,* LXV (Apr. 1960), 495-514.

16. Boorstin, *The Americans,* 185-205.

17. Forrest McDonald, *We the People: The Economic Origins of the Constitution* (Chicago, 1958); Hammond, *Banks and Politics;* Robert P. Sharkey, *Money, Class and Party: An Economic Study of Civil War and Reconstruction* (Baltimore, 1959); Robert H. Wiebe, "Business Disunity and the Progressive Movement, 1901-1914," *Mississippi Valley Historical Review,* XLIV (Mar. 1958), 664-85.

18. Charles V. Langlois and Charles Seignobos, *Introduction to the Study of History* (London, 1898), 279; Oscar Handlin, *et al., Harvard Guide to American History* (Cambridge, Mass., 1954); Jacques Barzun and Henry Graff, *The Modern Researcher* (New York, 1958). One exception is Allan Nevins, *The Gateway to History* (Boston, 1938), 235–a book written with unprofessional gusto and addressed to a wide audience.

19. Isaiah Berlin, *Historical Inevitability* (London, 1954); Friedrich Meinecke, "Values and Causalities in History," *The Varieties of History,* ed. Fritz Stern (New York, 1956), 267-88; C. V. Wedgwood, *Truth and Opinion: Historical Essays* (London, 1960), 47-54; David Knowles, *The Historian and Character* (Cambridge, Eng., 1955); A. J. P. Taylor, *Rumours of Wars* (London, 1952), 9-13. The most cogent arguments on the other side of the issue–denying to the professional historian an ethical function–are also by Europeans: Herbert Butterfield, *History and Human Relations* (London, 1951), 101-30; Marc Bloch, *The Historian's Craft* (New York, 1953), 139-41; Geoffrey Barraclough, "History, Morals, and Politics," *International Affairs,* XXXIV (Jan. 1958), 1-15. A valuable essay by an American philosopher, defending the exercise of moral judgment by historians, came to my attention too late for use in this paper: Arthur Child, "Moral Judgment in History," *Ethics: An International Journal of Social, Political, and Legal Philosophy,* LXI (July, 1951), 297-308.

20. Charles W. Eliot, *Educational Reform: Essays and Addresses* (New York, 1909), 104-106.

21. Henry C. Lea, "Ethical Values in History," *Annual Report, American Historical Association,* 1903 (2 vols., Washington, D. C., 1904), I, 53-69. This was the classic rebuttal, by an American scientific historian, to Lord Acton's famous protest in 1895 against the prevailing spirit of scientific neutrality: "I exhort you . . . to try others by the final maxim that governs your own lives, and to suffer no man and no cause to escape the undying penalty which history has the power to inflict on wrong." On this controversy, see Andrew Fish, "Acton, Creighton, and Lea: A Study in History and Ethics," *Pacific Historical Review,* XVI (Feb. 1947), 59-69, and John Emerich Edward Dalberg Acton, *Essays on Freedom and Power,* ed. Gertrude Himmelfarb (London, 1956), 41-52, 329-45.

22. Frederick Jackson Turner, "Social Forces in American History," in *The Frontier in American History* (New York, 1920), 323-32; James Harvey Robinson, *The New History: Essays Illustrating the Modern Historical Outlook* (New York, 1912).

23. For a parallel trend among philosophers, see Jay William Hudson, "Recent Shifts in Ethical Theory and Practice," *Philosophical Review,* XLIX (Mar. 1940), 105-20.

24. Although beset by such doubts in the 1930's, Beard fell back on an ultimate "act of faith" that history was moving "on an upward gradient toward a more ideal order." (Charles A. Beard, "Written History as an Act of Faith," *American Historical Review,* XXXIX Jan. 1934, 226.)

25. Louis Gottschalk, *Understanding History* (New York, 1950), 10-13.

26. René Wellek, "Literary Scholarship," in *American Scholarship in the Twentieth Century,* ed. Merle Curti (Cambridge, Mass., 1953), 111-45.

27. For a balanced summary of these competing views of history, see W. H. Walsh, *An Introduction to Philosophy of History* (rev. ed., London, 1958).

28. Wilbur J. Cash, *The Mind of the South* (New York, 1941); Hannah Arendt, *The Human Condition* (Chicago, 1958); Lewis Mumford, *The City in History: Its Origins, Its Transformations, and Its Prospects* (New York, 1961). Two recent efforts by professional historians are C. Vann Woodward, *The Burden of Southern History* (Baton Rouge, La., 1960), and William R. Taylor, *Cavalier and Yankee: The Old South and American National Character* (New York, 1961).

29. Charles H. McIlwain, *The American Revolution: A Constitutional Interpretation* (New York, 1923), and Robert L. Schuyler, *Parliament and the British Empire* (New York, 1929); Herbert Butterfield, *George III and the Historians* (London, 1957). A reviewer of the last book observed: "It is perhaps the strangest thing of all to find so impressive a controversy reared on the insoluble, and to some extent uninteresting question of what exactly were the relationships between George III, the Duke of Newcastle, and the Earl of Bute in the years following 1760." (*Times Literary Supplement,* Nov. 22, 1957.)

30. For an unusual and pioneering inquiry of this kind, see Eric L. McKitrick, *Andrew Johnson and Reconstruction* (Chicago, 1960).

Suggestions for Further Reading

The best comprehensive book on American historical scholarship is John Higham, *et al., History,* Prentice-Hall, Englewood Cliffs, N. J., 1965, which relates the writing of history to the climates of opinion in which it has been written. For an earlier and less comprehensive study, see Harvey Wish, *The American Historian,* Oxford, New York, 1960. A survey of historians of ideas is R. A. Skotheim, *American Intellectual Histories and Historians,* Princeton, Princeton, 1966. Historians of the Civil War are studied in Thomas J. Pressly, *Americans Interpret Their Civil War,* Princeton, Princeton, 1954, and historians of World War I during the 1920s and 1930s are the focus of Warren Cohen, *The American Revisionists,* Univ. of Chicago, Chicago, 1967. Richard Hofstadter has recently published *The Progressive Historians,* Knopf, New York, 1968. All these books are fundamentally concerned with the connection between historical interpretation and the climate of opinion. For a survey of presidential addresses to the American Historical Association up to 1945, see Hermann Ausubel, *Historians and Their Craft,* Columbia, New York, 1950.

There are few memoirs or autobiographies by American historians, and some of them are by "amateur" scholars. All their memoirs reveal the importance of the climate of opinion to the writing of history. See Claude Bowers, *My Life,* Simon and Schuster, 1962; Matthew Josephson, *Infidel in the Temple,* Knopf, New York, 1967; W. E. B. DuBois, *The Autobiography of W. E. B. DuBois,* International Publishers, New York, 1968; Samuel Eliot Morison, *One Boy's Boston, 1887-1901,* Houghton Mifflin, Boston, 1962, *By Land and By Sea,* Knopf, New York, 1953; Arthur M. Schlesinger, Sr., *In Retrospect,* Harcourt, Brace and World, New York, 1963. Dexter Perkins has completed his autobiography, *Yield of the Years,* which will be published in 1969 by Little, Brown, Boston. John D. Hicks has written his memoirs as *My Life with History,* U. of Nebraska Press, Lincoln, Nebr., 1968, and Roy Nichols has published *A Historian's Progress,* Knopf, New York, 1968.

Beard's intellectual biography is more complex than the brief introductory headnotes suggest, and can be traced at length in the following, and in the articles cited therein: Bernard Borning, *The Political and Social Thought of Charles A. Beard,* Washington, Seattle, 1962; Cushing Strout, *The Pragmatic Revolt in American History: Carl Becker and Charles Beard,* Yale, New Haven, 1958; R. A. Skotheim, *American Intellectual Histories and Historians,* pp. 87-109. The phrases quoted from Beard in the second introductory headnote are from Strout, pp. 89-90. The most recent discussion of Beard is in Hofstadter, *The Progressive Historians,* pp. 167-346.

Although Beard expressed a theory of historical relativism in the 1930s, as in "Written History as an Act of Faith," it was Carl Becker rather than Beard who consistently expressed the necessary relativism of written histories during the pre-World War I years, through the 1920s and into the

1930s. For Becker's statements on relativism, see: "Detachment and the Writing of History," originally published in *Atlantic Monthly,* CVI (October 1910), 524-536, reprinted in Phil Snyder, ed., *Detachment and the Writing of History: Essays and Letters of Carl L. Becker,* Cornell, Ithaca, 1958, pp. 3-28; "What Are Historical Facts?" originally read as a paper in 1926, printed in *Detachment and the Writing of History,* pp. 41-64; "Everyman His Own Historian," originally his presidential address to the American Historical Association, 1931, reprinted in Becker's *Everyman His Own Historian,* Appleton Century-Crofts, New York, 1935, pp. 233-255.

Parrington is analyzed in considerable detail in Skotheim, *American Intellectual Histories and Historians,* pp. 124-148, from which the quotations by Parrington in the introductory headnote are taken. The most recent discussion of Parrington is in Hofstadter, *The Progressive Historians,* pp. 349-434.

For studies which, like Crowe's essay, discuss progressive historians as a group, see: John Higham, *et al., History,* pp. 104-131, 171-211; David Noble, *Historians Against History,* Minnesota, Minneapolis, 1965; Lee Benson, *Turner and Beard,* Free Press, Glencoe, Illinois, 1960; Harvey Wish, *The American Historian,* pp. 181-208, 265-315; Strout, *The Pragmatic Revolt;* Skotheim, *American Intellectual Histories and Historians,* pp. 66-172; Hofstadter, *The Progressive Historians.*

The article which first located the distinctions between progressive historical interpretations and those of the late 1940s and 1950s, and which initiated analysis of the post-war histories, is John Higham, "The Cult of the 'American Consensus,'" *Commentary,* Vol. 27, February 1959, pp. 93-100. Higham's later views on post-war historians can be found in Higham, *et al., History,* pp. 132-44, 212-32. For a discussion of historians during the 1920s and 1930s who anticipated post-war interpretations, and also of post-war historians themselves, see Skotheim, *American Intellectual Histories and Historians,* pp. 173-288. Other recent treatments of the question of "consensus and continuity" in interpreting American history are: Richard Hofstadter, *The Progressive Historians,* pp. 437-466; Allen Davis and Harold Woodman, eds., *Conflict or Consensus in American History,* Heath, Boston, 1966; Burl Noggle, "Variety and Ambiguity: The Recent Approach to Southern History," *Mississippi Quarterly,* XVII, Winter 1963-64, pp. 21-35. The most promising comparative analysis of progressive and post-war historians is currently being undertaken by Gene Wise in a number of thoughtful and rigorous articles: "Political 'Reality' in Recent American Scholarship: Progressives versus Symbolists," *American Quarterly,* XIX, Part 2, Summer 1967, pp. 303-28; "Implicit Irony in Recent American Historiography," *Journal of the History of Ideas,* XXIX, October-December 1968.

The full references to other important works by Hartz, Boorstin, and Hofstadter, are: Hartz, *The Founding of New Societies,* Harcourt, Brace and World, N. Y., 1964; Boorstin, *The Americans: The Colonial Experience,* Random House and Alfred Knopf, New York, 1958, Vintage paperback and

The Americans: The National Experience, Random House and Alfred Knopf, New York, 1965, Vintage paperback; Richard Hofstadter, *The American Political Tradition,* Alfred Knopf, New York, 1948, Vintage paperback.

The Hofstadter critique of Populism as being in some sense anti-semitic was one version of a common view, other statements of which were: Oscar Handlin, "American Views of the Jew at the Opening of the Twentieth Century," *Publications of the American Jewish Historical Society,* XL, 1951; Victor Ferkiss, "Populist Influences on American Fascism," *Western Political Quarterly,* 10, June 1957, pp. 350-373. For other dissents, besides Pollack's, from the Hofstadter view, see C. Vann Woodward, "The Populist Heritage and the Intellectual," *American Scholar,* XXIX, 1959-60, pp. 55-72; Walter Nugent, *The Tolerant Populists,* Chicago, Chicago, 1963.

Irwin Unger's article is the only published study of New Left historians, but three recent important items should be added to those he cites: Staughton Lynd, *Intellectual Origins of American Radicalism,* Pantheon, New York, 1968; Lynd, *Class Conflict, Slavery, and the United States Constitution,* Bobbs-Merrill, Indianapolis, 1968; Barton Bernstein, ed., *Towards a New Past: Dissenting Essays in American History,* Pantheon, New York, 1968, which includes contributions by several of the outstanding young radicals and neo-progressives.

Allan Bogue's study of the behavioral movement among American historians is the only one in print, but two recent articles by Jerome Clubb and Howard Allen should be added to those illustrating the concern for quantification: "Computers and Historical Studies," *The Journal of American History,* LIV, December 1967, pp. 599-607; "Party Loyalty in the Progressive Years: The Senate, 1909-1915," *The Journal of Politics,* 29, August 1967, pp. 567-584.

BCDE69